# HOW TO RESTORE & MO

# CORVETTE

# 1968–82

Richard Newton

Motorbooks International
Publishers & Wholesalers ®

First published in 1995 by Motorbooks International Publishers & Wholesalers, PO Box 2, 729 Prospect Avenue, Osceola, WI 54020 USA

Motorbooks International books are also available at discounts in bulk quantity for industrial or sales-promotional use. For details write to Special Sales Manager at the Publisher's address

Library of Congress Cataloging-in-Publication Data

Newton, Richard F.
    How to restore and modify your Corvette 1968-82 / Richard Newton.
        p.   cm.
    Includes index.
    ISBN 0-7603-0052-6 (paperback)
    1. Corvette automobile—Conservation and restoration.
    I. Title.
TL215.C6N48  1995
629.222'2—dc20                                    95-13977

**On the front cover:** The much-feared 1971 big-block Corvette—hide the children and lock up the dog. Car owner is Tom Biltliff of Kutztown, PA. *Mike Mueller*

**On the back cover:** *Left:* A camshaft for a monster motor on its way in; very high lift and low duration add up to gobs of usable, eyeball-flattening torque. *Top right:* Patching fiberglass is a part of almost any Corvette restoration. *Bottom right:* A nicely restored front suspension.

Printed and bound in the United States of America

# Contents

# Introduction

Everybody has the dream. Some nice fall day you leave work early and take the back roads home. You're suddenly twenty-three years old again and your Corvette has these huge side pipes. This is the day you spend the afternoon driving every back road you've ever traveled. When you finally realize you're forty miles in the wrong direction, it doesn't even matter. You're riding in the Corvette you wanted ever since that day in junior high English class. This is what America is all about—nice days, winding roads, and Corvettes.

Many of us even have a plan that goes along with this dream. We'll buy an old used Corvette, preferably the kind we used to draw in our note-books during that junior high school English class. Then we'll carefully repair all the damage caused by the previous owners. At that point it'll be our Corvette. We'll honor it through sickness and health. We'll cherish it. Most importantly, we'll never sell it.

This book is all about that dream. In the next several hundred pages I'll show you how to make that dream real. I'll share with you how the dream can almost become a nightmare. I'll examine how I survived my Corvette marriage and never even had to enter a twelve-step program for Corvette addicts. The important thing is to simply realize that the Corvette dream can overcome our lives and that nothing will really make us happy except another dri-

This was the beginning of my relationship with Project Corvette. The car just barely ran. Nonetheless, it seemed to be a worthwhile project. It made most of the right noises, and it almost steered down the road. It would take ten years before it would ever be this good again.

The third-generation Corvette looked like this when it was brand new. Chevrolet had released the Mako Shark design for the general public. It was a revolution in Corvette design. No one imagined that this design would last fourteen years.

ve through the countryside with the sound of genuine Chevrolet power exiting the exhaust system.

A few years ago Chevrolet did a marketing study to find out what Corvette buyers were really like. What they found was that most of them have a Corvette imprinted on their brains. Corvette buyers, at some point, fixated on a particular Corvette. That impression defined for them how a real Corvette should look, sound, and drive.

This imprint usually takes hold when the Corvette groupie is very young. It never changes. It's the reason all Corvettes need V8 engines. It's the reason the power must be put down through the rear wheels. The idea of a twin turbo V6 in a Corvette causes a nauseous feeling in the bottom of a Corvette owner's stomach. The thought of a front-wheel-drive Corvette could bring on serious illness.

A lot of people came of age with the 1968 to 1982 Corvette. The good part is that these C3-generation Corvettes are also the affordable ones. While all the earlier cars have been restored to within an inch of their lives, the C3 cars are the ones you see driven on the road.

This book is an attempt to keep them on the road. Restored Corvettes are nice, but the ones you can drive are even better.

The Corvette is a car that never quite gets the respect it deserves. Yet, there is no other car quite like it in the world. Even my neighbors, who really don't like cars, have to come over to examine every new Corvette that pulls into the driveway. Corvettes do strange things to people. It seems that deep down everyone wants to spend at least one totally irresponsible afternoon in a Corvette.

Project Corvette actually started about ten years ago. I went to that great mecca of all Corvette sales in Carlisle. A green 1968 Corvette with a worn-out motor, a bad chassis, and three coats of paint came home with me. It was for the next book. At least that's what I told the family. The book never happened, and the green Corvette spent most of the next decade in a chicken shed in Bucks County, Pennsylvania.

Paul Zazzarine, of *Corvette Fever*, deserves a lot of the credit for getting Project Corvette out of the barnyard and into this book. When no one thought a C3 Corvette was worth rebuilding, he made the decision to feature Project Corvette in *Corvette Fever*. On a hot summer day in central Florida, Paul and I decided that people might be interested in rebuilding a 1968 Corvette.

The best decision we made on that hot sultry afternoon was to *not* restore the car. Instead we de-

Sure it looked a little different, but we all knew that under the skin it was still a 1968 Corvette. The emissions control lobby in Washington almost strangled the Corvette to death. Then, when they couldn't kill the Corvette with the emissions laws the safety czars took over. Even after that episode there was still a Corvette. Chevrolet continued to believe that if they built them people would come.

cided to focus on rebuilding the car for daily fun. If we thought modern technology would serve our purpose, we would use it. Project Corvette was going to be the car of our adolescent dreams.

Project Corvette was never going to be a slave to some judging manual. Very few people have ever dreamed of the day when they would haul their Corvette around in a trailer, being very careful not to get grass stains on the tires. Our Corvette dreams involved driving the car. These dreams involved doing things that bordered on being socially irresponsible. This was what Project Corvette was all about. Real men don't care about the stinking date codes on alternators.

The purpose of this book is to help you enjoy your Corvette, not restore it to within an inch of it's life. Enjoying Corvettes means driving them. If a fiberglass spring in the rear of the car means that I can go faster around the corner, then so much the better.

The only place where I drew the line was that Project Corvette had to at least look like a stock Corvette. The boy racer Corvettes with the big fender flares and the monster wings were totally out of the question. Cosmetic modifications not only do

nothing for the performance of the Corvette, but they generally make it very ugly.

While Duntov is widely praised for the engineering of the Corvette, we've totally neglected the design staff at General Motors. The looks of the Corvette have always sold as many cars as did the engineering. Dave Holls should get most of the credit for the looks of the Mako Shark-inspired Corvette.

I seriously doubt anyone in Warren, Michigan, expected the design to last for fifteen years. In fact it was the design that allowed the Corvette to carry on this long, even though the chassis design was actually getting old in 1968. It was how it looked that sold the car. It was the look that we remember.

That is why its foolish to add strange pieces of fiberglass to the body. *Corvette Fever* did a survey a couple of years ago and found that very few readers were interested in changing the looks of the Corvette they drove; however, they almost universally wanted more performance.

Project Corvette took the approach that more power is better. While the car should look stock, it would never be able to corner too well, nor have enough torque. This was how we created a small-block engine with the torque of a big block.

# Chapter 1

# Which Model is For You?

The dream won't be free; no dream is. The good part is that when you put your Corvette dream on the Richter scale of expense, the numbers aren't all that bad. The collapse of the Corvette market in the last decade has made it possible for more of us to own Corvettes.

The Corvettes built by Chevrolet between 1968 and 1982 are still the affordable Corvettes. These are also the cars you can have fun with. A 1970 Corvette can be acquired for less than the cost of putting your child in college for a year. Besides, the Corvette is more fun than paying for college.

The third-generation cars are not the mid-year Corvettes that the speculators drove into the price stratosphere several years ago. Neither are these the high-tech Corvettes that Chevrolet gave us in 1984. A quick look at the sales figures will remind us of one item—the third-generation Corvette is the car of the masses.

During the seventies, Chevrolet felt that average people should be able to own Corvettes. There was little interest in making the Corvette the exclusive car for the upwardly mobile yuppie. Chevrolet tried that marketing strategy in 1953, and it almost ended Corvette production.

The Corvettes built between 1968 and 1982 never required taking out a new mortgage on your home. The American sports car that Chevrolet built in the seventies were cars that average people could have fun with. And today, you can even play with the motors since a lot of the early cars were exempt from emissions testing. How's that for freedom?

There's always been therapeutic value in owning a car you can work on yourself. The latest model cars from around the world are for nothing but driving. All of us have opened the hood on our latest daily driver only to go back in the house to check out the warranty papers. Who even cares how quickly they accelerate? The thrill is gone.

With the older Corvettes there are only two things you'll need in order to have fun: time and courage. While I can't give you time, I can help you

The Stingray was back. The spelling was different, but after a year, Chevrolet decided to bring back the name everybody knew. Changes were limited to cleaning up all the mistakes made in 1968. The real question is did we really look like that in 1969?

It was 1972, the last year for the chrome bumper. A lot of people like these cars as they represent the end of an era. Everybody has a Corvette they refer to as the "last real Corvette." Don't let any of this influence your purchase decision. Just buy the one you believe is "the last real Corvette."

In 1970, the side vents, the grille, and the exhaust pipes were changed. There's so little difference between the 1969 to 1972 Corvettes you should only worry about condition. A good 1972 should always win out over a junk 1969. Indeed, junk Corvettes shouldn't even be considered as a possible purchase. Forget about what you think you can do for only a few thousand dollars. You're dreaming the wrong dream.

muster the courage to start working on your own Corvette.

It's worth looking at the production figures to see why the third-generation Corvettes are still so popular. Basically it comes down to one simple fact: Chevrolet built a lot of Corvettes in the seventies. The C3 Corvettes were built in the days when anyone with a steady job could buy a Corvette. It may have been a reach for the mechanic working in a gas station, but it could be done. Potential Corvette owners didn't need major-league incomes to qualify for a loan. Chevrolet gets all excited today when they sell 20,000 Corvettes a year. They forget there were years when they sold over 40,000 Corvettes a year on a regular basis. High-level technology may be wonderful, but Chevrolet sells a lot fewer cars these days. Following is a list of the number of Corvettes sold annually between 1968 and 1982:

| Year | Corvettes Sold |
| --- | --- |
| 1968 | 28,566 |
| 1969 | 38,762 |
| 1970 | 17,316 |
| 1971 | 21,801 |
| 1972 | 27,004 |
| 1973 | 30,464 |
| 1974 | 37,502 |
| 1975 | 38,465 |
| 1976 | 46,558 |
| 1977 | 49,213 |
| 1978 | 46,766 |
| 1979 | 53,807 |
| 1980 | 40,614 |
| 1981 | 40,606 |
| 1982 | 25,407 |
| TOTAL | 521,851 |

The current low prices on these Corvettes also point to one thing you really should consider. You're going to have to do most of the work on these Corvettes yourself since none of the cars can be properly restored without exceeding the value of the car. A basic fact of Corvette life is that the cost of a professional restoration is usually greater than the ultimate value of the car. You can either learn how to work on your own Corvette, or learn how to rob banks. Financial responsibility is a subject beyond the scope of this book; just remember that you're not working on your Corvette to make money.

The Corvettes built between 1968 and 1982 fall roughly into several categories. The Corvette went through a total transformation between 1968 and 1982. The amazing thing is that despite all the changes during those fourteen years, much about these Corvettes stayed the same.

The frame and the brake system changed so little that not many people can tell the difference between parts for the various years. If you've worked on a 1969 Corvette brake system, you can do the same things to a 1982 brake system.

This is all to our benefit since there are a lot of people in the world who can offer advice when you're working on your Corvette. Secondly, there are a lot of parts available for the seventies Corvette. Just take brake calipers for instance; Chevrolet produced over two million Corvette brake calipers.

Parts and expertise are not a problem with the C3 Corvettes. Whatever problems you might en-

## Corvette Judging and Clubs

### The NCRS

The National Corvette Restoration Society has done more for Corvette preservation than any other organization in the world. When the Corvette was just another cheap used sports car a few dedicated people not only decided that Corvettes should be restored but that they should be restored to a very specific standard.

The perfectly restored Corvette should be exactly the same as when it left the factory in St. Louis. When the NCRS says exactly they mean absolutely accurate—flaws and all. This group of enthusiasts firmly believes that Corvettes should not be restored to the standards that we might wish for, but rather the standards that were acceptable to General Motors during the seventies.

The best part here is that when you take your Corvette to an NCRS show you're never in competition with your friends. Everyone competes against "The Standard". It is entirely possible that everyone in the show can win a "Top Flight" award.

This manner of judging is now being copied by other clubs since it makes so much sense. Why should I restore a car only to be beaten by a person who's car is really no better than mine. All Corvettes should be judged against a finite standard.

The highest level Corvettes can then compete for the elusive "Duntov Award". In order to receive this award your Corvette must receive a "Top Flight" award at a succession of regional and national events. This award, named after the former chief engineer for the Corvette group, is the premier Corvette trophy in the country.

If you prize an authentic restoration, simply pay the money and purchase a car that's won a Duntov award. Restorations don't come any better than this. If you have any insecurities about your purchasing a Corvette then obtain a car that's won both a Duntov award as well as a "Bloomington Gold" award.

### Bloomington Gold

While the NCRS is a club, Bloomington Gold is a company that certifies Corvettes as being restored to original condition. The name comes from the fact they used to have a huge event at Bloomington, Illinois. A few years back this event was moved to the Illinois State Fairground in Springfield, Illinois.

A great many of the standards for being certified Bloomington Gold are the same as for the NCRS. After all, there is only one correct way to restore a part to original factory standards. Thus, a lot of the cars that win the Duntov award also make the trip to Illinois for Gold certification.

Ownership of "Bloomington Gold" changed several years ago, but the new owners seem to be following in the tradition set by the founders of the company. Having this company certify your Corvette is one excellent way to increase the car's value.

If you are buying a Corvette and have any doubts about your ability to judge quality then simply stick to the Bloomington Gold cars which have won the Duntov award from the NCRS. One magazine editor related as to how he only uses this type of car for magazine features. The main reason is that no one can question whether or not the car was properly restored.

### National Council Of Corvette Clubs (NCCC)

Compared to Porsches or Ferraris very few Corvettes ever reach the race track. Most of the attention surrounding Corvettes in the past few decades has gone towards restoration. While the Porsche Club of America sponsors hundreds of track events around the United States, the NCCC is the only Corvette club that provides opportunities for driving your Corvette. They don't have a lot of events but they are the only club in the country that will let you drive your Corvette at its full potential.

If you truly enjoy driving your Corvette then this is one group that you need to think seriously about joining. Especially since it's the only club around that encourages you to take your car on the race track and actually go fast in your Corvette.

---

counter, someone has confronted it before. Someone has solved all the same problems you're going to encounter.

The first decision you're going to have to make is to consider what kind of Corvette you want to drive. It may seem like splitting hairs, but there are a wide variety of used Corvettes available. There's everything from the outrageous big-block cars of the late sixties to the highway cruisers of the early eighties. Let's consider what each of these groups have to offer before rushing into any decision.

## 1968–72: The Chrome Bumper Era

The tires were too small, and the motors too big. These were the last of the hot-rod Corvettes, the final era of raw, unregulated power. Too bad we didn't know it at the time.

There are some very expensive cars in this group, as well as some very cheap ones. Not everyone likes these cars, but then again, do other people

The first soft bumper. The urethane technology was new, and Chevrolet had very little idea about what they were doing. The paint faded differently from the rest of the body, and the plastic warped. The alloy wheels on this press car were never really produced. After making four sets of wheels, Chevrolet gave up and pulled the option off the list.

Even though Chevrolet couldn't get the front bumper to look decent, they forged ahead and made the same urethane bumper for the rear. Chevrolet thought the optional wheels would finally be ready for production. Wrong. In 1974, not a single set of wheels was released to the general public.

really matter when you find that lonely country road in the fall?

The L88 Corvettes in this group are the King of the Hill. They have a type of raw power that will never be seen again. Forget about dual overhead cams and fuel management systems. We're talking great big cast-iron blocks with cylinder heads the size of your neighbor's Honda.

The L88s are the last of the really monstrous Corvettes. The raw unleashed power that Chevrolet created in the late sixties never quite returned. The latest Corvettes may be just as fast as the old big-block cars, but never as outlandish. After all, no one has ever terrorized their neighborhood with a 1994 LT-1, something an LS6 could do on a regular basis.

The base-engine Corvette is the least expensive car in this group. It's still capable of frightening people when you hit the accelerator. It's also capable of making some true Chevrolet sounds when you run the car up through the gears. These cars really define cheap thrills.

The large engines are the ones that provide excitement beyond the limit. This was the era when more power was better power. Such Corvettes were built for the thrill of it all. Gas was cheap, and foreign cars were a bunch of wimpy little four-cylinder cars from Europe.

The small-block cars will always be the best buy in this group of Corvettes. The 350ci engines will always be worth less than the big-block cars, but they can still provide more power than a truly responsible person can use on public highways.

Each era of Corvette reminds us of something special. The cars produced prior to 1973 remind us of a world when ozone was not a part of our basic vocabulary. The seventies Corvettes were not designed using Cray computer models and refined on the computer screen. In the future, Chevrolet would not be allowed to unleash racing cars for the street. The early C3 Corvettes were the end of the classic

By 1975 Chevrolet had finally given up on the aluminum wheels, and the big-block engines were gone. The mid-seventies were the low years for Corvette. The strongest available motor was rated at 205bhp. The Corvette had come a long way from the L88 days. The used Corvette market reflects this. Mid-seventies Corvettes are the least expensive Corvettes on the market.

Chevrolet finally made aluminum wheels that would hold air. In exchange Chevrolet gave the Corvette the steering wheel from the 1976 Vega. Then, as if to atone for the chintzy steering wheel, Chevrolet gave the L82 option an additional 5hp.

hot-rod era. It's just that none of us realized it at the time. These 1968–72 Corvettes take us back into that world of freedom and power.

### 1973–77: Middle Age

During this period the optional engines started to disappear. It was the end of the performance era, and it would take a decade for the power to return. The real problem here was that the power disap-

The 1977 Corvettes were really just more of the same. Actually, all of the 1973–77 Corvettes are nice cars. They just aren't performance cars. You can buy them at the right price and they offer everything except the performance that made the Corvette famous. Some people have described them as Chevrolet's answer to the Buick Riviera. Considering the traffic problems and the speed limits, these cars make more sense today than when they were manufactured.

peared, but the Corvette still wasn't a true touring car. In fact, Corvette's reputation began to get a little tarnished. The surprising part was that Chevrolet kept selling more Corvettes every year.

Today the Corvettes from the middle era are the cheapest Corvettes on the market. The problem is that the Corvettes that came before them had more power and the cars that followed them had more creature comforts. Yet, they're very easy cars to work on, and they still provide a Corvette driving experience. The 1973 to 1978 era can put you in a budget Corvette.

Here is one of the nicest Corvettes of the era. The Indy Pace Car Edition got all the publicity, but this Silver Anniversary Edition Corvette will probably be the most prized in the future. With the L82 engine, this is just a nice car. Buy the best example you can possibly afford and keep it well maintained.

The 1979 Corvette displayed very few changes. The pace car front spoiler was made an option for all the 1979 Corvettes. This car doesn't have it installed. When Chevrolet highlighted the dual-intake air filter, you just knew there wasn't much new on these cars. They're one of the best buys in the used Corvette market.

## 1978–79: More Changes

Pleasant is the only way to describe the 1978 and 1979 Corvettes. The only cars that even come close to having any horsepower are the L82 optioned cars. There are enough of these L82 Corvettes floating around out there to suggest you should confine your search to this car only.

One of the nicest cars in this group is the 1978 Pace Car, provided that you don't pay extra money for the car. These cars, which were supposed to be instant collector's items, were discounted long ago. There's nothing special about the Pace Car Editions, but they always attract just a little more attention than the average 1978 Corvette.

## 1980–82: The Final Glory

If a Corvette can ever be called refined, this era provided that type of Corvette. A lot of effort had gone into the Corvette by 1980. In fact, no one ever thought this body style would even be around by the early eighties, when everybody wanted a new Corvette but Chevrolet just couldn't produce it.

When Chevrolet couldn't produce the new Corvette on time, they had to give the customers a reason to buy the car they already had on the market. The answer was to make these models the smoothest and plushest Corvettes ever. Consequently, the 1980–82 models are some of the most comfortable Corvettes on the market.

Essentially, Chevrolet spent the final years refining the Corvette they already had, making the 1978 Corvette better. This is why you should seriously consider a Corvette from this era. You're not buying this Corvette for its outstanding performance;

that would arrive in 1984. Here, you're buying a Corvette for its looks and the fact that it's a high-speed touring car—even if it does lack luggage space.

The final years of the third-generation Corvette are just nice cars. Because they never had the performance of the early seventies cars they never fell into the hands of the boy racers, and what they lack in power they make up in smoothness. A 1982 Corvette with air conditioning is just a very nice car to own. This is confirmed by the fact that a good 1982 Corvette will cost you more than a 1984 or 1985 Corvette.

If you insist on having a special edition, the 1982 Commemorative Edition is possibly the best Corvette to own. There's really nothing special on these Corvettes except trim, but this special edition Corvette is just a little more interesting than the rest of the cars produced in 1982.

By now, the days of Corvette speculation are long over, and they probably won't return in our lifetime. Long gone are the days when people paid thousands of dollars for a trim package that was installed on just a few thousand cars. Besides, if you really want extra options on your Corvette, just add them. Very few people will ever know the difference.

The important thing in purchasing a Corvette is not to get carried away by individual years. There's not enough difference between a 1971 small-block coupe and a 1969 small-block coupe to fret over. The condition of the individual car is what you need to be most concerned about.

The first decision is to determine what sort of a Corvette you really want. Is your dream car a big block or a small block? Do you need a coupe or a roadster? Only after you answer these questions should you start to narrow the Corvette path.

## The Great Options Chase

Corvette options have become a joke. There's a group of people out there who have gone option crazy. A good example is the guy who proudly proclaimed an unrealistic value for his car because it was the first 1969 Corvette to have headrests installed. The sad part is that he actually thought this feature made his car valuable. He probably even kept it in a climate-controlled garage because of these "rare" headrests. People have to realize there are valuable options and options that have no relevance to anything in the real world.

Air conditioning is another good example of this principle. In 1968, less than twenty percent of all Corvettes had air conditioning. Ten years later, in 1979, almost ninety percent of the Corvettes left St. Louis with air conditioning installed.

The early C3 cars were performance cars. Air conditioning didn't matter. When the Corvette became a touring car, air conditioning was a whole lot more important. I really don't care if a 1969 roadster has air, but on the other hand, I wouldn't consider a 1982 without air conditioning.

Power windows are a option that is nice to have installed on any Corvette. Are they worth any extra money? This is the basic question you need to ask yourself when considering a highly optioned Corvette.

Actually there are two levels to this question. The first is whether this option will make driving a Corvette any more enjoyable. The second level is pure speculation. Will these options help you maintain your Corvette investment? In other words, will people pay you extra money for this option twenty years from today?

## Some Things You Should Start Considering

The most difficult thing is to walk away from a Corvette that's for sale. Your friend who purchased the perfect Corvette didn't just locate the perfect car—he or she walked away from some Corvettes that were very close to perfect. Knowing when to walk away from a car that you really like is difficult, but it's the most important aspect of getting the right Corvette.

It's not what you buy, it's what you turn down that makes you look brilliant. You'll run across a lot of cars that just need a few things to make them perfect. These few things can quickly add up to more than the original purchase price. This gap between "perfect" and "almost right" is going to cost you money, usually a lot of money.

Most of us have a certain Corvette imprinted into our brains. The psychologists have no idea how it got there, but it's there. You may want the same type of Corvette that used to cruise the local burger stands when you were in high school, or it may be the Corvette you saw in the dealer's showroom on that September day in 1974. Whatever Corvette is imprinted in your mind, it's the only one that you really want.

It's a lot like falling in love for the first time. We all overlooked the flaws and saw only what we wanted to see. That personal relationship cost us a lot of mental anguish. When you start overlooking flaws in your fantasy Corvette, that same sinking feeling will return, not to mention a declining bank balance.

When you start to rationalize about why a certain Corvette is a good buy, start walking away. This is not the car for you. There are a lot of Corvettes out there on the market. You should settle for no less than what you wanted in the very beginning.

If you can keep your emotions in check, you can purchase a very nice Corvette. Once you get emotionally involved with a car, you're in deep financial trouble.

A good rule for most of us is what I call the "Ten-Foot Rule." All Corvettes look good from fifty

The 1980 Corvette got a new front end and a new rear treatment. The 1980 Corvette couldn't meet the California emissions standards and for the first time a 305ci engine was offered in the Corvette. Just over 3,000 were made, and very few people make a big deal of owning one. Actually, it's just one more reason to check the serial numbers rather closely if you're buying a 1980 Corvette.

feet away. Very few of them look perfect when you get within three feet of the car. When you stand ten feet away from the average Corvette, however, you get a good appreciation for the general condition.

The end of the C3 Corvette came in 1982. The four-speed was gone, and there were no choices for the motor or transmission. The big news was that Chevrolet was trying out the new cross-fire injection system, offered only in 1982 and 1984. However, the cross-fire system is one good reason not to buy a 1982 car. Still, this car will always be worth more money than a 1984 fourth-generation Corvette. Other than the big-block Corvettes, the 1982 Corvette could be one of the most prized Corvettes in the next century.

With this rule, you can start to spot the bargains. The effort it takes to get a Corvette to look flawless from three feet away is considerable. You can expect to pay extra for all this effort.

If you want a Bloomington car, then go right ahead and check your bank balance. If you only want a Corvette for fun on the weekends, a "ten-foot" car is for you. The best part is that the ten-footer will cost less than half the price of a perfect car.

## What Is A Numbers-Matching Car Anyway?

The numbers-matching car is the great illusion. In 1960, Chevrolet decided to stamp the vehicle identification number (VIN) on Corvette engine blocks and transmissions. The purpose was to reduce the number of car thefts. We all know how well that idea worked. It was effective, however, in helping people determine whether the Corvette they were purchasing had the original motor installed.

The next step was deciphering the date codes on things like alternators and water pumps. This way a Corvette owner could easily determine which parts had been replaced. Even though these numbers may not match the VIN number, they should match the sequence of production. Basically, by using the codes an owner can tell when each and every part was made.

Matching numbers are still a key factor in Corv-ette values. This means that countless numbers of people have spent years assembling all the necessary bolt-on parts with the appropriate numbers. For most of us this numbers game gets a little ridiculous.

If you insist on purchasing a car with all the secret matching numbers, just keep in mind that these cars don't drive any better, or look any better, than a Corvette that has a non-original alternator. Every Corvette has had something replaced, at least once. If you're really serious about original condition, the 1972 Corvette with the original air in the tires should be the most valuable. Also, the most expensive.

You may think I've just made an absurd point. On the other hand, have you looked closely at some of the restored Corvettes on the market? There comes a time when you have to decide whether you're going to drive your Corvette or park it in the bedroom.

Restored Corvettes, whatever that overused term means, are now so common that the prices seem to get lower every year. The only Corvette that is guaranteed to increase in value is the original-condition, totally unrestored car. This will be the premier Corvette of the next century because anyone can restore a Corvette. Even numbers-matching cars are fairly easy if you have enough time and money. Money helps the most.

The original car cannot be recreated. There are only so many of them, and there will never be any more. These original Corvettes do have a serious problem, though. If you purchase one you are taking on a responsibility to preserve the car for future generations.

There's no shame in abusing a worn-out Corvette. If you damage a restored Corvette, there's nothing that money can't repair. Destroying an original car, however, is a serious problem. You've just damaged something that can never be replaced. On the other hand, look at how many people have destroyed original Corvettes simply to win various show awards. Just keep in mind that in order to restore a Corvette, you have to destroy every original item on the car.

*Chapter 2*

# Buying the Perfect Corvette

There are several ways to buy Corvettes. You can buy a certified prize winner, which is like buying a family dog with American Kennel Club papers. These Corvettes are complete with papers that authenticate their breeding. An NCRS Duntov or Bloomington Gold award winner, complete with all the special papers, is not going to be cheap. Plan on paying top dollar for these best-of-breed Corvettes.

Top-dog Corvettes are cars that numerous Corvette experts have carefully examined and declared to have the finest blood lines. In other words, someone else has already checked these cars over for you. Expect to pay for this extra service.

The one thing nobody has checked on these Duntov or Bloomington Corvettes, however, is whether or not they actually run well. These are

show cars, so nobody knows if they can really hunt. Several decades ago the Corvette world decided that appearance was more important than performance. Consequently, no one, except the National Council of Corv-ette Clubs, gives out awards for the high-speed operation of a Corvette.

It's entirely possible to purchase one of the top show winners in the United States only to find out that the car is terrible to drive. On the other hand, you can be absolutely certain that all the correct parts are attached to the car.

Even with this rather significant proviso you should seriously consider one of these Corvettes, especially if you have any doubt at all about your ability to select a good used Corvette. These Duntov cars also set the price standards for all Corvettes. Once

Remember Project Corvette from a few pages back? This is what it looked like after having spent ten years in a Bucks County barn. In ten years I managed to bring this Corvette's value down to about ten percent of what I paid for the car.

15

This type of project is designed to flatten your wallet and cause family stress. The owner of this abused Corvette wanted a totally unrealistic price for what was essentially a piece of junk. If you got this car for free, it would still cost more to repair than the car will ever be worth.

This sort of Corvette is a real problem. The owner has put a lot of money into the car, and all of the work is first class. The only problem is that once you make a personal statement like this, you'll find very few people who agree with your ideas. Corvette prices are a matter of supply and demand, and when few people want your personalized Corvette, the value of it goes way down. It doesn't matter how much money you may have invested in the car.

you know what one of these best-of-breed Corvettes will cost, you can calculate the rest of the Corvette market.

Even if you really don't want a certified top-quality Corvette, at least take the time to look at a couple of these cars. They can help you develop a price and quality standard. The thing you must absolutely keep in mind when you buy a Corvette is that there are a lot of them out there. So, there is no need to rush out and pay top dollar for any Corvette.

Just look for instance at the famous L88 big-block option. In 1968 and 1969 there were almost 200 cars produced. Consequently, at least a dozen L88s are for sale at any given time. If you pass up on purchasing one, it's no big deal, as another one will be for sale next week. Don't let yourself fall in love with that cute little puppy in the window. Make sure you're purchasing the best example of the breed before you take it home.

## The Basket Case Blues

Bringing a Corvette home in boxes is either the smartest thing you'll ever do in this decade, or the dumbest. However, the problem will be that you won't know until the project is almost completed.

The origin of Project Corvette was just such a project. Project Corvette was a venture that went completely out of control. The car was torn apart and then no one had the time or money to put it back together. After several years of sitting in a Bucks County barn, it was finally time for someone to resurrect the car. The constant question I went to sleep with every night was "Am I really this dumb?" I kept remembering something about fools rushing in where angels won't even open the door.

The only reason I even considered this 1968 Corvette basket case was that it was a numbers-

matching car with most of the components still around. Notice I said *most* of the components. It was well into this project before I actually found out what hadn't come with the car. Basket-case Corvettes are like icebergs—only ten percent of the problems are visible from the surface.

For instance, Project Corvette came complete with five rally wheels. But four of them were from a different-year Corvette, and 1968 was the only year that Chevrolet used a 15X7 wheel on the Corvette. Only the spare was NCRS-correct on Project Corvette. All the other wheels were 15X8, obviously from some unknown donor car.

If Project Corvette were going to be an NCRS car, I would have had to locate the correct wheels. Instead I opted for a set of American Racing Equipment Torque Thrust D alloy wheels. The classic sixties won out over the classic factory look.

This is simply one of the decisions that will have to be made when it comes to your Corvette. Sometimes it's easier to build an NCRS Duntov car for which no decisions need to be confronted—just make the car like it came off the assembly line.

## Buy The Best One You Can Afford

The cheapest used Corvette you can buy is generally the one with the highest original purchase price. The most expensive Corvette will almost always be the one with the lowest initial purchase price. Remember, the reason you got that lump of fiberglass so cheaply at Carlisle was that nobody else wanted it.

People with more knowledge, and usually a lot more money, decided that the broken car with the

The prices on the 1978 Indy Pace Cars are low enough that you have to give them some serious consideration. They're unique Corvettes. They work exactly the same as any of the others, but the uncommon paint and trim add that little extra touch. If you're considering a late-seventies Corvette you have to give the Indy Pace Car some serious thought.

This is one of the few bona fide, big-buck Corvettes. They just don't get any rarer than the ZL1. If you want one of these cars, plan on spending a lot of time, and a lot of money. Only two of these cars exist.

missing motor just couldn't be rebuilt within their budget. These are the smart people. Project Corvette is for the rest of us.

The best way to arrive at what a Corvette should cost is to find out what the really great cars are selling for. Take the current price of a Bloomington Gold or NCRS Duntov Corvette as the standard. Then take the Corvette you're considering and figure out how much money it's going to take to turn this frog into a Bloomington Gold car.

The value of the lesser car is determined by what the finest Corvettes are selling for. Here is the magic formula:

The Best Corvette = Beater Corvette + Labor + Parts

If the right side of the formula is greater than the left side, you're in trouble. Restoring a beater Corvette is often more expensive than simply purchasing a Bloomington Gold car in the first place.

When Corvette prices took a dive down to the basement, the price difference between the NCRS Duntov cars and the good street cars got much smaller. Today, the price difference between junk and quality is smaller than ever before in Corvette history, so there is no reason to buy junk. On the other hand, look at what I dragged home. Perhaps taking my advice is like getting diet advice from an overweight doctor.

## Does This Corvette Really Work?

One of the handiest ways to check the operation of a Corvette is the National Corvette Restorers Society verification form. When a car is certified for the highest NCRS award, the Duntov award, it must perform a road test. All of the original equipment

must be operational. This is truly one of the toughest operational tests that exists for a Corvette.

The beauty of this test is that it takes all the emotion out of the process. It's best to be emotionless before you start handing over cash in the middle of someone's garage; it's too easy to fall in love with a Corvette. Especially a bad one. The next few pages contain a modified NCRS verification test. Copy these pages and take them with you when you go for a Corvette road test. Also, never say anything good about the Corvette you're road-testing. Remember, you're trying to set the stage for some serious price haggling.

I suggest a three-part strategy for evaluating your future Corvette. The first part is evaluating the car before you even road-test the car. The second part is the actual road test. Since almost every Corvette is fun to drive, this a very dangerous test. You have to refrain from falling in love with Corvette performance. More than one person has bought a bad car because the sound of Chevrolet power caused them to lose control of their senses. It's like going on a first date and being so overwhelmed that you propose marriage.

Though you're probably very careful about your marriage proposals, it's easy to lose control when it comes to Corvettes. Remember, this whole Corvette deal is supposed to be about a long-term relationship. In fact, a lot of Corvette owners have found the car to last longer than their marriages.

The third part of the test is to double-check the exterior. This can also give you time to calm down after the test drive.

All these checklists have one other very important feature. They may help convince the current owner that he's mistaken about the true value of his Corvette, and he may realize that the prize car he described in the ad is actually in bad shape and that your offer is probably the best he'll ever receive.

The 1982 Collector Edition Corvette is one of my all-time favorites. If I ever get too old for side pipes and four speeds, this is the car I would own. There are a lot of near-perfect ones on the market every year. I'd buy the nicest one of the bunch and then spend the next ten years making everything absolutely perfect. The best part would be weekend trips to escape all the nonsense at work.

On the other hand, he may think you're totally crazy and throw you out of his garage. Remember, your goal is to pay as little as possible for this Corvette. The current owner, on the other hand, is trying desperately to get more money than the car is worth. These two strategies are in direct conflict, which is one reason you can seldom buy a car from a friend and remain friends after the sale.

The checklists are not only an attempt to ascertain the condition of a Corvette, they are also an attempt to intimidate the current owner into thinking you actually know what you're doing. Hopefully, by using the lists you can hide the fact that you have just met the Corvette of your dreams and are prepared to pay even more money than the owner is asking.

## Corvette Buyer's Checklist
### Before You Drive
Radio Volume and Controls (clear, no static) . . . . . P F
Radio AM-FM Selector Function . . . . . . . . . . . . . . P F
Radio Manual Tune & Push Button Tune . . . . . . . . P F
Stereo Reception Indicator Light. . . . . . . . . . . . . . P F
Speaker Control Balance (must play in stereo) . . . . P F
Heater Fan Speeds (3-speed w/o AC, 4-speed with A/C) . . . . . . . . . . . . . . . . . . . . . . . . . . . . . . . . . P F
Heater/AC Temperature Control (blows cool, hot). P F
Air/De-ice Control (non-AC; air blows to windshield). . P F
Air Conditioning (blows cold in norm, bi-level, and max) . . . . . . . . . . . . . . . . . . . . . . . . . . . . . . . . . P F
Seat Lap Belt Adjustment . . . . . . . . . . . . . . . . . . . P F
Shoulder Belts . . . . . . . . . . . . . . . . . . . . . . . . . . . P F

### Ten-Mile Road Test
Reset Tripmeter to 0000

Odometer Operation Begin_____ End_____ P F
Acceleration (no misfires or stumbles when secondaries open) . . . . . . . . . . . . . . . . . . . . . . . . . . . . . P F
Deceleration (no backfires) . . . . . . . . . . . . . . . . . . P F
Cruise Control Operation . . . . . . . . . . . . . . . . . . . . P F
Speedometer (no needle bounce) . . . . . . . . . . . . . P F
Tachometer (check for noise or needle bounce) . . P F
Oil Pressure (30–40lb is normal). . . . . . . . . . . . . . . P F
Coolant Temperature (160–230° F normal; 250° F max) . . . . . . . . . . . . . . . . . . . . . . . . . . . . . . . . . P F
Battery/Ammeter or Voltmeter. . . . . . . . . . . . . . . . P F
Fuel Gauge . . . . . . . . . . . . . . . . . . . . . . . . . . . . . . P F
Directional Turn Signal Cancel (left and right) . . . . P F
Directional Signal "Lane Change" Function . . . . . . P F
Sun Visors (must move freely but stay in place during drive). . . . . . . . . . . . . . . . . . . . . . . . . . . . . . . . . P F
Vents (Non-AC—check cable operation and vents) P F

### Manual Transmission
Excessive Noise. . . . . . . . . . . . . . . . . . . . . . . . . . . P F
Gear Engagement (no grinding) . . . . . . . . . . . . . . P F
Upshift and Downshift (must be smooth) . . . . . . . P F
Clutch Slippage (no slippage). . . . . . . . . . . . . . . . . P F
Clutch Pedal Adjustment (check for freeplay). . . . . P F
Acceleration and Deceleration (no popping out of 2nd or 3rd gears) . . . . . . . . . . . . . . . . . . . . . . . . . P F
Reverse Gear . . . . . . . . . . . . . . . . . . . . . . . . . . . . . P F

### Automatic Transmission
Shift Lever Detent Button . . . . . . . . . . . . . . . . . . . P F
Gear Engagement. . . . . . . . . . . . . . . . . . . . . . . . . . P F
Smooth Shifts . . . . . . . . . . . . . . . . . . . . . . . . . . . . P F
Manual Shifts . . . . . . . . . . . . . . . . . . . . . . . . . . . . . P F
Throttle Acceleration Kickdown . . . . . . . . . . . . . . . P F
Reverse . . . . . . . . . . . . . . . . . . . . . . . . . . . . . . . . . P F

## Rear Axle

Check for Axle and Wheel Bearing Noise . . . . . . . . P F
Check for Driveshaft Vibration . . . . . . . . . . . . . . P F
Check for Positraction Chatter (going around corners)
P F

## Brakes

Check for Squeal or Pedal Pulsation . . . . . . . . . . P F
Check for Pull to Left or Right. . . . . . . . . . . . . . . P F
Check for Low Pedal. . . . . . . . . . . . . . . . . . . . . P F
Check for Pedal Drop (hold foot on pedal firmly at
stop) . . . . . . . . . . . . . . . . . . . . . . . . . . . . . . P F
Check Power Booster (three pumps after car is turned
off) . . . . . . . . . . . . . . . . . . . . . . . . . . . . . . . P F

## Steering & Handling

Steering Wheel Centered . . . . . . . . . . . . . . . . . P F
Check for Steering Wander. . . . . . . . . . . . . . . . . P F
Check for Free Play in Steering Wheel . . . . . . . . P F
Check for Wheel Balance (vibration at about 55mph)
. . . . . . . . . . . . . . . . . . . . . . . . . . . . . . . . . P F

## General Performance

Check for Excessive Rattles . . . . . . . . . . . . . . . . P F
Check for General Tightness of Vehicle
(shakes and rattles over bumps) . . . . . . . . . . . . P F
Check for Drafts Around Windows and Top Seals . P F

## After The Road Test

Check for Automatic Transmission Parking Detent. P F
Check Automatic Driveline Clunk (shift from D to R,
checking for noise) . . . . . . . . . . . . . . . . . . . . . P F
Parking Brake Operation. . . . . . . . . . . . . . . . . . P F
Power Steering (check for squeals while turning). . P F

## Check Outside The Car

Check Engine Oil . . . . . . . . . . . . . . . . . . . . . . . P F
Check Power Steering Fluid . . . . . . . . . . . . . . . . P F
Check Brake Master Cylinder for Leaks . . . . . . . . P F
Check All Four Calipers for Leaks . . . . . . . . . . . . P F
Check Power Steering Lines for Leaks. . . . . . . . . . P F
Check Rear Axle Leaks (pinion seal and axles seals) P F
Check for Transmission Leaks . . . . . . . . . . . . . . . P F

## Condition Of Paint

Scratches and Stone Chips . . . . . . . . . . . . . . . . . P F
Check for Paint on Door Gaskets (indicates repaint)
. . . . . . . . . . . . . . . . . . . . . . . . . . . . . . . . . P F
Condition of Emblems and Trim. . . . . . . . . . . . . P F
Orange Peel . . . . . . . . . . . . . . . . . . . . . . . . . . P F

## Interior

Clock (works) . . . . . . . . . . . . . . . . . . . . . . . . . P F
Seat Track Adjustment . . . . . . . . . . . . . . . . . . . P F
Seat Back Tilting Mechanism . . . . . . . . . . . . . . . P F
Storage/Battery Compartment Doors (three). . . . . P F
Key for Locking Storage Area (oval key) . . . . . . . P F

Side Window Operation . . . . . . . . . . . . . . . . . . . P F
Inside Door Locks . . . . . . . . . . . . . . . . . . . . . . . P F
Cigarette Lighter. . . . . . . . . . . . . . . . . . . . . . . . P F
Condition of Seat Material . . . . . . . . . . . . . . . . . P F
Door Panels. . . . . . . . . . . . . . . . . . . . . . . . . . . P F
Carpeting . . . . . . . . . . . . . . . . . . . . . . . . . . . . P F

## Tires and Wheels

Size . . . . . . . . . . . . . . . . . . . . . . . . . . . . . . . . P F
Wear Patterns . . . . . . . . . . . . . . . . . . . . . . . . . P F
Condition . . . . . . . . . . . . . . . . . . . . . . . . . . . . P F
Stock or Aftermarket . . . . . . . . . . . . . . . . . . . . . P F

## Check For Rust

Frame Rails (Trailing Arm Pocket) . . . . . . . . . . . . P F

## Do The Lights Work?

Headlight Door Operation . . . . . . . . . . . . . . . . . P F
Headlights. . . . . . . . . . . . . . . . . . . . . . . . . . . . P F
Parking Lights . . . . . . . . . . . . . . . . . . . . . . . . . P F
Front Turn Signal . . . . . . . . . . . . . . . . . . . . . . . P F
Rear Turn Signals . . . . . . . . . . . . . . . . . . . . . . . P F
Brake Lights. . . . . . . . . . . . . . . . . . . . . . . . . . . P F
Back-Up Lights . . . . . . . . . . . . . . . . . . . . . . . . . P F

Serial Numbers (match VIN on body)
Engine. . . . . . . . . . . . . . . . . . . . . . . . . . . . . . . P F

Take a few minutes when you return from your road test and complete the exterior checks to make sure you've reviewed all the items on your list.

If you had problems on the road test, simply thank the owner and go look for the next candidate. You seldom marry the date who spoiled your expensive dinner. Why be any less discriminating about your Corvette relationship?

Don't waste time looking at sub-standard Corvettes. Don't even think about making some spectacular deal that will propel this Corvette into a good purchase. Remember, there are a lot of Corvettes for sale. Every Corvette owner knows what his car is worth, and is trying to get more than the value of the car. Whether or not he or she is successful can depend on you.

After you've completed your checklist, review your inventory and make a judgment about the amount of money you should offer for the car. Remember, you always work backwards when you figure price. How much money will it take to turn this car into a winner?

Estimate what it will cost to make the car you just road-tested into a Duntov winner. Subtract the estimated amount from the price of a certified Duntov winner and you've just figured out what to offer for your road-tested wonder.

Your Offer =
(NCRS Duntov Car Cost) - (NCRS-quality restoration cost)

I'm a sucker for old race cars. An SCCA Corvette, such as this car, was never seriously raced, which means it can be purchased for a reasonable price and can be a lot fun. However, some of the vintage racing groups are very fussy about which Corvettes are allowed to join in the fun, so be careful you don't purchase a vintage race car that you won't be allowed to race.

This is the all important trim plate. This number tells you colors and styles of the original interior trim and exterior paint. Some people put a great deal of stock in these codes and will pay extra money for Corvettes painted the original color. Matching numbers are important, but the condition of the car is equally important.

Don't worry about insulting the owner. After all it's your money he's trying to get. Also, remember that you'll pass up a lot of Corvettes with this strategy. The good part is that you won't be spending any more money than necessary, and unless you're dealing with a Gran Sport, there are a lot of Corvettes out there. The key is to not to fall in love with an unworthy suitor.

If you don't buy a Corvette this week, there will be several dozen more on the market next week. Corvettes are really not all that rare. More than a million of the cars have been built. Between 1968 and 1982, more than a half million drove off the assembly line. Just keep repeating the mantra: "Condition—Condition—Condition," and then keep telling yourself that the Corvette with the lowest purchase price will easily be the most expensive one in the long term.

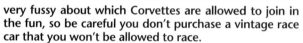

CHEVROLET C2

TRIM 408                                        974 PAINT

GENERAL MOTORS CORPORATION
CERTIFIES TO THE DEALER THAT
THIS VEHICLE CONFIRMS TO ALL FEDERAL
MOTOR VEHICLE SAFETY STANDARDS
APPLICABLE AT TIME OF MANUFACTURE

## Body And Trim Plate

The body and trim plate is stamped with the trim paint and time-built codes. This plate is attached to the left-hand door pillar.

### Example

C.............Month Built (October)
2 .............Day Built (2nd)
408.........Trim
974.........Paint

### Month

August ..................A
September ............B
October ...............C
November............D
December ............E
January.................F
February...............G
March ..................H
April ......................I
May.......................J
June.......................K
July .......................L

PAINT CODE is the key to the exterior paint. A complete listing is in the appendix.

TRIM CODE is the key to the interior color and material. A complete listing is found in the appendix.

Be careful of a Pace Car with paint chips. Painting a two-tone car can be even more expensive than a normal Corvette.

One thing you shouldn't get overly concerned about are the details of fit and finish. There is no such thing as an eighties Corvette in which all the panels fit properly. They came from the factory with the parts barely attached. Only in the nineties did GM realize they had to properly screw the car together if people were going to buy them.

It would be a terrible thing to take apart a Corvette like this one. Make the necessary repairs to the car and then drive it. Taking a Corvette off the highway should really be some sort of misdemeanor. This is especially the case with this particular Corvette, since it took me ten years to get it back in this condition.

# Chapter 3

# Evaluating Your New Car

The first rule of Corvette ownership is: "Don't take anything apart." Resist all temptation. It's easy to take your Corvette apart. I know, I've done it. I've also found that it's very difficult to put things back together. The best approach is to not do anything but routine maintenance for the first six months you own your Corvette. Then, and only then, should you take things apart—with a written plan.

I've tried to rebuild cars with a random approach. While this approach may work in financial markets, it certainly won't work in putting cars back together. The least frustrating and least expensive way to own a Corvette is to develop a plan of attack.

There are two things that limit most of our Corvette fantasies. First, most of us have a limited amount of money. Second, even if you have more money than you can ever spend in your lifetime, you'll still have a limited amount of time. Time and money are similar to the laws of nature when it comes to rebuilding Corvettes; violate them at your own risk.

Before you even start attacking your prize Corvette, you must develop a plan for how much time you plan on allocating for this project. When working on cars as a hobby, "next week" can easily turn into "a year from now," and the job you intended to do "someday" rapidly becomes "never." Call it the restoration time warp. You've just passed through real time and have entered restoration time. It's the time that never seems to end. Hour-long jobs become days of toil, monthly deadlines become annual events, and the Corvette eventually becomes "That Car." The only thing missing is Rod Sterling and strange music.

I'm always amazed at people who can set a goal and meet it exactly on schedule. I wonder if these people do normal things like eat and work? Do they have a life outside of their Corvette?

I suggest you set a realistic goal. Remember, this is still a hobby for most of us, which means the fun of it is that we don't have to have exact deadlines, just approximate ones. Make sure you make this clear to your spouse when you take over the family garage. It could save you from marital counseling.

The one item that will probably set the time schedule for a Corvette project is the financial picture. If you think working on Corvettes can be done cheaply, then start gathering some books on gardening. Before you have the chassis rebuilt, your credit card bill will approach the national debt, and your children will start complaining about their lack of designer sneakers. This is when the phrase "That Stupid Car" becomes a part of the family mantra.

The reason you see so many Corvettes advertised as "Ninety percent complete—forced to sell—no reasonable offer refused" is that the budget to rebuild the car went completely out of control. Those people spent so much time and money on the Corvette that they ran out of both, and it became time to write "The Ad."

There's an old rule of thumb as to how long a project car, or restoration, will take you to complete. First, carefully list all the jobs that have to be carried out. Then assign a time to each job. Next, carefully

Check the air filter. A dirty air filter can cause your Corvette to run rich. If your Corvette runs exceptionally rich, you could damage the catalytic converter. Air filters are so cheap that there's no reason to have a dirty one in your car. Some Corvette owners keep original AC-Delco filter locked away for show use only and use the Fram model between shows.

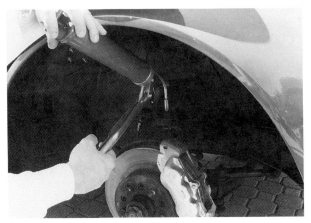

Grease all the fittings at least twice a year. Contrary to popular belief, you don't have to put so much grease into the fittings that it runs all over your front suspension. As soon as you see or feel the rubber boot begin to swell, stop. You've put in plenty of grease. It's better to grease your Corvette more often than to use too much grease in one application.

When you hold your hands at three o'clock and nine o'clock you're checking for steering play. If you find excess movement, you'll need an assistant to crawl under the car with a light to see where all the play is coming from. Just make sure you put a jackstand under the car before anybody crawls under there. More than one person has been killed when the car slipped off the jack.

add up all the individual time assignments. Having arrived at a total, double it. This might be close, though generally you'll still be well under the actual time you'll spend working on the car.

When it comes to calculating costs, you should do the same thing. Take the list of jobs that have to be done to your Corvette and sit down with your catalog collection. After double-checking the price of each needed component, multiply the number by four. Your Corvette project will probably end up costing you slightly more. Sometimes a lot more.

Once you've got the car home, having ignored everything in the previous chapter, you can actually begin to find out if the family savings were wisely spent. No matter how carefully you check out a car, it will take you at least a month before you find all the problems. During this time you must repeat the following statement every morning and twice on the weekends.

DO NOT REMOVE ANY PARTS OR REPLACE ANYTHING FOR THE FIRST FIVE HUNDRED MILES OF OWNERSHIP.

Starting to fix up your Corvette as soon as you get it home is a bad way to begin your Corvette relationship. A basic fact of life is that the first few problems you notice are not the most serious problems with the car. A corollary to this rule is that the first $35.95 you spend on your new Corvette will only make the serious problems more obvious.

## Paint and Chrome

The first month of ownership you should only deal with the very basic problems, like cleaning the

car and changing the oil. While doing this, have a clipboard handy so you can make a list of everything you need to fix. By keeping this list you'll feel that you're actually doing something, without spending a lot of time and money.

Paint may not be the most important area on your Corvette, but it sure makes a difference in your attitude. If the previous owner had any sense he would have had the car detailed before he sold it to you. Then, he could have gotten more money for it. But, chances are he didn't do that, which is not to suggest you paid any less than the car was really worth. You probably paid too much anyway.

This means you need to spend some time detailing, which is a handy way to postpone the inevitable, more expensive procedures. There are two nice things about detailing your Corvette. First, the car will look better when you're done. Secondly, you're going to find every little flaw and cosmetic problem that exists with your new prize.

This is the purpose of having the clipboard in your garage. List all the items you want to put further effort into in the days to come. I'm sure that you have a "TO DO" list at work. Now you have your own personal Corvette to do list.

## Stopping Power

Once you get through polishing your Corvette, you'll need to turn your attention to the brakes. First, you'll place your new Corvette on jack stands and remove all four wheels in order to look at the brakes. Besides the brakes, you'll want to examine a variety of items. The following checklist should help you.

## Brake System Checklist

| BRAKE PAD THICKNESS: | LF_____ | RF_____ |
|---|---|---|
| (Lowest Pad) | LR_____ | RR_____ |
| | | |
| ROTOR THICKNESS: | LF_____ | RF_____ |
| | LR_____ | RR_____ |

BRAKE HOSES:
MASTER CYLINDER:
PARKING BRAKE OPERATION:

### Caliper Leaks

All Corvettes made between 1969 and 1982 have, or had, leaking brake calipers. If your calipers are dry, then your calipers have already been replaced. Leaks are indicated by those dark spots you see on the calipers. Remember, we're not talking about drips, just slow leaks, the kind that make your calipers look very dark, and very dirty.

In some cases you'll actually find a set of brake pads soaked with brake fluid. This is cause for major concern and means you can start adjusting the family budget for a new set of brake calipers.

### Brake Rotor Condition

You should look for scoring and deep gouges on brake rotors and on the backside and the outside edge of the rotor. For some mysterious reason the worst problems always seem to be on the rear side of the rotor, the side you never checked before you purchased the car.

Another important point here is to check the

After jacking your Corvette up in the air, rock the front wheels to check for play. Hold your hands at twelve o'-clock and six o'clock and check for bearing play. Excess movement means you should tighten the front wheel bearings. If the car has a lot of miles, bearing play could also mean you should think about cleaning the wheel bearings and packing them with new grease.

overall thickness of the rotors. Chevrolet has stated that any rotor that measures below 1.215in should be thrown away. Remember at this point you're not going to get involved in a total brake project. All you're doing is attempting to figure out when you're going to have to perform the inevitable task of a complete brake system overhaul.

Replace the fuel filter once a year. The new reformulated gasolines contain so much alcohol that twenty-five years of varnish and crud are being set free every time you drive your Corvette. The new emissions gasoline will keep your fuel system nice and clean, but it will also clog your fuel filter. Just be certain there are no gas leaks after you change the filter.

Chevrolet wants you to tighten the wheel bearings to 12ft-lb, while rotating the wheel. Then back the nut off to the next hole which will allow for the installation of a new cotter pin. If you want to get very precise, you can use a dial indicator to check for end play, which should be between .001in and .005in.

## Brake Hoses

The four rubber hoses should be checked for cracks and splits. Once again, you're just trying to establish a baseline for future repairs. The key point here is that if you find cracks in the hydraulic hoses, plan on replacing them in the very near future.

Now that you have developed some knowledge about the stopping power of your Corvette, you need to focus some attention on how it drives down the road. At this point, though, you needn't be concerned about the power and handling finesse of the car. Instead, only pay attention to those items that will let you return from any journey upon which you embark. Coming home on the back of a flatbed truck does not count as a successful Corvette journey.

## Belts and Hoses

Belts and hoses have a finite life span. You need to look for cracks and tears in the belts, and feel for soft spots on the hoses.

No amount of Amor-All will restore worn-out heater and radiator hoses. You can polish those hoses to within an inch of their existence and they'll still rot out. The point is that all hoses deteriorate from the inside out. Only by checking and replacing them on a regular basis can you drive down the road with confidence.

## The Cooling System

People just love to ignore the cooling system. Until the steam comes out from under the hood, and the temperature gauge pegs the needle, nobody gives the cooling system a thought. Most Corvette owners worry more about the correct hose clamps

This was a little surprise I found in a big-block 1971 Corvette. The front springs had sagged to the point where the front of the car was dragging. The cheap fix, and the wrong fix, was using these spring spacers. These are so dangerous that most states have made spring spacers illegal. Imagine going around a corner and having the spacer drop out. Life would get very exciting, real fast.

than the muck inside the cooling system. The worst part of this neglect is that the condition of the cooling system can actually affect computer inputs, and drivability, on the eighties Corvettes.

You can save yourself a lot of headlight trouble if you simply lubricate the plastic slides every now and again. Vacuum-operated headlights are something Corvette owners have to live with. We might as well make it a little easier for the vacuum actuators to do their job.

While you're assessing your new possession, examine the sway bar bushings. The ones here are in fairly good shape. If your bushings are torn or cracked, replace them. Replacing the bushings is one job within everyone's mechanical ability.

The best approach is to assume that the last two owners did nothing. You can't go wrong with the pessimistic approach. The first step to cooling system recovery is to simply pour some dish cleaning soap into the cooling system and then drive the car for a couple of weeks.

Rather than use all the fancy cooling system cleansers, which really do nothing but eat holes in your radiator, use soap and hot water to clean the cooling system. You provide the soap, and the Bow-Tie motor provides the heat. This approach also gives you an excuse to drive your Corvette more often.

After a couple of weeks, put the car in the driveway and drain the old dirty coolant into a big pan. The first step is to remove the lower radiator hose and let all the gunk and filth run into the pan. After all the really nasty antifreeze is out of the system, rinse it with fresh clean water. Remove the upper radiator hose and keep running water into the radiator until clean water comes out of the lower hose. I've seen systems where this can take the better part of an hour.

If your cooling system is filled with mega-crud, simply fill it back up with plain water and add some more detergent. Drive the car another week and drain it the next weekend. You can keep doing this every weekend until you get clean water. At that point, add new antifreeze and you're all set.

### Engine Cleaning

The best way to clean your engine is to use an alloy wheel cleaner. These cleaners are not as harsh

When you pull the wheels off your Corvette, always look for dark spots on the calipers. These stains are caused by leaking brake fluid. If you have a caliper in this condition, you should replace it as soon as possible.

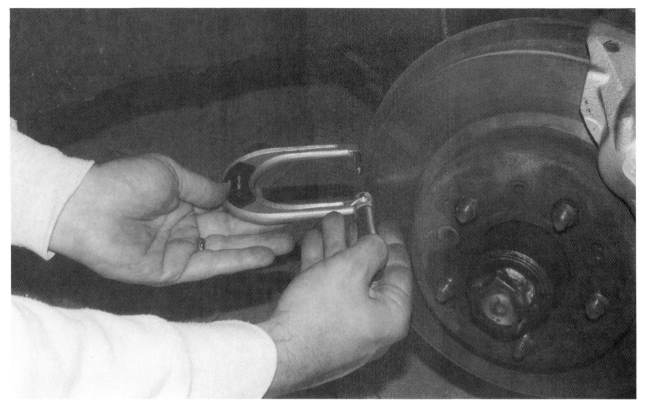

Measure the rotors with either a micrometer or a rotor thickness gauge. The micrometer is a little more accurate but a lot more expensive. If your brake rotor measures below 1.25in, it must be replaced.

as the engine cleaning solutions and do just as good a job. Remember, at this point you're not detailing the engine, you're just removing the oil film.

The whole purpose of this initial cleaning is to ascertain where the oil leaks begin. If you own a Chevrolet engine that doesn't leak oil you're very lucky. Most of the leaking oil will be dripping out of the valve cover gaskets, but you'll also probably find a couple other minor leaks.

### Valve Cover Gaskets

The valve cover gaskets will probably have to be replaced. In 1955, Chevrolet decided that four bolts were all that were necessary to hold down a valve cover. For the next three decades, all of them leaked. If yours is a 1968 or 1969 Corvette small-block, this is no major task. If you own a 1982, be prepared to spend some serious time on this job. For that model, Chevrolet seems to have placed every available part just above the valve covers.

### Fuel Filter

Fuel filters are typically neglected. You generally don't see them, so why should you change them? More importantly, you have no idea when the last owner changed the fuel filter. This means you should do it at the first opportunity.

One point to be very careful about is gas leakage. More than one person has burned their car to the ground after having changed the fuel filter. What happens is that the new filter develops a leak. In a relatively short time this leaking gasoline results in a

A warped brake rotor will cause the brake pedal to push back at you. A dial indicator can tell you how bad the situation really is. Any variation beyond .005 is a good reason to replace the brake rotor. Sometimes, warpage can be removed by machining the rotor. Often, the only solution is to replace the rotor.

It's always a good idea to check the engine's compression before you spend a lot of money on ignition parts and carburetors. You should be concerned about a variation between cylinders rather than an absolute number. A variation greater than ten percent can be caused by burned valves and blown head gaskets. No amount of tuning will fix a motor with a compression problem.

If you have a miss, and the compression is good, check for bad wiring. Use a volt-ohm meter to check the condition of the spark plug wires. You're looking for a wire with excessively high resistance.

fire, which can leave a lot of melted fiberglass in the middle of your driveway.

After you install a new filter, run the car in your driveway for about five minutes and carefully check for leaks. If gas starts running out of the fuel filter/line shut the car off and start over again. This simple procedure could save you from a lot of paperwork with your insurance company.

## Oil Change

This is real easy. You've done this a number of times in your life without drastic results, and this time should be no different. Any of the major brand oils work just fine for this purpose, as well as any major brand oil filter.

The one basic fact that most Corvette owners refuse to recognize is that no one has ever blown up a Chevrolet motor because of the brand of oil they used in the motor. People have destroyed motors because they let the oil level get too low; motors have

expired because the oil was too dirty; and bearings have been destroyed from detonation, but no one ever lost a motor because they believed the wrong oil advertisement. Just use a quality-brand oil and leave the advertising myths to Madison Avenue.

However, the one oil you needn't consider is the latest synthetic oil. First, your 1968 to 1982 Corvette simply doesn't need this type of oil. Secondly, the old engine gaskets aren't compatible with synthetic oil, which can also produce some major oil leaks on your garage floor.

The main idea behind all this maintenance work is for you to learn about your Corvette. Over the first year you own your Corvette you should only work on one item at a time. You bought the car to drive, not to frustrate your life.

You have to develop a relationship with your Corvette. You'll need time to locate the problem areas and time to figure out where your money can be best invested. In short, you should do exactly the opposite of what we did with Project Corvette.

# Chapter 4

# Tools and Plans

You're going to need some tools to rebuild on your Corvette. Not just wimpy little wrenches but real tools. Tools that make noise and create dirt. Big powerful tools. Men's tools.

The first item is a solvent tank. Okay, so it doesn't make noise, and the new solvents don't really smell, but a good solvent tank is still necessary. You're going to be removing over twenty years of grease and dirt from the old parts. When we were growing up and the Beach Boys were young, we would wash parts in gasoline and then throw all the dirty gasoline down the sewer.

This is no longer socially responsible, not to mention unwarranted. You can get a good quality parts washer tank for about $200 at your local parts store. The solvent can be recycled, so everybody's happy. The best part is that this new technology actually does a better job of cleaning your parts than the old gasoline trick.

The next item you want to consider purchasing is a small bead blasting cabinet. These small units are now within the budget of the home shop. We found a marvelous one that fit on our workbench at The Eastwood Company.

The biggest problem with a bead blasting unit is that it creates dust. It's best kept in a corner where you can collect the dust with some sort of vacuum arrangement. The other secret to keeping the dust to a minimum is to use fresh blasting media.

Cleaning is done by crashing the blasting media into your Corvette parts. While removing rust and paint with this action, the blasting media also becomes smaller each time it strikes a part. Eventually the media becomes dust particles that will infiltrate every nook and cranny of your garage.

Purchasing a bead blasting cabinet also means you'll need an air compressor large enough to run the blast cabinet. Now we're talking about the kinds of tools that your spouse may never understand. This new cabinet won't require a lot of air pressure, just massive volume. When purchasing the compressor, be sure it will produce enough air volume. Make sure you discuss with the people who sell you the blasting

cabinet just how much air you're going to need. There's nothing worse than having too little air volume to do the job.

Another item you must have in your shop is a good fire extinguisher. If you work on cars long enough, you'll set one on fire. Most professional shops have had cars catch fire. The important point is that the pros have the proper fire fighting equipment, and so a big Corvette melt-down can easily be contained to a few singed strands of fiberglass.

You probably already get enough grief from your family about taking cars apart and putting them back together. Think about what your family life might be like after you burn down the garage.

## Basic Hand Tools

People spend too much money on tools. You shouldn't buy a single tool until you've determined how it will be used in the completion of your Corvette project. You can take a Corvette apart with a set of combination wrenches, a 3/8in socket set, and a 1/2in socket set. Everything else you buy will

Money is the most important tool of all; it can overcome all sorts of obstacles. Whatever amount you initially budget for your project, it won't be enough to complete the car.

You'll need a parts washer. Check out several of the units currently on the market before your make your purchase. While you don't need one large enough to scrub an engine block, you will need one large enough to accept a Chevy cylinder head.

just make things easier, although they aren't really necessary.

The secret to your Corvette rebuilding budget is to depend on friends and used hand tools. Remember, every dollar you spend on a tool means you get to spend less on Corvette parts. Life is full of hard choices.

## Tools For Inside The House

Some of the most important tools for this project will be kept on a bookshelf. Rebuilding a Corvette without a basic library would be like rebuilding your Corvette with vise grips and a set of adjustable wrenches.

The basic Corvette library listed below is what you will need to start the project. Before the car is done, you'll have obtained several shelves of Corvette books, since reading about Corvettes will help ease the frustration of working on Corvettes. Besides, reading at least puts you inside the house with the rest of the family.

*Chevrolet Power* by Chevrolet Motor Division

This is the first book you'll need to read if you are even considering the slightest modification to your Corvette. It contains all the stuff Chevrolet recommends. It's hard to go wrong with the basics.

*Fact Book of the 1968-1972 Stingray* by M.F. Dobbins

If you want to know what original Corvettes look like, this is the book. Dobbins has spent the best part of his life photographing original Corvettes, and there is no part on a Corvette that Dobbins can't describe. I really think he could tell you the day of the week the part was produced, just by touching it.

*Chevrolet Corvette* by Haynes Publishing

This is the best shop manual on the market. Don't even think about rebuilding your car without this book. The authors carefully laid out all the steps for removing every part from your Corvette. The best part is that they didn't write this manual by simply copying the factory manual—they actually took apart a Corvette.

*How to Rebuild Your Small-Block Chevy* by David Vizard

Vizard gives you all the basics. This book is the best step-by-step manual you'll find for assembling small-block Chevys. It shows how all the parts go together—even the smallest parts—and what all those different parts numbers mean. This volume is one of the best books you can have on your shelf.

*How to Rebuild Your Big-Block Chevy* by Tom Wilson

If you've got a big block in your Corvette, this is the book you'll need on your shelf. Don't even think about taking your motor apart without this book.

*Assembly Instruction Manual* by General Motors

This is the book of drawings that was used by the assembly people to assemble Corvettes. If you want to know how all the little parts fit together, you'll want this book. I think of it as an appendix to the Haynes manual.

## Why Am I Doing This?

Once you've passed your first six months of Corvette ownership and still have a family left, you can start giving some consideration to major projects. You are hopefully developing an appreciation of what Corvette ownership entails. The children are now well aware that they don't need clothes with designer labels and your spouse is beginning to believe that Corvette posters are really art.

Now is the time to start asking some serious questions, such as, "What am I trying to do here? What will I be driving when this project is done?" Before you park your Corvette in the garage for a major project, give a lot of thought to what you really want to drive out of that garage. Keep asking yourself, "Do truly rational people take Corvettes apart?"

A sand blaster is not really a luxury. If you pay to have every little part professionally cleaned, the price of your project will go up considerably. The cost of small bead blasters is so low that every home can have one. Make sure you set some money aside for the optional vacuum system. Without a good vacuum system, your house will soon be filled with silica dust.

Too many people spend all their money on big horsepower motors, only to find that the car won't stop. What has stopped, however, is their cash-flow. They may have a big horsepower Corvette, but their Corvette won't go down the road straight or stop in a straight line, and their bank balance resembles the national debt. Make sure you know what you want and how much it's going to cost—before you start removing parts.

With Project Corvette the goal was to apply current technology to a car that was over twenty-five years old. What could we do with a car that's a quarter of a century old? How could we improve the Corvette's performance without changing the way it looked?

The idea with Project Corvette was to keep the appearance as stock as possible. The external appearance remained the way God and the Chevrolet Design Studio intended it. No big fender flares, no fancy air dams or wings. Corvettes look nice the way they left the factory in St. Louis. Why gild the lily?

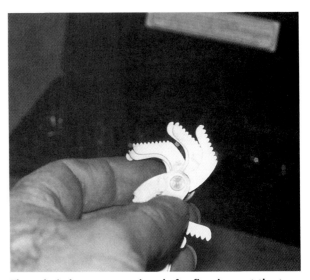

Thread pitch gauges are handy for figuring out the type of nut you need. Threads are described by the number of threads per inch.

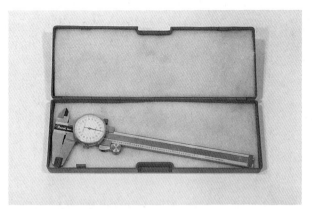

Precision measuring devices are nice to have around the garage. Dial calipers can be used to measure everything from bolts to exhaust pipes. Since you generally won't be dealing with real precision, purchase a dial caliper that is reasonably priced. If you think you'll have trouble learning to read a dial caliper, simply purchase one of the new digital calipers.

The interior also remained the same. I've yet to see the first real improvement on the interior of a third-generation Corvette. Granted, if I were designing a car from scratch I might move some things around, but there was no need to modify the interior, except in the interest of high-speed safety.

The chassis received a major amount of work, though. The chassis is one area we've learned a few things about how to make a car go fast. In the late sixties, life was simple and people paid less attention to basic physics. Since that era, chassis technology has become more scientific, and modern cars go faster as a result of this scientific approach to design.

The world of engines has become even more highly evolved. There's no more leaded gas, and the government monitors what comes out of your tail pipe and even checks whether you've changed the parts on your motor.

The engine in Project Corvette not only had to put out horsepower, it had to be socially acceptable. That's the equivalent of bringing Madonna home to meet your mother. A good trick that requires a lot of thought.

Another way to look at Project Corvette is to consider the cost of the total project. Corvettes don't run on gas, they run on money. Unless you want to sell your children to a group of gypsies, you need to have a rough idea of how much your Corvette affair is going to cost.

If you have a $10,000 budget, you can plan on spending one-third of it on the motor. Approximately $3,000 will get you all the motor you really need for a street car. You really don't need a $35,000 NASCAR motor. I'm not even sure what you would do with that much horsepower; probably hurt yourself.

The brakes will easily wipe out another $2,000. For any Corvette built between 1968 and 1982, plan on replacing the master cylinder and all the lines, and installing four new calipers. This is the absolute minimum. Throw in four new rotors and watch Visa raise your credit limit.

The chassis will end up costing another $2,000. Add a very basic $2,000 paint job, and the budget is shot. We haven't even added on the extra little items like sandblasting and powder painting. In fact, so far we haven't even touched a bolt and we're over budget.

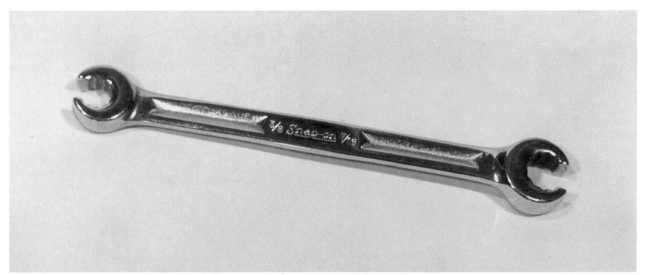

These are called line wrenches, or flare nut wrenches, and they're designed to work on brake and fuel lines. This is one type of tool that is worth paying for a top-quality wrench. Snap-On seems to produce the strongest, and thinnest, wrench on the market.

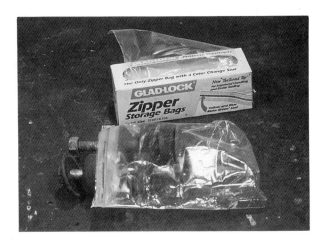

Whenever you take something off your Corvette, place it in a labeled container. You might think you'll remember where all these little nuts and bolts belong, but five years from now you won't have a clue. I know.

You have to have a plan. One of the nicest Corvettes I've seen was completed over a five-year period. Each winter the owner would attack a major area. The first winter he took on the engine and transmission. The second year it was the chassis. The third winter he worked on the paint. Finally during the fourth and fifth years, he tackled the interior. The best part was that he never gave up using the car for more than three months at a time.

Restoration, or simply rebuilding a car, is actually a matter of disassembly and reassembly. You'll take things off the car—until there's very little car left—and then you'll put the reconditioned parts back together. That's really what you're doing with all your time and money. Think of your Corvette as a drivable jigsaw puzzle.

A great deal of the actual rebuilding process is going to done by somebody else. Not only that, but it might be done far away from your actual worksite. We're talking about items like chrome plating and painting—things you can never do properly in your home garage.

There are still a great number of people who take pride in doing as much as possible in their two-car garage at home, but let's be realistic about using time and money. Very few of us can afford to build our own plating tanks and high-tech downdraft paint booths.

You're now as much project manager as a craftsman. You have to decide who to allow near your Corvette. Chrome platers, painters, and alignment specialists come in all shapes and forms. Some do quality work, and others misplace your parts. It's your choice as to the type of shop you'll work with.

The key is to have a good idea as to how your final product will look and perform. Next decide how many members of your family you're willing to sell to achieve your dream Corvette.

## Body Off?

With a restoration project, everybody talks about removing the body from the frame. Most people speak about this as if it's an everyday occurrence, yet there's one major problem. What do you do with the body when you still have a rolling chassis on the garage floor where your complete car once resided? More importantly, where do you put the body?

When you do a body-off restoration you end up with two cars. Think about what this will do to your basic two-car garage. Think twice about what this situation will do to your marriage when your spouse is outside the garage scraping snow off her car before she goes to work.

Even if you leave the body and frame united, your biggest problem will be dealing with all the parts. There are two problems here. First, where do you store all the parts once you've taken them off? Second, how are you going to remember where they go?

Furthermore, this project will never be completed on your original time schedule. I currently have the ignition shielding for my 1958 sitting on a shelf in the basement. It was taken off to polish. That was five years ago. Now I'm afraid to check where all the wingnuts might reside.

When you put something away—even for five minutes—use a system. Mixing a lot of Corvette parts on the shelf may not seem like a big deal—until you try to make a car out of them someday.

Two important tools to purchase for a rebuild are a Polaroid camera and a magic marker. Before you take anything apart, make sure that you take several pictures of the part in its place. Also, take pictures that make sense. You're not creating art here, you're just trying to file information. You could use 35mm color prints, but you'll lose the instant aspect of the pictures.

Never trust your memory. Even if you really think you'll remember how the headlights go together, take several pictures of them. Remember, if you had a sound mind you never would have started this project.

If you're going to have problems rebuilding your Corvette, this is the place where you'll make mistakes. Any time you spend taking parts off the car and putting them away properly will pay huge rewards several months, even years later.

A lot of parts are going to come off your Corvette, and there's no way anyone can possibly remember where each nut and bolt goes. Consequently, store each set of nuts and bolts together and label them so you can remember which components they hold together.

Having tried most approaches over the years, I've taken to putting parts into two types of containers. Ziplock sandwich bags are good containers because you can see what's inside of them, which saves you from taking the lids off cans every time.

There are two ways to store all these baggies. First, you can simply lay them on a shelf, which is what I've done on several occasions. Even better, randomly spread them around on different shelves in your garage. This provides a real challenge when you try to find the bolts for the rear axle.

A second approach, and the one I used for the first time on Project Corvette, was to put all the baggies from one component area in a box and then clearly label the box. While this system should have been more efficient, there were whole months when the system broke down. Keeping Project Corvette parts organized was a far greater challenge than I was prepared for.

Another all-purpose parts system is the plastic deli container. Once again you can look into the container without taking the lid off, but only if you buy your food from the right sort of deli and purchase all your food in clear plastic containers, not the frosted kind. Once again, the idea is to be able to actually see your parts without removing lids.

## The Component Theory

The best way to approach Corvette rebuilding is to think in terms of one component at a time. For instance, do not take the engine apart until you have the chassis all together. Having several major components apart at the same time is simply asking for trouble. Don't ask how I know this.

I now operate on the theory that the fewer parts I have lying around the garage, the greater the chances are that I'll remember how they go back together. For instance, I did exercise a tremendous amount of restraint when I left the motor and transmission alone until I had the chassis completed.

The interior doesn't need to be touched until the chassis is together and the motor installed in the car. Besides, on those long winter nights in the garage, you can slip behind the wheel and pretend you're driving down the road listening to the magic sound of a Chevy V8.

In the major restoration shops, the drivetrain is pulled from the car and sent to the engine team. It doesn't come back until it's time for installation. In the shop, the engine crew is usually in a separate area, where head bolts do not get mixed up with spring bolts. With Project Corvette, and with your project, we're talking about a one-man team and a shop with only one area. Never take any more components apart than you can reassemble without a team of Corvette experts. Remember the KISS principle—Keep It Simple Stupid.

## Save Everything

Remember, we don't own our Corvettes, we're simply custodians of them. The day will come when Project Corvette will be placed in the custody of another individual. That person may want to restore the car to NCRS standards, and so we need to make it as easy as possible for that individual.

Save every single part you remove from your Corvette. Nothing should be thrown away. This rule is absolute, whether you're restoring your car for NCRS competition or improving it the way we are. Everything that is not going back on the car should be saved.

When working on a numbers-matching car, save everything possible, even though some of the parts may be missing, for the day will come when the car passes on to a new individual. Who knows how many generations this car will survive? This Corvette has historical value, and nothing should be done to the car to prevent it from being returned to the condition it was in when it left St. Louis.

*Chapter 5*

# Front Suspension

There are two ways to make a Corvette go fast. The first way is to use mega-horsepower. This will make up for a lot of ills, as you can use the horsepower to simply overwhelm an evil chassis. The car will seem quicker than most other cars, but it will never be as fast as it could be. Most likely this sort of Corvette will be downright scary. After trying to drive it at the limit, the owner usually slows down and takes up bench racing. He may even think it's all this horsepower that makes his Corvette so frightening to drive.

The best way to make your Corvette go fast is to get all the wheels pointed in the same direction. Instead of adding horsepower, simply reduce the rolling resistance of the car. Now you can go just as fast, probably even faster, as the ill-handler with monster-horsepower. You just do it with a lot fewer horses, not to mention a whole lot less anxiety.

The front suspension on your Corvette is really the same as that found on the Chevrolet Impalas of the era. One story has it that when Duntov was designing the chassis for the 1963 Corvette, he was told he could have independent rear suspension only if he took the front part of the chassis directly off the Chevrolet parts shelf.

The upside of this deal is that your Corvette's front suspension is very easy to understand. It's also very easy to work on. The front suspension consists of an upper and lower control arm connected with a steering knuckle. The steering knuckle is connected to the upper and lower control arms with ball joints.

The ball joints not only carry the weight of your Corvette, they also allow the front wheels of the Corvette to turn. The first thing you need to examine is how your ball joints are connected to the control arms. When your car left the Corvette plant, the ball joints were riveted to the control arms.

Your Corvette's suspension looks like this after you remove all the brake and steering parts. Don't proceed any further until you've read the Haynes manual and talked to several friends.

Removing the control arms involves separating them from the front spindle. Notice the spring compressor is already installed on the coil spring. If you should ever remove a spring without the compressor attached, you could have a serious problem. The best method is to find a friend who's done this job on their own car. Invite them over for lunch and ask if they have a few extra minutes to help out a little bit. Don't do this job on your own the first time you attempt a front suspension overhaul.

This is the lower control arm prior to bushing removal. After you bead-blast the control arm, check carefully for cracks in the bushing area.

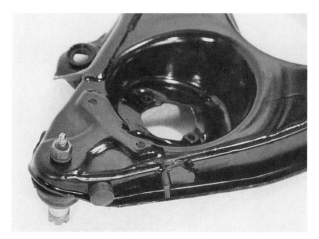

This is the lower control arm with a new ball joint installed. The control arm was cleaned in the abrasive cabinet and then painted with Eastwood chassis epoxy. The control arm looks better now than the day it left St. Louis.

When the ball joints wore out, these rivets were cut out, and a new ball joint was bolted in place. The replacement bolts work just fine, so the only possible reason you might not want bolts is if you're entering your car in NCRS competition. The NCRS wants everything to look the same as when Chevrolet completed your car. Function is not an important NCRS criteria.

Worn ball joints go bad very slowly. If you've had your car for several years you may not even notice that they're worn. I know of one Corvette owner who won an SCCA national Solo I championship while chasing a bad ball joint for three months. Only after he replaced the entire front suspension did he realize that a bad ball joint was the source of his handling problem.

The wheel bearings are often another overlooked area of the front suspension. We all realize that wheel bearings allow the wheels to turn. What we don't seem to understand is that when wheel bearings wear out, or get loose, they can cause a lot of handling problems.

The good news is that Corvette front wheel bearings are very easy to work on. Compared to what you have to go through with Corvette rear wheel bearings, the front wheel bearings are an absolute picnic. Corvettes use two tapered roller bearings for each front wheel. Considering the low price on these bearings, you shouldn't use a wheel bearing with the slightest sign of wear.

The first step in making a Corvette handle well is to make sure the entire front suspension is absolutely perfect. It makes absolutely no sense to change some parts while others are worn to the point of being hazardous. First, you'll never get any benefit from super-trick improvements. Second, you

might degrade your Corvette's handling beyond it's already worn-out state.

Improving how your Corvette corners involves two things: Getting the car to go around corners as quickly and consistently. Above all else, a Corvette chassis must be predictable. When you're rushing into a corner, you certainly don't want to be surprised by what the car does. A good Corvette will never surprise you; it will do exactly what it did the last three times you entered that corner. This predictability is far more important than any mystical G number. Consistency is what lets you drive your Corvette at the limit—all the time.

## Physics 101

Your Corvette chassis will never overcome physics. Physics happens. Remember this fact and your Corvette will go around corners faster. You'll also save a lot of money by not buying the trick suspension part of the month.

There are really only three ways to make a car corner faster. First, you can widen the track, which simply increases the distance between the tires. Second, you can lower the center of gravity. Third, you can reduce the weight of the car.

Sway bars, spring rates, and bushing materials are all simply tuning devices. They never really change the mechanical energy used in cornering. The largest gains in handling come through lower weight, a wider track, and a lowered center of gravity. Keep this in mind as you start making changes in your Corvette.

## Springs

The front springs on your Corvette really have only one purpose. They should hold the car up in the

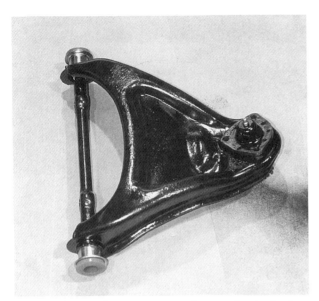

Pictured here is the upper control arm prior to final assembly in the Corvette. The bolts for the ball joint have not been installed, and the control arm bushings have not been pressed on. The Eastwood epoxy paint may not be NCRS correct, but it looks nice and holds up very well.

air while the wheels go up and down over the surface of the road. Generally this means that the softest possible springs are the best. A soft spring lets each wheel move up and down while having minimal effect on the driver. A proper Corvette will have a soft ride, at least relatively soft.

Remember Physics 101. A stiff spring will not make the car handle better. The spring only needs to be stiff enough to keep the bottom of the car from hitting the road. Watch the F1 cars on ESPN and observe how they all bottom out at some point on the track. Perfectly set-up suspension will be as soft as possible; the car will bottom out once or twice each lap.

A proper chassis will keep the wheels in touch with the road at all times. The softer spring allows the wheel to follow the undulations of a normal road surface. Stiff springs simply allow the tires to skip over the road from bump to bump—not a good idea since you really need to keep the rubber on the road.

With the C3 Corvettes there are three basic chassis configurations. The first is the basic street suspension, which is more than adequate for any street-driven Corvette. If all you ever do is drive your Corvette on the street, then you've never really reached the limits of this suspension, which has always been the best compromise between ride comfort and handling.

The next option on the suspension list is the F41. This option provides you with the springs that Duntov didn't believe you could live with on the

With the coil spring still compressed and the lower control arm bolted in place, you can raise the entire assembly and slide the spring into the frame pocket. Usually, the real obstacle is getting the spring properly seated in the frame pocket. Take your time and be very careful.

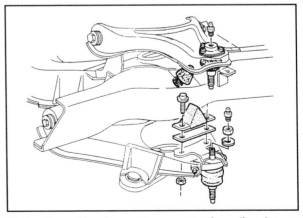

Notice the rubber bump stop next to the coil spring on the lower control arm. This rubber bumper stop strikes against the frame to keep the spring from fully compressing under severe load. The bump stops are key parts of the suspension, and both bump stops should be replaced when you rebuild the suspension.

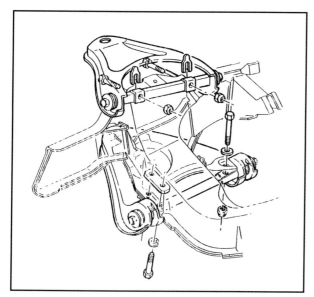

Here's a good drawing of how the control arms attach to the frame. In order to get the upper control arm to bolt up to the frame, you'll have to install several alignment shims. Without the shims installed, you won't be able to tighten the nuts that hold the upper control arm to the frame. When you have the car aligned you can worry about installing the proper amount of shims.

street. This suspension wasn't offered as a separate option until 1973. Until that time, Duntov wrote the option list in such a way that you couldn't get the F41 unless you ordered an outright racing Corvette. Before you put F41 springs under your Corvette, ask

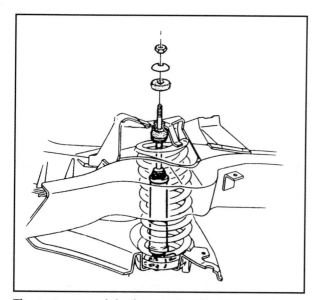

The upper part of the front spring fits into a pocket on the frame. The lower part of the spring fits on the lower control arm. The secret is to get the coil properly situated on both the frame and control arm.

yourself, "Do I know more about Corvettes than Zora Duntov?"

There is yet another set of springs that are stiff beyond belief; the Daytona package. This package was designed to keep the back end from dragging on the high banks of Daytona. A spring package that is this stiff is beyond the pale for the street, or even normal racing. There's no reason to ever use the Daytona package, unless you're racing the high banks of Daytona.

|  | Front | Rear |
|---|---|---|
| Standard Springs | 280lb/in | 140lb/in |
| F41 Springs | 550lb/in | 305lb/in |
| Daytona Springs | 860lb/in | 450lb/in |

With the F41 springs you get better transient response and a little less understeer at high speeds. The only time you'll really need this F41 suspension is on the race track.

In the early seventies, the ride quality of the F41 was so bad it wasn't worth the trade-off. My first idea was to try to use the F41 springs and get the ride quality back with the latest chassis technology. Gary Gonzalez of Vette Products talked me out of that idea. He felt that the ride quality just wouldn't be satisfactory. He suggested I compromise and use 460lb front springs, pointing out that I would be giving up very little handling at the limit, and Project Corvette would be a whole lot more comfortable on the street.

## Bushing Selection

Selecting the proper chassis bushings is one area where you must be sure of your choices. If you intend to drive your Corvette on the street, new stock rubber bushings make a lot of sense. If you don't push your Corvette very hard, the stock bush-

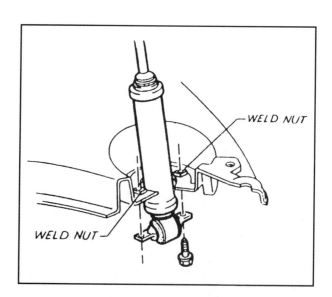

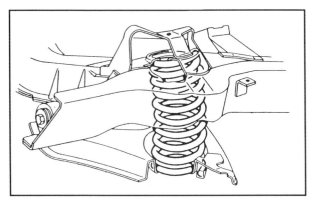

The lower shock mounts are easy to remove and install. However, on occasion, the weld nut on the lower control arm breaks loose. Your local parts house will have a little clip designed to function as a nut. You can also reach through the spring and put a regular nut on the mounting bolt. The top bolt can be a real problem because too often the nut is rusted to the shaft. I've cut them off, and I've burned the nut off with a torch. The upper nut can be a real aggravating problem on these occasions. Also, when you get the new shocks in place, make certain you have enough clearance between the shock and the frame. Clearance can be problem with heavy-duty, or larger, shocks.

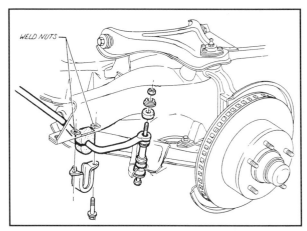

The front sway bar is very easy to attach. As was mentioned previously, make sure all the rubber bushings are in good condition.

ings will work just fine. If you intend to do anything besides drive it back and forth to car shows, then you need to pay attention to the bushings.

What you want to do is eliminate suspension bushing deflection, and new rubber bushings will work fine in a street car, at least for a while. If you intend to use your Corvette in anger, then you'll push the suspension to the point where the factory bushings will deflect, giving you imprecision at the furthest edge of handling. What happens is that when you turn into a corner, the tires stick to the ground and the rubber bushings compress. It's the classic tale of the weakest link. The less movement you have in the suspension, the greater the force on the bushings.

The more your high-tech sticky B.F. Goodrich tires adhere to the pavement, the more the bushings will deflect. The problem, however, is that they don't deflect exactly the same way all the time. Hence, the suspension will be unpredictable.

Everything will work just fine until you get to that final ragged edge of handling. When nothing else will move, the rubber bushings will compress and give you that feeling of instant excitement. Worn-out bushings will make your Corvette even more exciting. Every time you enter a corner, the bushings will deflect a little differently.

If your Corvette has more than 30,000 miles, you should consider replacing all the bushings. You'll need to choose the type of material you want to use. Since I've decided to use Project Corvette for high-

speed events, I wanted to eliminate all the imprecision I could, which meant using poly bushings. Remember though, not all polyurethane is created equal. A cheap set of bushings will be sloppy and make a lot of noise. Energy Suspension has been making bushings for a long time now, and they know how to do it right. After all, Doug Rippe has used the same set for two seasons of serious racing. Do you really need anything better?

## Sway Bars

The best way to control body roll is with a set of big sway bars, not stiff springs. With the Corvette there's a lot of body lean since there is very little anti-roll effect built into the independent suspension. Basically, this means that when you go around a corner, the outside of the car lifts up in the air, and the side of the car toward the inside of the turn pushes down toward the pavement.

All this body roll is a bad thing because, other than scaring your passenger, you'll want very little camber change when going around a corner. When the body of the car rolls, the tires follow, reducing the amount of rubber you actually have on the ground.

When your Corvette is leaning through a corner, the tires make contact with the road with only their edges. If you can minimize the body roll, then you can keep the tires perpendicular to the ground and get the maximum cornering power.

Sway bars control body roll by requiring that the sway bar be twisted before the body rolls. The bigger the diameter of the sway bar, the more it resists this twisting. The best part is that sway bars have very little effect on the vertical movement of the chassis.

In the old days people tried to control body roll through the use of stiff springs. They had forgot-

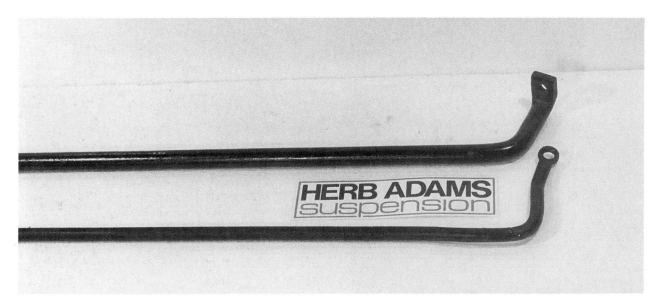

This is a comparison of the Herb Adams front sway bar and the standard sway bar that came on Project Corvette. The bigger Herb Adams bar is used to increase roll stiffness. The idea is to use a combination of soft springs and large sway bars. This combination will provides the best possible blend of ride and handling. The sway bars control body roll, and the springs keep your Corvette from dragging on the pavement.

ten basic physics. A spring so stiff that it controls body roll in a turn is stiff enough to cause the tires to lose contact with the pavement every time you hit a bump.

I'm a big believer in soft springs and huge sway bars. This is the best way to make your C3 Corvette handle. Herb Adams, who makes some of the best Corvette chassis parts in the country, uses the same technique.

Combining soft springs with big sway bars should also give you a more comfortable ride. If both front wheels go up and down together, then the entire sway bar simply rotates in the bushings, offering no resistance. Thus, you get a decent ride with very little roll in the corners.

Notice that I said "decent" ride. In theory, a big anti-roll bar shouldn't change the ride of the car at all. As long as both wheels go up and down to-

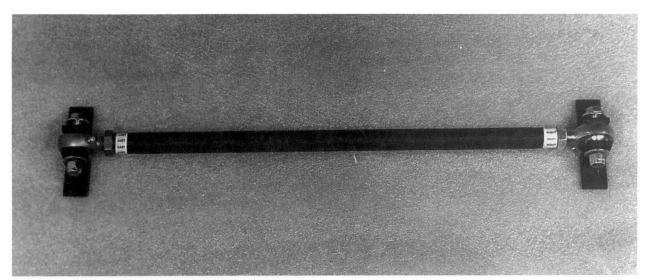

This is a bar that fits between the two front spring towers. The purpose of this bar, from Vette Brakes & Products, is to keep the front spring towers from moving under heavy side loading. The new modern tires stick so well that the Corvette chassis moves under the load. This bar is designed to keep that movement to a minimum. The outer brackets must be welded in place.

Pictured here is the completed front suspension prior to installation of the brake system. Notice the rather large heim joint for the front sway bar. Obviously there will be some tremendous forces generated by the new Herb Adams front sway bar. The disc-brake dust shield is from Caledonia Classic Cars. There's really no reason fooling around trying to make a twenty-five year old part, like a dust shield, look new when you can get an exact reproduction for a reasonable price. You constantly have to make judgments about the effective use of time and money when you're rebuilding your Corvette.

This is the front suspension fully assembled. The front sway bar is the original stock Corvette unit.

gether, then the sway bar simply rotates, never acting as a spring. With today's lousy roads, the right wheel is always bouncing up and down differently from the left wheel. This means the sway bar is acting as spring, giving you a slightly turbulent ride. The bigger the diameter of the bar, the more you'll feel it. The worse the road, the more you're going to feel it. I'm willing to give up some ride comfort to limit body roll in a corner.

| | Front Sway Bar Size |
|---|---|
| Standard | 3/4in |
| 1973–74 FE7 | 15/16in |
| 1975 FE7 | 1-1/8in |
| Vette Products | 1-1/4in |
| Herb Adams | 1-1/4in |

The Herb Adams sway bars, available from Moroso, use heim joints for links, which gives you a very solid connection. Using sway bar links with poly cushion, such as Vette Products uses, is just as good for street use.

I like heim joints mainly for the way they look, but also because they provide a more direct force on the sway bar. With a polyurethane bushing, the bushing must first be compressed before the total force of the sway bar starts to act on the car. With the heim joint, the action is instantaneous.

You should keep in mind, however, that if you only use your Corvette on the street, the standard Corvette bars, or the Vette Products items, with poly cushions from Energy Suspension, are probably all you really need.

You really can't drive your Corvette fast enough on the street to tell the difference between heim joints and polyurethane bushings. If you intend to use your car at the race track for high-speed NCCC events, then you'll notice the difference.

# Chapter 6

# Rear Suspension

Before you decide which rear spring to purchase, remember what this spring really does. The rear spring really only has one purpose: to hold the body steady while the wheels go up and down over the surface of the road.

Generally, just as I said in the previous chapter, this means that the softest possible spring should be the best. A soft spring lets each rear wheel move up and down while having minimal effect on the driver, and remember, a proper Corvette has a soft ride.

With the older Corvettes, there were three basic chassis configurations—as previously discussed, which means there will be three different rear springs available.

| | Rear Springs |
|---|---|
| Standard Spring | 140lb/in |
| F41 Spring | 305lb/in |
| Daytona Spring | 450lb/in |

The easy part in choosing a rear spring is to use fiberglass monospring. There's no reason to carry around a big heavy steel spring today; technology has gone beyond that level. Fiberglass springs come

The third-generation Corvette's rear suspension was designed in the late fifties. It's big and it's heavy. What you see here is a rather successful attempt to bring the third-generation Corvette into the nineties. The spring bushings are from Energy Suspension, the spring from Vette Brakes & Products, and the sway bar from Herb Adams.

A rear sway bar only came on the big-block Corvettes. Sway bars should be matched front and rear. If you put a big anti-roll bar on the rear and leave the front alone, you'll have some major handling problems. Pictured is the Herb Adams sway bar, available from Moroso. It uses heim joints and is adjustable, as well.

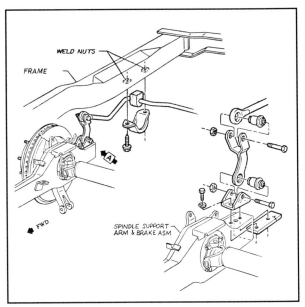

The original factory sway bar used mounting brackets with rubber bushings. The rubber bushings give a slight delay in reaction, since they must first compress. On the other hand, they are a lot quieter than heim joints. Generally, for street use, the factory rubber bushings are more than satisfactory.

in four different weights: 300lbs/in, 330lbs/in, 360lbs/ in, and 420lbs/in.

My original idea was to use the 360lb spring, but Gary Gonzalez, of Vette Brakes & Products, felt the ride quality just wouldn't be satisfactory with a spring that stiff. He suggested we use a 330lb rear fiberglass spring to match our 406lb springs on the front of the car. He pointed out that we would be giving up very little handling at the limit and Project Corvette would be a whole lot more comfortable on the street.

If you glance back at the chart you'll notice we actually used a rear spring that's stiffer than the old F41 steel spring. The difference is that the fiberglass material doesn't give up any ride quality. This is also known as having your coffeecake and eating it too. Isn't technology wonderful?

The fiberglass rear spring gets rid of the chop and harshness you get from conventional steel springs. Besides, the spring weighs so much less than a steel spring that I can't understand why everybody wouldn't use them. Leave the big old heavy springs for the NCRS and Bloomington crowd. After all, they don't even drive their cars.

### Rear Sway Bars

The rear sway bar made its debut with the big-block and heavy-duty chassis options. All Corvettes have pre-drilled holes for this optional rear sway bar, so adding one to your car is no big deal. Both Herb

Adams and Vette Brakes & Products offer sway bar kits in case your Corvette didn't arrive with one.

|  | Rear Sway Bar |
| --- | --- |
| Standard | none |
| 1973–74 FE7 | 9/16in |
| 1975 FE7 | 7/16in |
| Vette Products | 5/8in or 3/4in |
| Herb Adams | 1in |

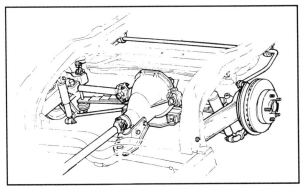

This drawing gives a good idea of how a sway bar works. In order for the left rear wheel to rise, it has to twist the sway bar. The larger the diameter of this bar, the harder it is to twist. The stiffer the bar, the harder it becomes for the wheel to move. If both wheels move at the same time, the sway bar simply rotates in the rubber mounts on the rear frame rails.

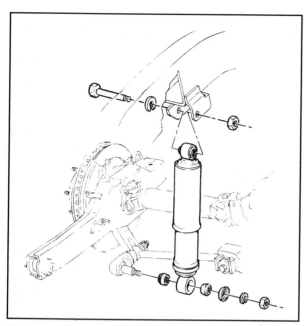

The rear shock is one of the easiest parts to remove. Switching to a quality shock, such as Koni, won't perform a miracle, but it will make a big difference in both the ride and handling of your Corvette.

Once again, you can take the body roll out of the Corvette chassis by linking the two sides of the car; the rear sway bar unites the right and left sides of the car. The result is a Corvette that will corner much flatter than any stock C3 Corvette. The bigger the

The lower end can be twisted out of place after you've removed the top mount. The critical part is to not damage the lower mounting bracket. The lower end can be difficult to remove, and you might try to knock it off with a hammer, which will damage the threads. Several companies make a tool that covers the threads in case nothing but a large hammer will do the job.

sway bar, the flatter the car will go around corners. The ride will also feel a little harsher, so be careful.

You need to consider the fact that the rear sway bar will give you improved handling at the price of increased road harshness. Whenever you connect the left side of the car to the right side, you're actually increasing the effective spring rate, which means that every time you hit a pothole, or drive across railroad tracks, you'll know you have a rear sway bar.

A rear sway has absolutely no effect if both rear wheels go up and down at the same time. But whenever one wheel moves at a different rate from the wheel on the other side, the sway bar comes into effect, which is the reason the effective spring rate is raised with a huge rear sway bar.

**Rear Locating Arms**

One area where you can improve the handling of your Corvette and give up very little ride quality is by replacing the rear locating arms. The rear arms on the stock Corvette are pretty meager items. They're made from stamped sheet metal welded together. The first problem is rust. Water and salt from the highway reside in these rear arms and can rust away the sheet steel.

The only solution for a rusted locating arm is replacement. If the arm is structurally sound, you can probably get by with simply replacing the bushing, which means you'll need to make some decisions.

The easiest way to remove the arm is to simply disconnect the brake line at the caliper and the bolt that runs through the frame, located directly forward of the rear tire. This whole unit is bulky, and fairly heavy, but I usually save some time by taking it out of the car in one piece.

With the entire assembly on your workbench you can remove the brakes and rear hub assembly

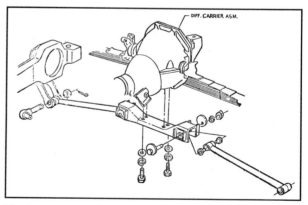

The lower control arm links the rear suspension together and adjusts the rear tire camber. The ends of the control rods use rubber bushings. One economical upgrade is to replace these bushings with the polyurethane versions from Energy Suspension.

These eccentrics adjust camber. You can purchase these new, or you can simply clean up the old ones. Either way, you should use some silicone lube where the bolt runs through the bushing.

from the locating arm. This is all fairly straightforward. The next step, however, depends on the choices you've made.

With Project Corvette, I did all of the rear bearing work myself. This took a lot of time, effort, and money. A better choice would have been to send the whole bearing assembly to Art Dorsett at Van Steel in Clearwater, Florida. I would have saved a lot of time and effort, and spent only a little more money. I also would have been absolutely sure the job was done correctly.

While all your bearing assemblies are enjoying the sun of Clearwater, Florida, you need to make a decision regarding the rear control arm bushings. Poly bushings can be installed without a press. This is good.

Actually the best replacements are the whole kits from Vette Brakes & Products. They sell whole

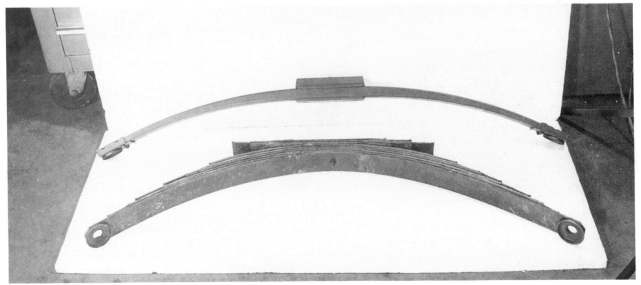

The fiberglass spring from Vette Brakes & Products is much lighter than the steel spring and will produce a better ride. Considering that Chevrolet has been using fiberglass springs for almost twenty years, it doesn't make any sense to keep using an old steel spring for your 1969 Corvette.

The easiest way to lower your Corvette is to lengthen this bolt. Also, these are the stock rubber bushings. You'll need to use a new cotter pin at the bottom of the bolt.

The rubber bump stop directly above the control arm and brake shield is an important part of the suspension. The engineers at Chevrolet thought about the firmness of the rubber they used for this bump stop. Leaving these or similar items to this off your car is not a good idea. Replacing the bump stops with new ones is a better idea.

kits that include all the parts you're going to need, including a flaring tool. Energy Suspension has nice bushings as well, but that's all you'll get from them. Pay the extra money and get the whole package. It's worth it.

## Polyurethane vs. Rubber Bushings

The trick of the year is to use polyurethane bushings for both the rear leaf spring and the rear control arms. There's very little question that these bushings will improve the handling of your Corvette, but you have to keep in mind that there is a price. The chart below might help you make up your mind.

Despite all the problems, Project Corvette was the second car on which I've used poly bushings. If you use the proper grease, and install the bushings properly, the squeaking is kept to a minimum. Poly bushings seem to need new grease every few years, but this is a problem I can live with. The only significant problem is a slight increase in harshness and road vibration. As long as I get Project Corvette to Pocono Raceway once or twice a year though, I can tolerate this minor irritation. Basically it's a question of "How fast do you really want to go?" and "Are you willing to pay the price?"

## The Shocking Truth

The next item that helped Project Corvette was the Koni gas shocks. I have a blind prejudice about Konis. Every time I've used them, they've

| | Polyurethane Bushings | Stock Bushings |
|---|---|---|
| Wear | Improved resistance to oil and heat | A life span of 60,000 miles |
| Appearance | Non-stock | Stock |
| Installation | Can be time-consuming | Standard shop procedure |
| Handling | Improved | ZR-1 uses rubber bushings |
| Ride Quality | Slight harshness | Softer ride |
| Problems | Squeaking | Rapid deterioration |

Pictured here is the backside of the control arm. The bracket on the left side is where the rubber brake line is

attached to the hard steel brake line. New locking tabs are available from your local Chevrolet dealer.

worked. Something else might work just as well, but why take a chance?

If you drop your front coil spring on the garage floor, you'll notice it bounces around a lot. In

techno-talk it's called oscillation. When you put a spring into motion, it tends to stay in motion until all the energy is used up.

It's not a good idea to have your Corvette bouncing up and down the road like a slinky toy.

This picture shows the pocket where the control arm bolts to the frame rail. It also illustrates how the rubber flex line attaches to the frame. The end hanging in space will connect to the hard line on the trailing arm.

The parking brake cable is attached to the outside of the control arm. You can also see the hard steel line on the rear of the arm. If you use tires and wheels wider than stock, you'll want to make sure the tires do not rub on this parking brake bracket. There are times when you might have to cut this bracket completely off the car in an effort to get maximum clearance.

The trailing arm is removed from the frame with one bolt. Inside the frame pocket are the alignment shims. Before you get in big hurry, make certain you carefully remove the alignment shims, noting their location. You'll still have to align the car once you replace the arm, but at least you'll have a baseline. This one little effort can cut your alignment time in half.

What you'll need is something that dampens the movement of the spring.

Shocks have three basic tasks to perform. First, they have to control the rate at which the spring compresses in reaction to bumps in the road. Second, they have to control the reaction as the spring releases the energy from the bump in the road. Third, they have to control the rate at which the unsprung weight of your Corvette responds to any dynamic energy when turning corners.

Shock absorbers are the high-tech wonders of the eighties. Racing teams spend more time selecting the right shock absorber than they spend on spring selection. The latest Corvettes have shocks that can be adjusted from the center console.

For seventies Corvettes the situation is much easier. For these, you simply buy a pair off the shelf. The only variable is brand name. I've never seen a comprehensive shock test for any of our cars, instead we've only gotten impressions as to which shock feels best.

Two items do need consideration though. If you use a fiberglass spring, Koni shocks seem to work better than most other shocks. *Corvette Fever* did a spring swap a few years ago and found that the Bilsteins just didn't work that well. This was a highly impressionistic test with no real data, but when they installed the Koni shocks, the car rode a lot better.

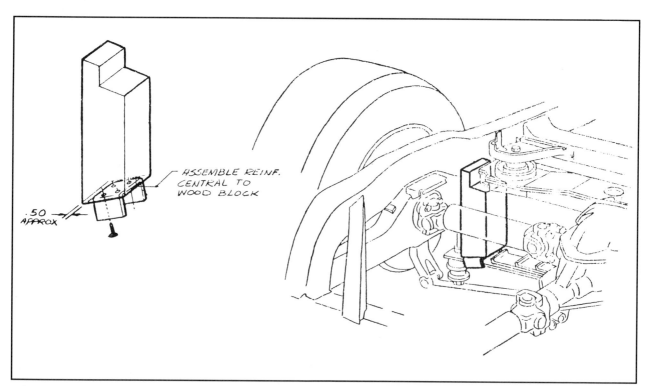

ASSEMBLE REINF.
CENTRAL TO
WOOD BLOCK

.50
APPROX

When your Corvette left St. Louis, Chevrolet installed a shipping block in the rear suspension. This block kept the suspension from moving while the car was in transit.

This seems like it could be just as worthwhile today if you trailer your Corvette.

The second point to consider is that C3 Corvettes respond well to gas shocks. With gas shocks there's more ride comfort coupled with the extra firmness. Unless you're building an NCRS Corvette, there's just no reason to use anything but a gas shock on your Corvette.

The shocks are very easy to change, and the only problem I encountered was getting the new Koni through the front lower control arm. The Koni is larger in diameter than the original Delco shocks, and for some reason it didn't want to line up properly. When everything was finally in place, there was no problem. Perhaps this was just one more weird Project Corvette problem. Nothing is surprising when it comes to our abused '68.

The fiberglass rear spring first appeared in 1981 and was used with the automatic transmissions and bse suspension. The spring here weighs 8lb; it replaced the 44lb steel spring.

# Chapter 7

# Steering System

It's very basic—when you turn the steering wheel, you want your Corvette to go in a specific direction. The problem is that too many Corvettes seem to have a mind of their own. This is because the steering system has been worn to the point where what should be a very precise operation becomes a vague and random activity.

If you're one of those Corvette owners who find themselves steering their car all the time, you understand what I'm talking about, and if you've put the latest high-tech oversize tires on your Corvette in the past year, you've probably noticed the steering got even worse. Don't blame the new tires for your problem. The trouble is that the new tires work so well, all the little flaws in your steering system become more noticeable, which is one reason you should never put big sticky tires on your Corvette until you're absolutely certain the steering system is in first-rate condition.

Remember, the steering wheel is not connected directly to the front tires. When you turn the wheel you're simply moving a lot of parts that even-

This is a close-up of the rag joint. The bolts holding the two parts together are different sizes. It's impossible to install a rag joint improperly because of the many different sizes of nuts and bolts used. Chevrolet tried very hard to make this joint assembly-line-proof, and that helps us all when we finally get around to restoring our Corvettes. If you're rebuilding the total steering system, it doesn't hurt to replace this coupling. They seldom wear out, so it isn't necessary to replace it until the complete system is being overhauled.

The best way to separate the tie rod end from the steering knuckle is with a tool called a pickle fork. Several blows with a 5lb hammer on the end of the fork and the tie rod end should be separated from the steering arm. The only problem is that you'll most likely rip the rubber boot. Energy Suspension has non-stock polyurethane replacements.

tually transmit a message to the front tires. All the wear in the steering system can be cumulative. There doesn't need to be a single horrible part in the system, just a series of marginal parts that add up to get a lot of steering play.

In other words, no single part may be totally worn out on your Corvette. What's happened is that each component is worn a little bit, and when you add up all the excess play in the system, the result is lousy steering response. You might never notice this in your family car, but in your Corvette it becomes a real hassle.

You bought your Corvette because you wanted a different sort of driving experience. A worn-out steering system will be different all right. It just wasn't quite what you had in mind when you turned all that money over to the previous owner.

You need to think about exactly what happens when you turn the steering wheel in your Corvette. This will help you understand where all the wear begins.

The steering wheel is connected directly to the column that goes down through the firewall to the steering box. Just before the steering box, there's a big rubber disk with four nuts and bolts. This is usually called the "rag joint." The purpose of it is to allow some flex in the steering column.

Remember, the top of the steering column is connected with bolts under the dash of the Corvette. It doesn't move. The steering box is connected to the frame of the car. There's no movement between the box and the frame. If there's any movement between the body of the car and the frame, it's the job of the rag joint to deal with this flex. Rag joints usual-

It's amazing what a few minutes in the blasting cabinet and some paint will do for old parts. The Eastwood Chassis Black may not match the original finish, but it provides a lot stronger finish than the more commonly used products. The trick is to use several light coats for a high-gloss finish. A heavy coat will result in a flatter, more original finish.

ly don't wear out, and it's rare to replace them. However, given the age of your Corvette, and the way it may have been driven, this universal steering joint should be replaced. It's very easy to do, and it can add a little more precision to the steering.

The steering box can be a major source of wear, depending on how many miles are on your Corvette. A steering box is really used to change the direction of motion; it takes the steering wheel motion and forces it into a right-angle turn. While the motion changes direction, the ratio of the turning wheels is also altered. A full 360° turn on the steering wheel obviously doesn't turn your front wheels 360°.

When people talk about steering ratios they are referring to the number of turns of the steering wheel it takes to turn the pitman arm from left to right. This is also referred to as lock-to-lock. In other words, how far must you turn the steering wheel to get from a hard right turn to a hard left turn.

The upper tie rod uses the adjuster sleeve available from Vette Brakes & Products. The boots on the upper sleeve are from Energy Suspension. If you drive fast and have big sticky tires, you should have the stronger unit. The stock factory unit is fine for normal driving but lacks the strength of the Vette Products unit.

With all the gears and balls moving around the steering box, you might consider the steering box a major source of steering wear. Actually, it is one of the more reliable items on your Corvette—if the previous three owners have taken care of your Corvette.

This Corvette steering box generally works so well that we often ignore it until something drastic happens. Wear that does occur in the steering generally happens so slowly that you don't even notice the deterioration—until you actually rebuild the box.

Leaks are the most common problem with the steering box. The seals are the first item to wear, and then all the gear oil runs out on your garage floor. Worse yet, the steering box becomes empty of all lubricant, and the gears, not to mention the ball bearings, begin to wear rather rapidly.

One way to fix this is to fill your steering box with bearing grease. The only disadvantage is that if you try to drive your Corvette on a cold winter morning, the steering is going to be a little stiff.

You should remove the three cover bolts on the steering box with a 9/16in socket and pack all

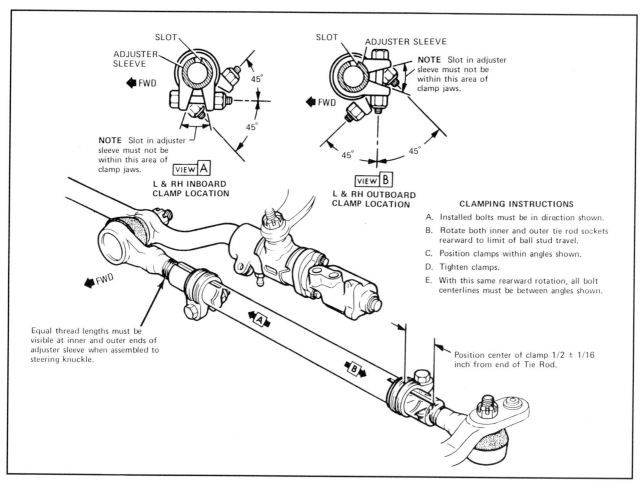

If you're using the stock Chevrolet tie rods, this is the way they were installed at the factory. You'll note that the factory used the forward-most hole in the steering arm when power steering was used.

Rebuilding a steering box is for the advanced restorer. Very few shops will even go inside the steering box. On the other hand, it's seldom necessary. Adjustments to the gears can be made with the nut and screw on the top of the gear box. Consult your Haynes manual for the exact procedure.

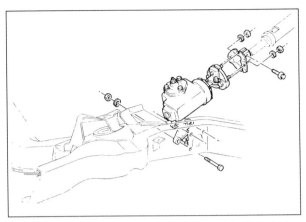

The steering box is bolted to the frame with three bolts. In order to remove the steering box you have to disconnect the pitman arm, the rag joint, and the three bolts that run through the frame. It's a fairly simple job.

the grease into the box. You may want to turn the wheel several times to pack the grease around all the gears. Sometime in the next decade you can actually rebuild the steering box.

At the bottom of the steering box is a big steel bar-shaped device called the pitman arm. This arm never, or very seldom, wears out on the Corvette. When you start working on the steering, it's worth checking the pitman arm, but there's usually no reason to replace it.

The pitman arm is connected to the center link. In the old days this was called the drag link or, in some manuals, the relay rod. A stud is used to attach the left side of the center link to the pitman arm. The ball on the end of the stud rests in the center link and should be lubricated through the normal grease fitting.

Now there's this long bar, or center link, connected to the left side of the Corvette steering. The

## Key Steering Parts

### Lower Ball Joints

The lower ball joints are a constant wear item on the C3 Corvettes since they carry the weight of the car. Next to the idler arm, these ball joints are the fastest wearing part of the steering. The good part is that high-quality ball joints are cheap, even the best ones. The bad part is that they can be a real hassle to replace, especially since you have to remove the original factory rivets.

### Upper Ball Joints

Upper ball joints seldom wear out. They carry no weight and seem to last forever. Just because you're changing the lower ball joint doesn't mean you need to change the upper ball joints. The only time these uppers need replacement is when you're doing a complete front-end rebuild.

### Tie-Rod Ends

Loose tie-rod ends will cause steering wander. Any play in these rod ends will have a direct effect on the front toe settings. Check them every time you grease the front end of your Corvette.

### Idler Arm

The stock GM unit uses rubber bushings and wears out very quickly. You always check for vertical play on this part. If possible, the stock unit should be replaced with an idler arm that uses needle bearings.

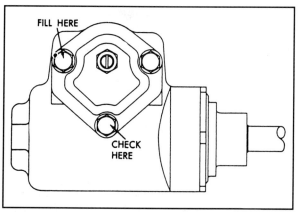

This is about as clear as it gets when it comes to the steering box. Check the fluid level on a regular basis, especially if you notice leaks.

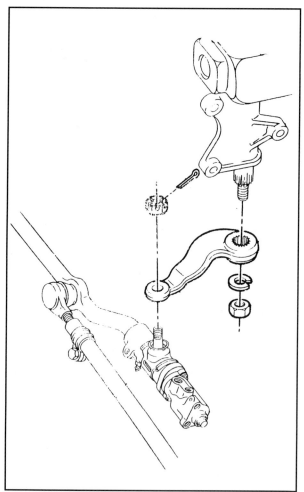

The pitman arm connects the steering box and the relay rod. In order to disconnect the pitman arm from the steering box you'll need a special tool called, yes, a pitman arm puller. A pickle fork is used to remove the pitman arm from the relay rod. The best solution is to remove the arm from the relay rod first.

This is the relay rod with the tie rods attached. The relay is a non-wear item. If you find you have to replace this item you have a seriously abused Corvette. Make sure you use the grease fittings at least twice a year, so you will never have to do this job again. The aluminum foil in the transmission tunnel is from Caledonia. It prevents engine heat from migrating into the passenger compartment. Caledonia stocks a complete set of all the various heat shields that belong under your Corvette. Install them before you situate the motor. Once the motor and transmission are in place, this is an impossible task.

next step is to find a way to connect it to the right side of the frame. For this purpose we use an idler arm. Basically all the idler arm does is hold the right side of the center link. The idler arm provides a nice steady support for the steering.

Too often the idler arm is worn out and needs to be replaced. This is the most common source of steering wear in the Corvette. You check idler arm wear by having a friend move the steering wheel

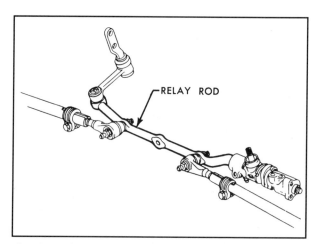

The tie rods are attached to the relay rod. Remember the left hand of the relay rod is held up by the pitman arm, while the right hand of the relay rod is held in place by the idler arm. The idler arm just stands idle. See, all this makes sense if you think about it for a minute.

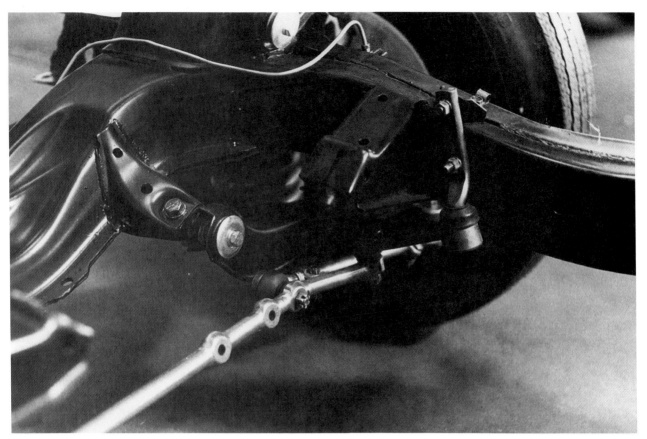

The idler arm bolts to the frame with two bolts. Most professional shops can replace the idler arm in about fifteen minutes. Make certain you're getting a MOOG or TRW replacement, which hold up a lot better than the standard item.

while you check for vertical play in the idler arm. Any more than a 1/4in of vertical play is enough to throw the idler arm in the trash can.

The big problem is that the bushings inside the idler arm are constructed of rubber. This is not quite up to the job, especially if you use wide tires. The secret is to locate a replacement idler arm that uses needle bearings in the shaft. That will usually solve the problem for the coming decade.

Now you've got a Corvette that steers. Move the steering wheel and the center link moves across the car. The only thing left is to connect this center link to the wheels. This is done with tie-rods, which literally tie the front spindle to the center link. Corvettes use a studded ball joint system to make this connection. There are two ball sockets on each end of the tie-rod ends, and they are, you guessed it, a major source of wear.

The proper way to check the tie-rod ends is raise the front of the car off the ground so the front suspension hangs down. Then grasp the tie-rod end near the end of the bar and push the tie-rod end up and down. If you feel any vertical movement, the tie-rod end should be replaced.

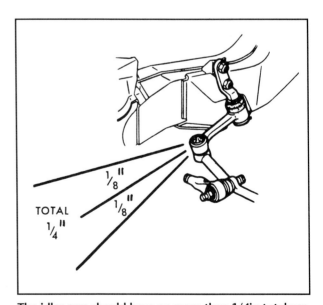

The idler arm should have no more than 1/4in total vertical play. Check this by having your helper turn the steering wheel while you watch the idler arm. If the idler arm moves vertically before transmitting any movement to the tie rod ends, it should be replaced.

In order to adjust the steering lash, loosen the nut on top of the steering box and turn the screw in the center. I've seen cases where an impact air gun was necessary to loosen this nut. Be careful. You should check the fluid level in the steering box by removing the bolt nearest the frame.

These polyurethane replacement boots from Energy Suspension can save you from a lot of headaches. It used to be that if you ripped the rubber boot removing the tie rod end you had to replace the entire rod end. Now you can save some money, unless of course you're building an NCRS car. If you insist on factory replacements, you still pay the extra money.

A second check for these tie-rod ends is to have someone rock the steering wheel back and forth while you pinch the rubber dust boot between your fingers. You must perform this check with the weight of the car resting on the tires. You must not have the car raised in the air for this type of examination. This is one situation where the K-Mart drive-on ramps are handy to own.

The tie-rod end is simply a pivot point. The ball socket should rotate, not jump sideways, when your friend turns the steering wheel. The second check should always be done in conjunction with the first test we outlined. It's entirely possible to have play with the wheels hanging free, and no play when the wheels are resting on the ground. Of course you might have just the opposite situation. In any case make sure you check the tie-rod ends both ways.

These tie-rod ends are connected by adjuster sleeves. These sleeves allow for changing the distance between the center link and the wheels, which means they're used to change the toe specification on the front wheels. The sleeves usually rust before they wear out. In fact I've never seen any wear out.

The steering can be adjusted by using the different holes in the steering arm. The front holes give you faster steering but require more effort. The rear holes will slow down the steering ratio but make it easier to steer the car at slow speeds. The slower steering ratio is just fine unless you insist in taking your car to Watkins Glen several times a year.

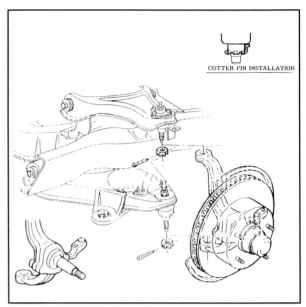

The upper and lower ball joints are what allows the wheels to turn. The steering knuckle is attached to the upper and lower control arms through the use of these ball joints. The lower ball joint is the one that takes most of the stress and will usually need replacement. The upper ball joint can outlast several lower ball joints.

They just rust so much that they can't be adjusted. When they get to that point, the alignment shop can't get the front wheels pointed properly. This is when it's time to replace them.

Have the sleeves cut off, but don't allow them to be replaced with the standard Chevrolet item, unless you're building an NCRS car. It's best to use the heavy-duty adjuster sleeves available from Vette Brakes & Products, since these will not flex during performance driving. The difference in price between the stock items and the performance sleeves is so small it's not worth quibbling over it.

One difference between the 1963 Impala steering assembly and your Corvette's front-end parts is that the Corvette's steering arms, which are connected to the front spindles, have two holes for the tie-rod ends. If you use the front hole you get a quicker steering ratio (17.6:1). If you use the rear holes, you get slower steering (20.2:1). In other words, when you use the rear holes, it takes more turns of the steering wheel to go around the corner. But the quicker ratio makes it lot harder to turn the steering wheel, since you have less leverage.

The problem become even worse when you have wide tires on your Corvette, but there's a very simple solution. First, unless you drive your Corvette at the race track a great deal, use the slower steering ratio. The fast steering ratio is good only when you're trying to make it through a series of turns at the fastest possible speed. For ordinary driving it just isn't worth the trouble it would take to park your car.

Corvette steering is all very basic Chevrolet. When Duntov was making a case for an independent rear suspension (IRS) in the late fifties, General Motors said he could have the expensive IRS if he would use standard Impala front-end parts. If that was the only way Duntov could get the fancy rear suspension then that was what he would do. You don't survive all those years at General Motors without being a pragmatist. The good part is that this decision, made in the early sixties, has made Corvette steering a very easy car to work on.

### Power Steering

Power steering gives you all the leverage you need for parking your car. There was a time when only wimps used power steering. Today you can find power-steering units on just about every race car at the track. When Kyle Petty and Dale Ernhardt use power steering, we have to reconsider all our old prejudices—especially when almost all of the late seventies and early eighties cars came with power steering.

Corvette power steering uses three main components. First, there's the power-steering pump, which is driven by a belt off the crankshaft pulley. The second unit is a control valve assembly that's connected to the pitman arm by a ball stud. The

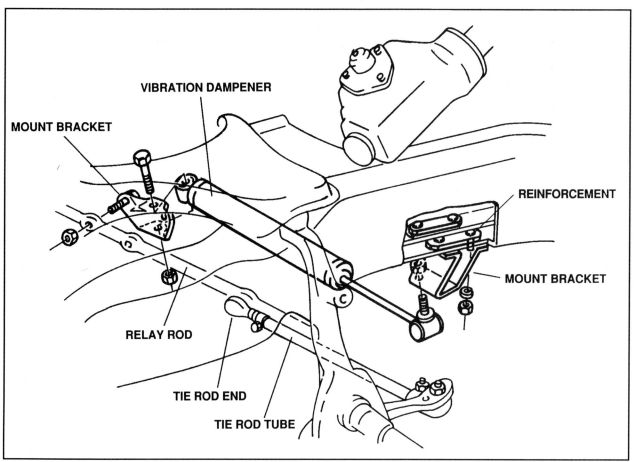

VIBRATION DAMPENER

MOUNT BRACKET

REINFORCEMENT

MOUNT BRACKET

RELAY ROD

TIE ROD END

TIE ROD TUBE

Steering vibrations have always been a Corvette problem. One way to counteract this problem is to use the steering damper, which is nothing more than a shock absorber bolted between the relay rod and the frame. The early version used an adapter that bolted to the relay rod. Later, Chevrolet made a slight revision.

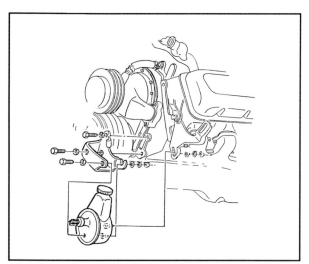

Pictured here is the power steering pump and accompanying brackets. About the only thing that ever goes wrong with this pump is that it develops a leak from a blown seal. This pump seldom wears out from normal use.

third component is the power cylinder connected between the frame and the center link. Everything else is the same as the manual steering system.

The most common power-steering problem is leakage, which generally occurs because the power steering hoses are dying of old age. This means they'll drip power steering fluid all over your driveway. In some cases the problem is that the hoses have been rubbing up against some stray part and have actually burst. If the problem is aging hoses, you lose your power steering fluid slowly, but if the hoses burst, you lose the fluid all at once.

Another source of leaks may be hose fittings that have loosened ever so slightly. In this case, fluid begins to drip out and spread itself all over the steering components. This can usually be repaired by simply tightening the hose fittings. The big problem here, however, is locating the point at which your power steering system is leaking. You already know that if you keep all your power steering parts clean, the job isn't all that hard. Think of power steering

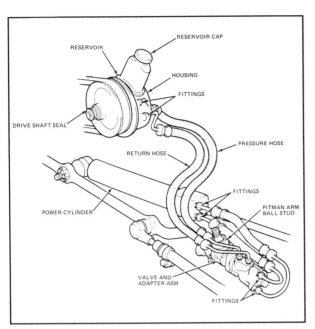

Power steering hoses leak on a regular basis. The trick for tracing a leak is to clean the hoses as much as possible. Then spray talcum powder all over the hoses. Any leak will be readily apparent as it leaves a trail through the talcum powder.

leaks as just one more reason you should keep your Corvette looking good.

In the next chapter we'll discuss how to get the front wheels pointing in the proper direction.

This is what it looks like when you're all done. A job like this represents hours of standing next to the bead-blasting cabinet and being very careful when everything goes back together.

This is called alignment. Once the wheels are properly connected to the steering wheel, it's important that all four wheels roll down the road without scuffing or dragging on the pavement. In other words, you'll want all four of your wheels going in the same direction.

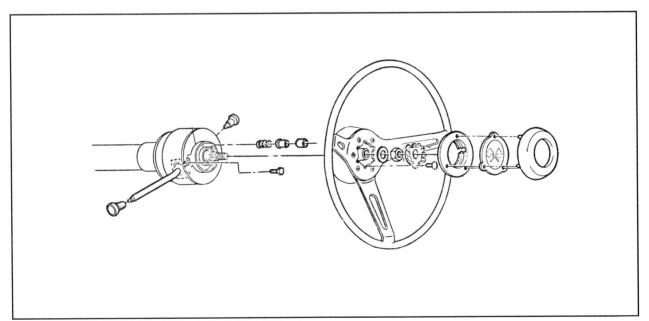

The steering wheel is not a big deal to remove, unless you have a tilt wheel, in which case leave it alone. There are simply too many parts in a tilt wheel to deal with on a rational basis. You're even going to have problems finding a professional willing to rebuild a tilt steering column.

# Chapter 8

# Alignment

A properly aligned Corvette goes down the road without dragging one of the tires along for the ride. Most of the time Corvette owners have at least one wheel that wants to go in a different direction from the other three. This makes the car hard to drive, wears out your tires, and does absolutely nothing for the speed that made us all buy Corvettes in the first place.

The problem is sometimes aggravated when you take your car to the average alignment shop. They usually know what they're doing, but don't seem to care. An alignment that's good enough for the average Geo Storm won't do for a Corvette.

What usually happens is that the alignment technician, or worse yet the service advisor, hands you a computer printout with a bunch of numbers. They quickly confuse you with all of the numbers and they add that insidious comment, "Everything is within factory specs." All you know is that your Corvette doesn't drive properly.

Factory specs are not good enough. The best way to have your Corvette aligned is to specify exactly what you want and then have the alignment shop deliver it. Too often the factory specs have too wide of a range.

There are two items you should take care of before you even start the drive to the alignment shop. First, make sure you have the tire pressures properly set. If one tire is very low on pressure, that corner of the car is going to set lower than it should.

This big-block Corvette is dragging a rear tire down the road. Tire wear is a result of poor alignment. Lack of alignment will not only wear out your tires, but it'll also make your Corvette slower than it should be.

A major source of Corvette rust is the frame pocket where the rear trailing arm is installed. These pockets usually fill with dirt and water, setting up the perfect rust situation. Make sure you clean the entire area and thoroughly undercoat the complete pocket.

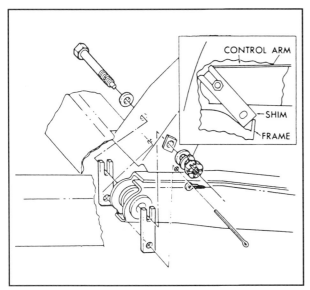

This shows how the rear arm comes together with the frame. The shims come in a variety of thicknesses. The correct combination of shims will give you the correct rear toe setting.

Check all four tires yourself. Don't count on the alignment shop to do it for you.

Second, make sure you don't have any unnecessary items in your Corvette. Extra weight will also make the car sag abnormally. If you carry cement blocks or tool chests in your Corvette, remove them before heading to the alignment shop.

Now let's try to illuminate some of the terminology that the alignment shops use to perplex you.

## Ride Height

This simply refers to the height at which your Corvette sits above the ground. The ride-height check verifies that none of the springs are sagging. If one of the corners of your Corvette is beyond the factory specifications, tell the shop to stop right there. No alignment in the world is going to cure your problem. Don't let them align the car "as good as we can get it." You want it done right, not "close."

The alignment shops have complete ride-height information in their computers. All you have to do is make sure they actually use this information. Too often alignment shops simply use the equipment as a way of selling you new tie-rod ends and ball joints. Don't get caught.

## Toe-In

Toe-in is quite simply the distance between the front edge of the tires and the back edge of the tires. If you have zero degree of toe, then the distance is equal and both of the tires are exactly parallel. If the fronts of the tires are closer together than the backs

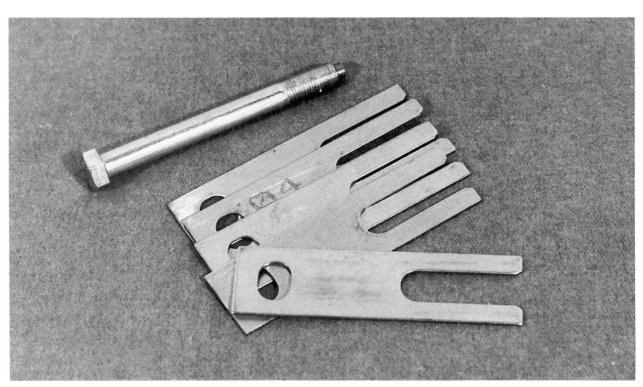

These shims, from Mid-America, are stainless steel reproductions of the original Chevrolet parts. When you finally get around to aligning the rear of your Corvette, it would be foolish to use the original rusted parts.

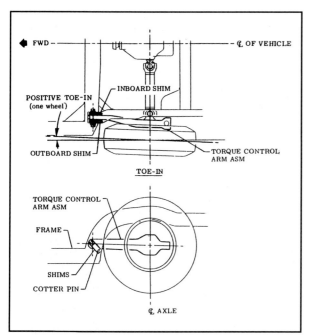

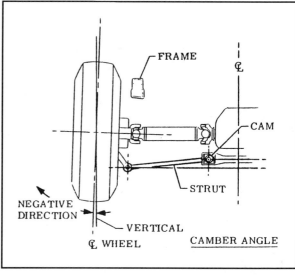

This photo illustrates how the shims actually set the toe on the control arm. If you move shims from the inboard position to the outboard position, the rear tire will toe-in at a greater angle.

The camber is set by changing the length of the rear strut. If you lengthen the rod, it pushes the bottom of the tire out, or in the direction of negative camber. The standard Chevrolet part is adjusted by rotating the bolt at the inboard position. This bolt is actually an eccentric, and turning the cam changes the position of the strut rod. Before you even start aligning your Corvette, check to make certain the strut rod is not bent.

of the tires, you have toe-in. If the distance between the fronts of the tires are further apart than the backs, then you have toe-out.

The Corvette is generally set so there's a slight amount of toe-in. The idea is that when you actually get going down the road, this small amount of toe-in will change to zero toe. This is also referred to as the difference between dynamic and static alignment.

Another point to remember is that your Corvette has settings for both front and rear toe. Both of these settings have to be accurate in order for your car to drive down the road in a straight line without wearing out the tires.

Bad toe settings account for almost all of the excessive tire wear on Corvettes. Camber and caster can cause problems and wear out tires, but neither of those settings will eat your tires away like a poor toe setting.

## Camber

This is a measurement of how far the top of the tire leans in, or out. Camber is normally measured in the degree of the angle between the wheel and a true vertical line. For instance, with two degrees of negative camber, the tire is leaning inward two degrees off of vertical.

Camber is always a compromise between performance and tire wear. If the tire leans too far in, or out, you're going to have excessive tire wear. On the other hand if you want maximum performance you're going to want the tire leaning in at the top. This is called negative camber. Negative camber means that when you go around a corner, the tire will actually be on a vertical angle, and the maximum amount of rubber is coming in contact with the road. The only way to get a tire vertical in a corner is to have it at an angle when the Corvette is sitting still

## Alignment Specifications (in degrees)

|  | Warranty Repairs | Periodic Alignment | Resetting |
|---|---|---|---|
| Caster | +1.25 to +3.25 | +0.25 to +4.25 | +2.25 to +/- 1 |
| Camber | 0 to +1.5 | -0.75 to +2.25 | +0.75 to -0.5 |
| Toe-In (total) | +0.125 to +0.375 |  |  |
| Toe-In (deg. per wheel) | +0.12 to +0.36 |  |  |
| Cross Caster | No More Than 1 Variation | No More Than 1/2 Diff |  |
| Cross Camber | No More Than 1 Variation |  |  |

Here is the outer strut mounting arrangement. At this point you should make certain the rubber bushing is in good condition. Energy Suspension makes polyurethane replacement bushings that are an improvement over the stock bushings, without being too harsh.

on the alignment rack. I'll get back to this whole idea of negative camber when I talk about modifying the alignment settings on your Corvette.

## Caster

This is the hardest one too understand. It's also the one that most alignment shops try to ignore. Technically, caster is the pivot angle of the front wheels. It helps if you think about your bicycle. All bicycles have positive camber. If you take a look down the front forks of your bike and draw an imaginary line down the forks, you'll notice that this line hits the ground way out in front of where the tire actually meets the road. This is positive caster at the extreme.

The more positive caster you have on your Corvette, the more self-centering and responsive the steering will feel. The downside is that the greater the positive caster, the harder your Corvette will be to turn at slow speeds and the harder it will be to park your Corvette.

Just in case you don't believe alignments vary depending on who does the work, check out the Chevrolet shop manual. They give one set of specifi-

cations for warranty and another for a normal alignment, and they have a third set of specifications for when you're just getting your vehicle checked.

## Aligning The Rear Tires

The rear tires on your Corvette have alignment settings just like the front tires, but they cause even more problems than the fronts. In particular, some of the rear specifications are more difficult to set than the front, which means the person aligning your Corvette must have a great deal of skill. More importantly it means you'll be paying this technician a lot more money.

## Changing The Settings

The specifications Chevrolet developed for the Corvette are still the best all-purpose alignment numbers you can use. If you never drive your Corvette fast, these settings work very well. The car will feel stable and you'll get decent tire wear. What you won't get is maximum performance at high-speed NCCC events. Consequently, it pays to take a look at

For Project Corvette I used a Vette Brakes & Products tie rod connection. This rod has left-hand threads on one end and right-hand threads on the other end. If you turn the rod clockwise, you create toe-out. If you turn the rod counterclockwise, you can reduce the amount of toe-out. The big advantage is that the rod is a lot stronger than the stock Chevrolet part. If you drive fast and use large sticky tires, this is the best arrangement.

Once you adjust the front toe to the desired setting, you simply tighten the jam nut on the end to hold the setting.

what happens when you deviate from the stock Corvette alignment numbers in an effort to get even more performance from your Corvette.

### Tire Pressures

Changing the pressure in your Corvette's tires can make a big difference. A higher tire pressure will decrease the amount of tread surface that's in contact with the road. When you lower the tire pressure, more of the tire will be in contact with the pavement. However, if you get the tire pressure too low, the tire will roll right off the rim when you go around a corner.

There are two ways to determine tire pressure for maximum performance. First, we have the cheap way, or the old trick of putting white shoe polish on the sidewall. After you come back into the pits, you can check how much tire tread you used by the amount of shoe polish that has been rubbed off. Though unscientific, this approach will at least get you a ballpark estimate.

Your goal is to use every bit of tread of this high speed tire. When the shoe polish wears off at

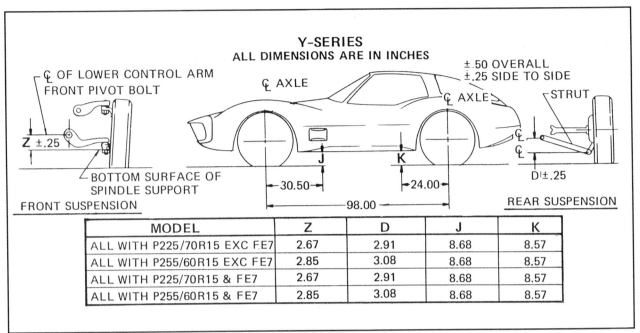

**Y-SERIES**
**ALL DIMENSIONS ARE IN INCHES**

| MODEL | Z | D | J | K |
|---|---|---|---|---|
| ALL WITH P225/70R15 EXC FE7 | 2.67 | 2.91 | 8.68 | 8.57 |
| ALL WITH P255/60R15 EXC FE7 | 2.85 | 3.08 | 8.68 | 8.57 |
| ALL WITH P225/70R15 & FE7 | 2.67 | 2.91 | 8.68 | 8.57 |
| ALL WITH P255/60R15 & FE7 | 2.85 | 3.08 | 8.68 | 8.57 |

Before attempting any alignment, make sure the ride height is accurately set. Notice the frame height is always the same, regardless of tire size and suspension options. Also note that ride height is given in hundredths of an inch. When was the last time the local tire store checked that carefully? I suggest you copy this page and take it to the alignment shop with your Corvette.

the very edge of the tread, you've reached the optimum tire pressure. The best way to do this is to sneak up on the correct pressure. Start with the factory tire pressure, and drop the pressure by 2lb intervals until you reach the edge of the tread. If you start too low, you run the risk of ripping all that expensive rubber directly off the rim.

The second way to determine tire pressure is to actually measure the temperature of the rubber after you do a couple of laps at the track. You'll need at least 90° of heat in the tires to do this. If you go above 220°, you've got a real problem, and you'd better talk to a tire professional.

The temperature should be even at three points on the tread. The only hitch is that caster, camber, and toe settings can also affect tire temperatures. The best time to play with these settings is when the B.F. Goodrich Team T/A folks are around. Listen to them rather than all your Corvette friends.

## Changing Caster
Earlier I pointed out that the more caster your Corvette has, the more self-centering and responsive the steering will be. Increased caster will also give you more negative camber on the outside front wheel in a turn, not a bad thing. But increased caster also creates two problems. First, the car is going to be harder to steer at slow speeds, and this—combined with wide tires—will give you strong arms, or force you to install power steering.

The second problem is that at high speeds your Corvette will feel nervous, too responsive, and you'll need to steer the car all the time. The correct caster for a National Council of Corvettes event will not be the best setting for the street. Chevrolet uses very little caster. They feel that as little as 1/4 degree of caster is quite adequate. Dick Gulstrand, who knows more about Corvettes than any ten people,

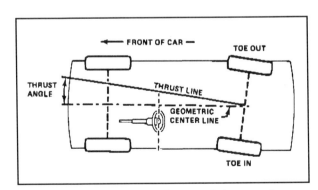

In a four-wheel alignment the toe of the rear tires are measured against the geometric center line of your Corvette. Ideally the thrust angle and the geometric center line of your Corvette is the same line. Since rear toe is adjustable, make certain the rear is properly adjusted before you let the alignment shop begin on the front toe settings. Once the rear toe is properly set, the front wheel toe can be set so all four wheels are tracking the geometric center line of the vehicle.

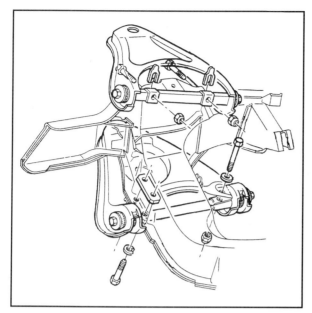

The front camber and caster is set with the use of shims. If your front end starts to make noise, check to make sure the bolts are tight. It's not uncommon for the bolts to loosen and the shims to fall out on the road.

goes all the way to 3° of positive caster in his racing Corvettes.

The net result of this discussion is that you can stick with the factory settings only if you drive your Corvette on the street. Changing the alignment settings, though, can do wonders for your Corvette at the race track. Just remember that you'll never drive fast enough on the street to utilize any deviations from the stock Chevrolet settings. The next part of this chapter is really for the people who use their cars at NCCC or SCCA track events.

## Race Track Alignment

### Camber

Everyone talks about negative camber wearing out tires. In my experience this really isn't a big problem. For a high-performance street Corvette, you really don't need much negative camber. But, if you're involved in any sort of motorsports, then you'll want to dial in a lot of negative camber. A lot of people are running about 3° of negative camber with the new radial tires. This is a whole lot of negative camber. The downside of high negative camber is that your Corvette will be less stable under braking, since only part of the tread will be in contact with the track during straight-line braking.

You can easily live with 1° or 2° of negative camber on the street. With Project Corvette I went to 1° of negative camber for the street. When I take it up to Pocono, I use 2.5+ degrees of negative camber at the rear, and about 2° of negative camber on the front tires.

### Toe

Remember, the perfect car will have zero toe all the time. Yet, this just isn't possible. Adjusting the toe-in should be the last adjustment you make on an alignment, and always bear in mind that the static toe setting and the dynamic toe settings are usually quite different.

Since merely driving down the road pushes the tires apart, we compensate by adjusting the tires toward each other (toe-in) when the car is on the alignment rack. When you drive down the street, all the dynamic forces push the tires to zero toe.

By changing the toe settings on your Corvette, you increase tire wear, high-speed instability, and problems under braking. There is no perfect alignment setting; everything is a compromise. You'll find that playing with alignment setting can give you more performance than all the carburetor adjustments combined. The best part is that when you're done, your Corvette will be a lot more fun to drive.

Now that we've spent a lot of time looking at a variety of Corvette alignment settings, it's worth spending a few minutes looking at where Dick Gulstrand sets up Corvettes.

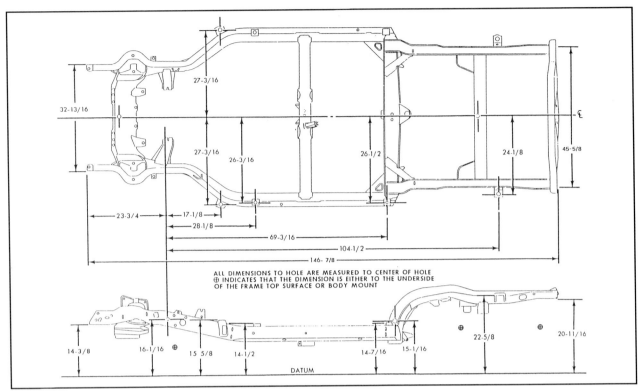

ALL DIMENSIONS TO HOLE ARE MEASURED TO CENTER OF HOLE
⊕ INDICATES THAT THE DIMENSION IS EITHER TO THE UNDERSIDE
OF THE FRAME TOP SURFACE OR BODY MOUNT

Occasionally it's impossible to align a Corvette. The car may have been crashed and the frame is bent. The only way to check for this problem is to locate a good collision shop and have all these dimensions checked very carefully.

Clearly there are a number of different alignment settings that can used for a variety of purposes. Dick Gulstrand's recommendations for street use are probably the best all-around numbers.

When you go to the alignment shop, take thse settings with you. You'll have to convince them that these are the settings you want on your Corvette—with no deviation, or range, on these settings.

I've also learned the hard way that you'll want to keep the printout from the computer. Most alignment shops will tell you anything, but the printout doesn't lie, so it will be the only way of knowing your settings are correct.

Basically, you want your Corvette to go straight down the road with as little effort as possible, and you want it to stop in a straight line without darting from side to side. On a street Corvette this means finding an alignment shop that knows how to use all their fancy computerized alignment equipment.

## GULSTRAND ALIGNMENT SETTINGS

|  | Camber (in degrees) | Castor (in degrees) | Toe (inches) |
| --- | --- | --- | --- |
| RACING | | | |
| Front | 1/2 to 1 neg | 2 to 3 pos | 0 to 3/16 |
| Rear | 1/2 to 1 neg | —— | 0 to 1/4 |
| AUTOCROSS | | | |
| Front | 1/2 to 1 neg | 1 to 1/2 pos | 1/8 to 1/8 |
| Rear | 1/2 to 3/4 neg | —— | 0 to 1/4 |
| STREET | | | |
| Front | 1/4 to 1/2 neg | 1 1/2 to 2 1/2 pos | 1/8 to 3/16 |
| Rear | 0 to 1/2 neg | | 1/16 to 1/8 |

# Chapter 9

# Wheels and Tires

I like tires. Since no one really knows very much about why the latest high-tech tires work so well, everyone can be an expert. All you have to do is bolt a set of the latest tires on your Corvette and people will start asking you about the best cornering technique. Put a set of F70x15 reproduction tires on your older Vette and people will start asking you about the NCRS.

The latest high-tech tires are better than your car. Very few people ever use these new high-tech tires to the limit. Modern tires are simply faster than most cars and drivers. They contain more dry-weather performance than you could ever use on the street.

At some race tracks, these DOT-approved tires are faster than racing slicks. If you take the average Corvette and switch from the latest BF Goodrich Comp T/A R1 tires to racing slicks, your lap times might even increase. That's how good the latest single-purpose tires stick to the pavement. How's that for modern technology? Street-legal tires as fast as racing slicks.

To achieve the potential of these tires, however, your chassis has to be in perfect shape. Put a set of the latest BF Goodrich T/A R1 tires on a rusted-out Corvette and the frame will start breaking from all the stress. Seriously.

Single-purpose tires stick so well that everything comes under tremendous pressure. Bushings that could take the pressure a few years ago will now deflect into some strange shapes. You'll also find your cornering will take some strange shapes when these bushings deflect.

Project Corvette got the best of both worlds. I used the latest all-season tires, installed on a set of Corvette rally rims for normal use. This makes a lot of

Chevrolet used this classic Corvette steel wheel from 1968 to 1982. Less than 2,000 Corvettes were built in 1982 with the standard rally wheel. Steel wheels may be the rarest of the 1982 cars. No one even remembers seeing a Corvette with steel wheels in 1982.

One of the trickiest jobs is removing the center trim section without scratching the outer rim. The best technique is to remove it with your hands. When it finally pulls off, be careful you don't drop it and scratch the outer trim ring.

This is an unusual combination—a black car with the rally wheels painted black. You could easily do the wheels in body color for a different look. Considering how easy it would be to customize these wheels, I'm surprised more people haven't tried it.

Chevrolet introduced this wheel in 1973 but was never able to actually install it. A few sets were made by American Racing Equipment but never seen on an actual car. It's possible that four customers got the wheel, but even that seems remote. Finally, in 1976 Kelsey-Hayes and Western produced this wheel for factory installation.

sense because tires can only do three things: They can produce dry traction, they can be wonderful in wet weather, or they can wear forever. The only problem is that a tire can't do all three things at the same time; at least one will be compromised for the others.

I've chosen the BF Goodrich HP/4 all-season tire because these give me some traction in wet weather, as opposed to the latest dry-weather single-purpose R1 tire. These latest all-season tires will also be faster than we'll ever be able to drive on the street with Project Corvette.

When Project Corvette goes to the racetrack, I can install the latest DOT street-legal race tire on a set of American Racing Equipment mags. This is called having your Hostess cupcake and eating it as well.

When it comes to tire sizes, let's start with the tires that the 1982 Corvettes arrived on—the 255/60R15. The best part is that they still fit on the Corvette. I tried to jump to 275/60R15, but they really didn't fit under the fiberglass. There is a limit, and I found it.

## Wheels

You should learn to like the wheels that came on your Corvette. The 1968 to 1982 Corvettes have a very limited supply of wheels. You actually have two choices. You can put a set of stock wheels, either alloy or aluminum, on your Corvette, or you can spend some very serious money for larger wheels. There is nothing in between.

The stock Corvette rally wheel is the most popular wheel ever made. They're on everything Chevrolet ever manufactured. I'm sure some Ford owners have even tried to put them on cars with the blue oval. The good part is that these stock Corvette wheels fit without using wheel spacers.

### Stock Corvette Wheels

The 1968 to 1982 Corvettes have a major problem: The brake calipers get in the way of most wheels and the edge of the brake caliper sticks out

The Special Commemorative Edition aluminum wheel for 1982 fits right in with the GT image of the final third-generation Corvettes. The only problem is that they're very difficult to keep clean. The classic white letter tires are rapidly becoming a thing of the past. Most of the major tires manufacturers no longer make a tire with white outline letters.

Even though a quarter of a century has passed, most people still feel this classic American Racing Equipment wheel is the best-looking wheel you can put on a Corvette. The only problem is that it won't clear the brake caliper. You have to use wheel spacers in order to mount the wheel, which can present a lot of problems.

beyond the hub face. Everything goes very well until you try to rotate the wheel and the caliper rubs against the back of the wheel. Wheels that don't go around are not a good thing.

Chevrolet found this out in 1965. The 1965 Corvette wheels are slightly different from the 1964 wheels, because the new brake calipers hit the inside edge of the old wheel. It only took me three decades to catch on. Worse yet, though, a lot of the aftermarket wheel manufacturers still haven't caught on.

Some of the aftermarket wheel suppliers solve this problem through the use of wheel spacers—a controversial idea. In fact, companies like Moroso and American Racing even refuse to sell spacers for this application. The problem with spacers is that the lug nuts can loosen after driving. Spacers also put a lot of extra strain on the wheel studs, causing the studs to break and your wheel to fall off. Not a good situation, but racers have had acceptable results with sticky BF Goodrich R1 tires on the American Racing mags for high-speed NCCC events. Mr. Gasket makes a set of spacers that seem to work just fine for this application.

Every time I've used spacers, I've gotten in the habit of checking the lug nuts with a torque wrench

Crager also made a wheel for the third-generation Corvettes. The Crager wheel gives the Corvette the classic hot-rod look of the early sixties, but these wheels have the same problem with the brake caliper as the American mag wheel. You'll need to use a wheel spacer in your effort to get adequate clearance.

The problem with all the aftermarket wheels is that the brake caliper hits the wheel spokes. Some of the vintage race car people have been known to machine the caliper to get the wheels to fit, something I didn't want to get involved with. The other alternative is to install a spacer between the brake rotor and the wheel.

This is a wheel spacer from Mr. Gasket, the only company that still produces wheel spacers. Lawyers have scared all the other companies out of the business. Remember to check the torque on the lug nuts every week if you're going to use a wheel spacer. People have been known to have problems with using spacers, so be very careful.

every fifty miles. Not a big deal at the race track. If you don't have the desire to tighten your lug nuts every fifty miles, then you can simply use the wheels that Chevrolet originally sold with your Corvette.

The rarest of all stock Corvette wheels is the rally wheel on the 1968 Corvette, the only year 7in wheels were offered on the Corvette. All of these 1968 7in steel wheels seem to have disappeared over the last few decades. Most 1968 Corvette owners took the 7in wheels off their cars and installed 8in rally wheels. The old 7in wheels are now either installed on Monte Carlos, or buried in a landfill in New Jersey.

If you're intent on building an NCRS or Bloomington Gold car, start looking for these wheels as soon as possible. Stock 1968 wheels may be the most difficult part of your restoration, since there are no reproductions.

In 1969 Chevrolet went to the 8in Corvette rally wheel. They stayed with this wheel right up to the very end of C3 production in 1982, which was also the last year a steel wheel was ever offered for the Corvette. Aluminum wheels became more popular, and less than 2,000 Corvettes were produced with steel rally wheels in 1982.

From 1969 to 1982 all Corvettes had the same steel wheels. The chart below shows the different offsets for the rally wheels manufactured between 1967 and 1982.

| Size | Part Number | Year | Offset | Comments |
|------|-------------|------|--------|----------|
| 15x6 | 3968773 | 1967 | 1/8in | Stamped DC |
| 15x7 | 3910799 | 1968 | 9/32in | Stamped AG |
| 15x8 | 327708 | 1969–82 | 1/2in | Stamped AZ |

The part numbers in the chart are from an old 1972 parts book and may have changed several times by now. This shouldn't be a problem for your local Chevrolet dealership. They can simply punch this number into their computer system and tell you what is currently available from the factory.

## Aftermarket Rally Wheels

There are a lot of aftermarket rally wheels available. These reproduction wheels work just fine unless you're interested in NCRS or Bloomington awards. There doesn't seem to be a totally accurate rally wheel on the market. The good part is that these replacement wheels are very easy to identify. The bad part is that all the judges in the world also know the difference.

All the original rally wheels were made by Kelsey-Hayes and had the rims welded to the center of the wheels. Kelsey-Hayes also makes most of the reproduction wheels on the market, but the reproduction wheels have the center of the wheel riveted to the rim. In every other respect, original and reproduction wheels are exactly the same.

## Date Codes

If you want an NCRS Duntov award or Bloomington Gold Corvette, you have to pay attention not only to the way the center is attached to the rim, you must also notice the date code. This date code will

Compare the width of these three wheels: the one on the right is the stock 1968 Corvette wheel; the wheel in the middle is the 1969 to 1982 Corvette steel wheel; and the widest wheel, on the left, is from American Racing Equipment.

This is called the backspace, or offset. Before you buy any aftermarket wheels for your Corvette make sure you do some careful measuring. Very few companies will allow you to return a wheel once it's had a tire mounted or had balance weights installed.

Here's a case of what happens when you get too wide of a wheel. This wheel and tire will never fit into the fender. The first time the car is driven hard, the fender will squat down onto the tire causing all sorts of damage to both the tire and the fender. Even if this Corvette never goes fast, the road debris will make a mess of the paint. Here was a Corvette owner who went over the edge with a tire/wheel combination.

usually be stamped into the hub, or drop-center, of the wheel. It'll look like this: K-1-8.

The K means Kelsey-Hayes, while the first number (1) means the Chevrolet Division, and the second number (8) signifies year, which, in the case of Project Corvette, is 1968. The other four wheels on Project Corvette are stamped K-1-70, which means they were originally installed on a 1970 Corvette. Somewhere out there in the world is a 1970 Corvette either setting on four milk crates, or more likely four strange wheels.

### Balancing

One of the most difficult tasks is matching the factory balancing. Chevrolet never used wheel weights on the outside of the rim. The clearance between the wheel and the trim ring is very tight, and

The tire on the right is a BF Goodrich 255/60R15. The tire on the left is an F70x15 reproduction tire. Both are roughly the same height. The overall diameter, or height, of the tire is critical. People get too involved with tire width when they should be concerned about how tall the tire is and how well the tire fills the wheel well.

it may have been that Chevrolet didn't feel there was enough room for the balance weights. On the other hand, Chevrolet never used balance weights on the outside of alloy wheels either.

B. F. Goodrich taught me the trick to balancing wheels. In my effort to keep a Corvette looking

Reproduction tires are great for shows but they do very little for your driving pleasure. Tire technology has gone so far beyond what the reproduction tires offer that I really can't understand why people continue to use them. On the other hand, if your Corvette is a trailer queen, why not put out-of-round tires on the car?

The tire on the left is the latest BF Goodrich all-season tire. The tire on the right is the single-purpose R1 BF Goodrich tire.

This is the tread pattern for the BF Goodrich R compound tire. These are street-legal racing tires. If you compete in NCCC events, you're already on a first-name basis with these tires. If you want to go really fast, you should be dialing 1-800-847-8475 to find out more about the latest hi-tech rubber.

stock, and without putting wheel weights on the outside of American Racing Equipment wheels, I started asking questions about how to balance tires without the balance weights showing.

The trick is to use tape weights stuck to the center of the wheel. Set the balancer the same way as if you were going to use weights on both sides of the wheel. When the wheel balancer gives you instructions about where to place the weights, simply put the tape weights in the center of the wheel. The balance won't be perfect so you'll have to do it a second time with smaller weights. With your second attempt, or maybe the third, the tire should show a perfect balance.

The only thing to be concerned about is that the brake caliper doesn't hit any of the weights, but this shouldn't be a problem with the Corvette. This is an especially good trick with alloy wheels since the ugly clamp on weights won't destroy the look of your wheel.

## Chevrolet Alloy Wheels

The first alloy wheels were offered by Chevrolet in 1973, but there were problems. Very few sets,

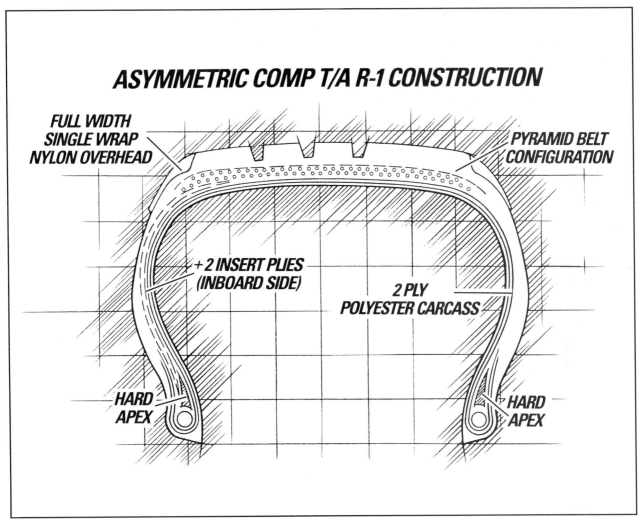

## ASYMMETRIC COMP T/A R-1 CONSTRUCTION

FULL WIDTH
SINGLE WRAP
NYLON OVERHEAD

PYRAMID BELT
CONFIGURATION

+2 INSERT PLIES
(INBOARD SIDE)

2 PLY
POLYESTER CARCASS

HARD
APEX

HARD
APEX

This drawing shows why the T/A R-1 tires let you go so fast.

possibly only four sets, ever made it to the dealers. In 1976 Chevrolet tried once again. This time they got it right, and the alloy wheels became an option.

These aluminum wheels will fit any of the Corvettes up until 1982, and they seem to be just about the only alloy wheels on the market that don't require using wheel spacers.

The trick to keeping these wheels looking good is to make sure you don't let brake dust and dirt build up on the wheels. However, never clean them when they're hot and always use a wheel cleaner with a low PH value. When it comes to alloy wheels you should start reading the labels on the wheel cleaners very closely.

### Tires

This is where the real revolution in performance has been happening. Corvette owners spend a lot of time talking about engines, but most of the big performance gains in the last ten years have been happening where the rubber meets the road.

The only problem with this tire revolution is that you need to be very well-informed about tires. The technology of the new high-tech rubber has surpassed the ability of your local tire dealer to keep informed about the product. Only about six tire stores in the United States really know anything about the latest high-performance tires.

The average tire store sells very few high-performance tires in the course of a year. The majority of people still want a long-wearing all-season radial tire, and the average tire store is geared to help this customer. When you drive in with your Corvette and start asking about dry weather traction and extended tread life, you're just confusing the issue, not to mention the tire salesman.

Making a decision about tires for your Corvette requires that you either locate a store, like NTW, that

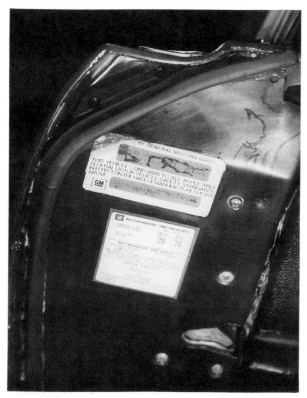

There should be a tire pressure decal on the driver's side door. This sticker will tell you that tire pressure should be 20lbs in the front and 26lbs in the rear. This decal also states that tire size should be GR70x15. M. F. Dobbins has any decal you could possibly want for your Corvette. A properly finished Corvette will have all new decals.

has a performance tire specialist on staff, or learn about tires by asking people in the tire industry a lot of questions.

Things got complicated when different race-sanctioning groups decided that the way for racers to save money on their hobby was to mandate the use of street tires on the race cars. This was just one more failed effort to hold down the cost of racing. To no one's surprise, racing just kept getting more expensive, and the cars got a whole lot faster.

The tire manufacturers, especially BF Goodrich, saw the DOT tire requirement as an opportunity to promote the sale of high-performance street tires. It was all part of the old idea, "win on Sunday, sell on Monday." The good part is that we now can purchase street-legal tires that are just as fast as the slicks of three years ago.

BF Goodrich has always been the leader in the quest for the highest performance street tires. A host of other tire companies have competed with BFG over the years, with the result that today we have street tires that stick so well they'll rip your chassis apart.

These new tires, like the ones we installed on Project Corvette, will bring out every weakness in your Corvette chassis. With the old street tires, the first thing that broke loose was the rubber on the tire. Now the tire stays glued to the ground so well that every half-worn part in the chassis is noticeable.

BF Goodrich, Yokohama, and occasionally Goodyear, have decided that the high-performance market is where they want to be, and they're willing to risk everything on this marketing strategy. Corvette owners are the ones who benefit.

There shouldn't be any tire tread sticking out past the top of the fender line. This means that the best all-around tire for the third-generation Corvette is a 255/60R15. You really can't go much larger than this size. Even with this size you might have trouble with the front fender hitting the tire. No one has ever been successful at installing the 275/60R15 on these Corvettes. Both BF Goodrich and I have tried. Believe me—it won't fit.

The best way to deal with rally wheels is to have them sandblasted and then painted using the wheel paint from Eastwood. The stock wheels were first painted black on the back, and then silver on the front. No taping was carried out at the factory, so on a show car, silver overspray should be found on the backside.

This is a 245/60R15 on a Western wheel. Not all tire companies make this tire size.

Here we have a 255/60R15 on an aftermarket wheel. I believe these rough-cast wheels were made by Western. There are no polished areas on this wheel. Getting a high-performance tire that fits the third-generation Corvette can be a problem. The 15in wheel is consid-ered an antique, hence getting modern ultra-perfor-mance tires is becoming a real problem. All-season tires, such as this BF Goodrich are readily available, but not the Z-rated racing compounds.

One big problem with alloy wheels is the use of wheel weights. First, if you insist on using wheel weights on the outside of the wheel, then at least use the plastic covered weights. You could also use tape weights on the inside of the wheel. Place these weights as close to the center of the wheel as possible. It may take several attempts to get the wheel balanced, but when you're done the tire will be perfectly balanced, and no ugly wheel weight will be showing on the rim.

Other companies like Dunlop, Bridgestone, and Pirelli have tried to compete in the high-performance market and went running back to the shelter of all-season tires. The competition is so fierce that you can have the fastest tire in June only to be beaten every time you leave the starting grid in September. There have been years when the whole process was referred to as the "Tire-Of-The-Month Club."

Before you purchase these truly serious tires you have to ask, "Do I really need these R compound tires?" These tires have performance capabilities you will probably never use and are way beyond what any person needs for street driving. These are race car tires that happen to be street legal. They're also a lot of fun when you go fast at the racetrack.

Even if you decide you don't need a tire BFG R/1, you should join BFG's Team T/A, which costs absolutely nothing to join, and they'll send you the only newsletter in the country dedicated to high-performance tires. Even better, they give you an 800 number you can call for advice about the best tire for your Corvette. If you ever go to an NCCC national event, you'll see the Team T/A tractor trailer rig loaded with the latest and fastest street-legal tires in the world.

## The All-Season Tire

There is no technical definition for an all-season tire. "All-Season" is a marketing term that means

This shows what happens when you use a wheel weight without the plastic coating. These stains are almost impossible to remove.

you don't need snow tires. If you only intend to use your Corvette on the street, these are probably going to be the best all-around choice.

Street usage demands a tire that can handle rain. The R compound tires may be fast, but they are miserable in the rain. If they act like slicks in the dry, then they will also act like slicks in wet weather. If you intend to drive your Corvette in the rain, you should seriously consider a set of high-performance all-season tires.

The other problem with C3 Corvette tires is that the 15in wheel is rapidly becoming obsolete. The true ultra-performance tire is becoming difficult to find in this size, which is one more reason you might want to consider using a V-rated all-season tire on your Corvette.

## Reproduction Tires

These are probably the worst tires you can put on your Corvette—unless you're going to enter a car show. If you plan on taking your Corvette to an NCRS meet, or to Bloomington to collect the coveted gold award, then you must purchase these reproduction tires for your Corvette. Just don't try driving to the show. As good as these tires are for shows, they're equally bad for actual driving.

Reproduction tires are for owners who want their Corvettes to look just like they did the day they left St. Louis. The problem is that reproduction tires won't allow you to enjoy the performance of the Corvette you install them on. I have never met an owner of a Corvette who enjoyed driving on reproduction tires. It seems to have something to do with the fact that they're not really round.

Here's a good example of what's possible with the alloy wheels from Chevrolet. The owner polished the wheel to a high luster and probably went directly through the clear-coat finish. The price of this luster is a wheel that will take a lot of maintenance. You decide if it's worth the weekly effort.

The object of Project Corvette was to enjoy driving the car. As great as repro tires look, I just can't deal with them on a street car. The solution is to have a set of all-season tires mounted on rally wheels.

Next, I purchased a set of the all-out banzai R1 Comp TA tires from B. F. Goodrich for excursions to Pocono and Watkins Glen. These tires have to be mounted on a set of American Racing Equipment mags. Even if Project Corvette isn't a vintage racer, I can have the all-important look. Just as you alternate wearing both suits and sports jackets, why should your Corvette wear only one set of wheels and tires?

**Changing Tire Sizes**

If you have a pre-1978 Corvette, you're going to change tires sizes. You have no choice. Once upon a time there was a tire called a GR70 installed on your Corvette. They don't make them any more. The best approximation of this old tire is the 255/60ZR15, which is slightly wider but is the same height as the GR70.

There's a possibility that the front tires might hit some fiberglass, so check very carefully before you go on some midnight banzai run. The rear tires present no problem. As I mentioned earlier, I tried installing 275/60ZR15 tires on the rear of the car, but they were just a bit too big.

Another thing you shouldn't do is try and install fifty-series tires on these third-generation Corvettes since the diameter of the tire is just too small. The 255/60ZR15 tire used on Project Corvette have an overall diameter of 27.1in. If I were to install a 265/ 50ZR15, the overall diameter would be only 25.4in.

A reduction of almost two inches in diameter does two things. First it lowers the car one inch—not all bad. Secondly, it leaves an extra inch between the top of the tire and the bottom of the fender opening. You end up with a Corvette that has problems with reduced ground clearance, altered final drive ratios, and looks like it has baby-buggy tires installed.

Basically, with third-generation Corvettes, you have almost no choice when it comes to tire size. The wheels are also very limiting. But when it comes to settling on the type of tire, the choices are tremendous.

The only black cloud on the horizon is that most tire companies are in the process of phasing out 15in tires in the ultra-performance category, so buy yours today, or hope that someone comes to the rescue with a 17in wheel. Perhaps even a 20-in wheel would be nice on our Corvettes—anything with an overall tire diameter between 27in and 29in.

# Chapter 10

# Brakes

Brakes have always been a problem with Corvettes. The cars are heavy and they go very fast. Remember how in high school physics you learned that energy couldn't be destroyed, it could only be converted? Well, the energy of a Corvette going 90mph can't be eliminated, it can only be converted to heat energy. And you wondered why your brakes got so hot? Now you know.

The job of the brakes is to take all the mechanical energy from your Bow-tie power and convert it into heat. After you've created all this heat, the next trick is to dissipate it. The key to a good brake system is to do everything possible to spread the heat, generated by stopping the car, into the air around your car.

The legendary J56 brake option offered on the L88 Corvettes was simply a way of dealing with the heat generated by braking. The brakes on the L88 racing Corvettes would get so hot that the steel backing plate on the pads would actually warp, at which point the brakes were non-existent.

The extra lip on the J56 brake-pad backing plate was designed to keep the plate from warping. Chevrolet wasn't able to dissipate the heat generat-

Most master cylinders go bad because people never change the brake fluid. Since brake fluid is hydroscopic, moisture builds up and rust starts. Stick your hand down to the bottom of the master cylinder. If you come up with sludge, it's time to change the brake fluid. If you've owned your Corvette for more than a year and haven't changed the fluid, it's time. Changing the brake fluid is nothing more than bleeding the brakes until brand-new clean fluid comes out of the bleeder screws. The key to bleeding the brakes is to keep the master cylinder filled with fluid. If you let the master cylinder run dry, you'll have to push air completely through the system.

If you have to install a new master cylinder, you must bleed it prior to installation in the car. Over one-half of the master cylinders that professional mechanics return as defective are really quite good. The service technician simply neglected to bench bleed the master cylinder.

The little bleeder hoses are sometimes in the box with the new master cylinder. If they're not present, purchase a set from the parts house that just sold you the master cylinder.

ed by racing quickly enough so they simply built a backing pad, that could deal with the tremendous heat.

Today there's no real use in having the J56 brake option; technology has gone beyond that

point. Leave the dual pin brakes for the restoration crowd—they get extra points when they counterfeit all those L88 Corvettes. I talked to Andy Porterfield, who has raced more Trans Am Corvettes than most of us have even seen, and he suggested I deal with

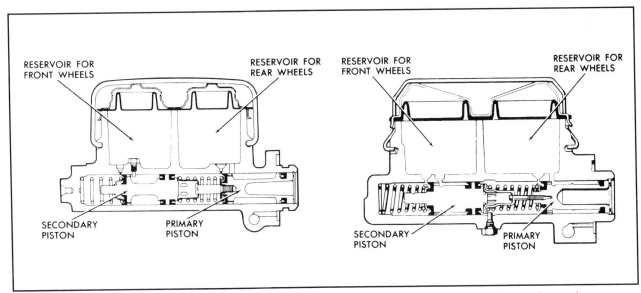

When a master cylinder is defective it's because the little rubber seals on the secondary or primary piston have started to leak. This can be because they just simply wore out, or more often, they were torn by a piece of

rust in the master cylinder bore. If you change your brake fluid on an annual basis, you'll never have a master cylinder problem.

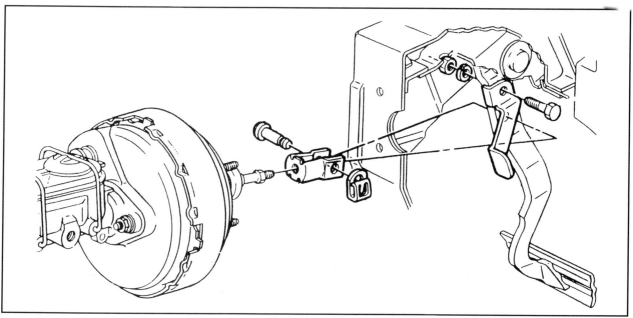

This sequence of drawings show how a power brake assembly goes together. The booster assembly seldom goes bad, so you usually don't have to worry about replacing the entire assembly. If the booster does fail, you'll need a whole new assembly. Caledonia Classic Cars used to rebuild boosters so it's worth a call to see if they still offer this service. As with most restored parts, it'll probably cost more to have your unit restored than to have a new non-original part installed.

the heat problem through the use of modern brake fluid and high-tech brake-pad material. This led me to the hottest name in racing pads in the U.S.—Performance Friction.

If your name is Kyle Petty and you drive your car at places like Daytona, Richmond, and Watkins Glen, you use brake pads from Performance Friction.

Indeed, everybody in NASCAR is using Performance Friction brake pads, as do about ninety percent of the Indy Car teams. Should Project Corvette use anything less? Of course not.

Normally, we depend on the rotors to get rid of the heat built up in braking, but Performance Friction pads dissipate heat better than any other brake

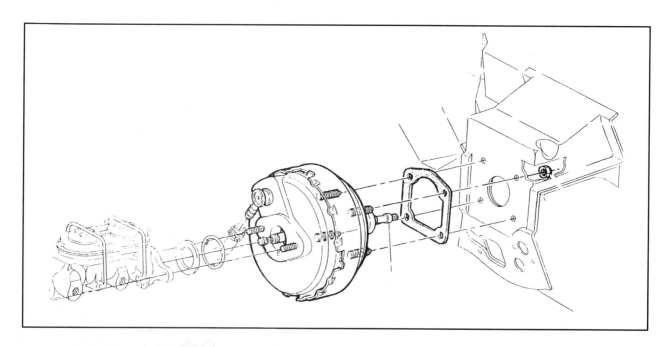

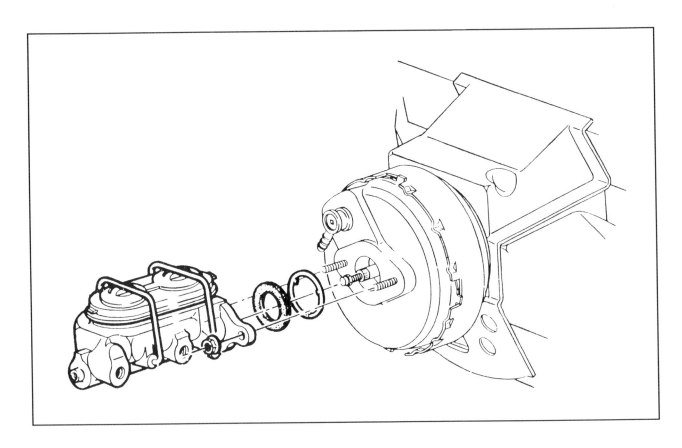

pad on the market. Performance Friction has developed a pad material that gets rid of heat quicker than any other material on the market. I don't quite understand how it all works, I just know that if all the big dogs use them, I want the same brakes on Project Corvette.

## What Brake Fluid Works Best?

Before you buy brake fluid, you must decide how you intend to drive your Corvette, as this really determines whether or not you're going to be able to use silicone brake fluid. If you plan on using your Corvette on racetracks, skip the silicone fluid; it just isn't appropriate.

First, silicone brake fluid will compress. This means that as your brakes get hot and the pedal will go away. Secondly, silicone fluid is very hard to bleed. If you ever have to bleed your brakes at a high-speed club event, you probably won't have enough time left in the day to race.

On a similar note, if you drive one of the new Corvettes with ABS, skip the silicone implant. The pressure of the ABS pump will aerate the fluid and you'll get a very spongy pedal, not to mention the possibility of losing your brakes altogether.

Silicone fluid is best for a car that gets driven very little and spends a lot of time in storage. Silicone brake fluid is also the best choice for show cars, and cars that only get driven a few hundred miles a year.

The brake booster draws vacuum from the engine. Before you rush out and replace the vacuum booster, check all the vacuum hoses for leaks. Some of the later-model Corvettes use a filter on the vacuum, which can also cause leaks.

If you intend to drive your Corvette at any high-speed events, stick to the glycol-based brake fluid. In my never-ending search for the finest products, regardless of cost, I discovered the best surprise of all.

Project Corvette uses the very same brake fluid that most of the IMSA, INDY CARS, and NASCAR

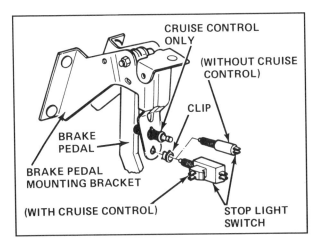

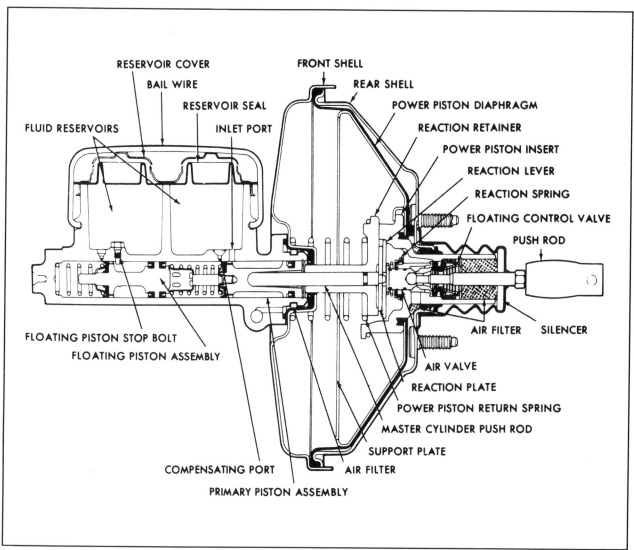

RESERVOIR COVER
BAIL WIRE
RESERVOIR SEAL
FLUID RESERVOIRS
INLET PORT
FRONT SHELL
REAR SHELL
POWER PISTON DIAPHRAGM
REACTION RETAINER
POWER PISTON INSERT
REACTION LEVER
REACTION SPRING
FLOATING CONTROL VALVE
PUSH ROD
AIR FILTER    SILENCER
AIR VALVE
REACTION PLATE
POWER PISTON RETURN SPRING
MASTER CYLINDER PUSH ROD
SUPPORT PLATE
AIR FILTER
FLOATING PISTON STOP BOLT
FLOATING PISTON ASSEMBLY
COMPENSATING PORT
PRIMARY PISTON ASSEMBLY

This is a cross-section of your vacuum booster. Any repairs will require separating the front shell from the rear shell. Home repairs are not the answer.

race car teams use—Ford Heavy Duty brake fluid. Most of the major race teams use this Ford fluid, even if they have to wrap tape around the label. After hiding the logo from Project Corvette, I simply did the same. There's brake fluid on the market that's just as good, but plan on paying about four times as much as you're going to give the Ford dealer. There are times when you just have to admit that Ford does make a good product.

### Getting The Fluid Around

The key element in your Corvette's brake system is moving this Ford brake fluid from the master cylinder to the piston bore in the calipers. This is what makes your Corvette brakes work. Chevrolet uses all sorts of steel lines, rubber lines, and brass

blocks to route this fluid from the master cylinder to the four corners of the car, which also means there are all sorts of places for fluid to leak. Remember, one leak and you have no brakes.

The biggest problem with old Corvette brake systems is rust in the lines. Even worse is the fact that they rust from the inside out. The major rust problem area is the line that runs across the rear of the car, the one that goes past the differential. Since, water is heavier than brake fluid and this line is the lowest point in the brake system, water naturally settles at this point and starts to eat its way to the outside of the line after a few years.

There are two ways to prevent rusting in this line. First, flush your brake fluid often enough so there's no moisture-laden brake fluid resting at this

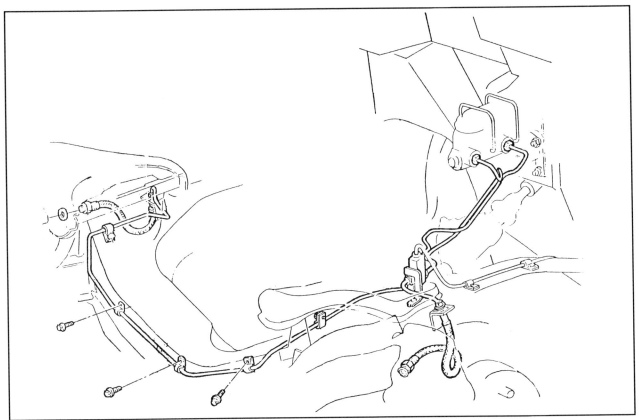

The first stop for the brake fluid will be at the proportioning valve or, on early cars, the distribution block. The 1967 Corvette was the first year that two separate brake systems were present on the Corvette. In the 1968 Corvette, a proportioning valve was installed directly off the master cylinder. The Corvette front brakes have a hydraulic system totally isolated from the front brakes.

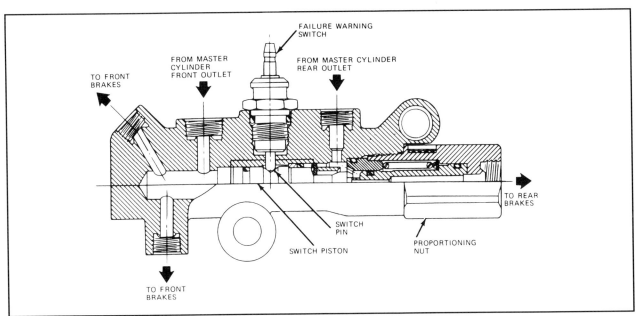

This is a cutaway of the combination valve. These valves are some of the most reliable parts on the braking system and seldom give Corvette owners problems. If you do need one of these valves, you're probably going to make a trip to your Chevrolet dealer. The aftermarket parts people generally don't carry these items.

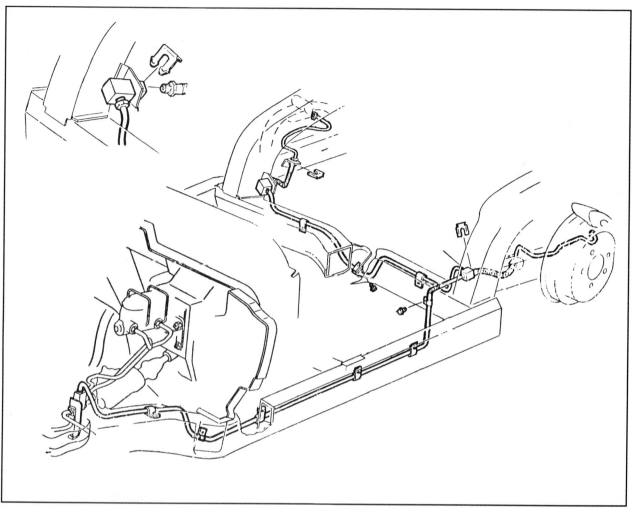

The rear brake lines are rather straightforward. Never remove the brake line on the left frame rail, however. If you remove this brake line, and it's easy to remove, you'll have to pull the body to install the replacement.

The rubber flex hoses at the rear of the car should be carefully checked during the first month you own your Corvette.

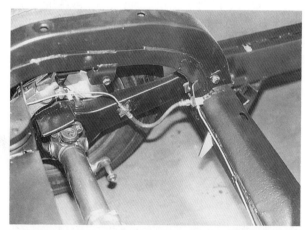

Note the routing of the rear brake lines. The little brass block, known as a distribution block, distributes the brake fluid to the rear calipers.

point. Annual brake fluid flushes are the best way to avoid any line and caliper problems. Second, replace all your hard brake lines with stainless steel brake lines. I did both with Project Corvette. I replaced all the steel lines in Project Corvette with new stainless steel brake lines from Vette Brakes & Products. The cost wasn't all that great, and the lines were actually fairly easy to replace. I have this thing about wanting to replace systems only once each decade. As long as I was playing with brake fluid and rusty fittings, it made sense to do them all at one time. Sure. Wrong idea.

The biggest problem with Project Corvette was that I replaced *all* the brake lines. On the Corvette, there is one brake line that runs from the front to the rear along the inside of the left frame rail. This is a very serious brake line. It's also very easy to remove. The only problem is that you have to remove the

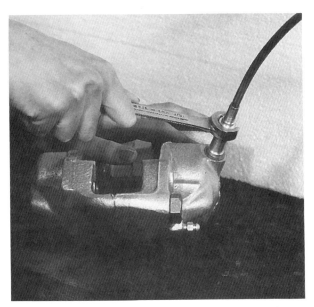

Brake hoses should be installed on the calipers prior to installation on the car. When you install the lines, make certain you use new crush washers between the brake line and the body of the caliper. Any effort to recycle old crush washers is simply foolish and will result in a brake-fluid leak. Also, use a "line" or "flare nut" wrench; a standard wrench will eventually round off nuts. Note the braided stainless steel lines, which look wonderful and improve brake feel, as well. Good quality sets of stainless steel lines bolt up just like the stockers; don't waste your time with kits that require adapters.

body from the frame to replace the line. The problem was nobody got around to telling me.

You know the feeling. I have this very long brake line in my hands, trying to figure out just the right angle for installation. After about thirty minutes of deep contemplation, I start calling people all over the country to find out the correct way to install this one lousy brake line. No one had the answer I wanted to hear.

Every single Corvette restorer in the United States said, "Yeah, The brake line along the frame. You're going to have to pull the body to install that line." The fact that they were so matter of fact about this statement upset me the most.

The one thing I did not want to do was pull the body, yet I did it. I worked out a system for raising the body about eighteen inches and quickly positioned the line. I will never do this again. Do *not* remove this line unless brake fluid is running out of the rust holes. All the stuff about the "Joy of Pulling Corvette Bodies" is wrong. It is not fun. The new axiom for my Corvette work is: "I will never again separate a fiberglass body from a frame that Duntov brought together."

Some of the old steel brakes lines might be rusted so badly that they break and twist when you

We finally get to the infamous Corvette calipers. Most of these calipers developed a leak early in their life. By this time almost all of these calipers have been sleeved, some more successfully than others. There was a time when everybody got in the business of installing stainless sleeves in Corvette brake calipers. Most of the shoddy operators are long gone. The downside is that when your caliper starts to leak it may not be repairable. On the other hand, why worry about things that haven't happened yet?

The rear calipers are just as prone to leaks as the front calipers. Also notice that the rear brake rotors are riveted to the hub assembly. A lot of the problems blamed on the calipers are really a problem with warped, or improperly installed rotors. If the rotors are warped or installed improperly, the caliper pistons will be pushed back into their bores. On occasion they'll suck air. This means you'll have to bleed the brakes. If you find you have to bleed your brakes on a regular basis, start checking for rotor run-out.

Rotors are about more than thickness and run-out. They also have to look good. I threw the old rotor in the Eastwood bead-blasting cabinet and cleaned the rust off. Next, I sprayed them with the Eastwood "Spray Gray." After touching them up on the brake lathe, I left one setting on the work bench. A veteran mechanic stopped by the shop. His first question was "Why did you buy new rotors?" If I could fool him, I knew the effort was worthwhile.

The trick to installing brake pads is to use these special retaining clips from Vette Brakes & Products or Mid-America. These clips hold the pistons into the caliper so the pads can be slid into place. Without these little clips you'll spend hours trying to hold both pistons in place. Spend the money on the clips and save yourself the frustration.

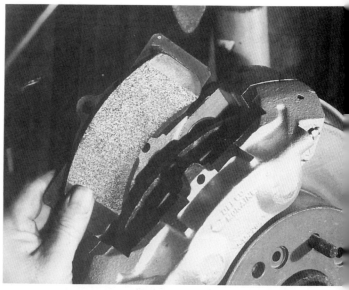

Project Corvette uses Performance Friction brake pads. They dissipate braking heat to the atmosphere better than any other brake pads on the market. A brake pad must do three things: Stop the car, have a long life, and not produce noise. Many of the brake pads on the market are superior at only one of these three objectives. Your Corvette needs the combination of all three items.

A major drawback of disc brakes is figuring out how to get an operating parking brake. Chevrolet created a miniature drum brake for that purpose. This miniature drum brake operates inside the rotor. Thus, the backside of the rear brake rotor functioned as a brake drum.

Here is the backside of the rear brake rotor. The inside of the rotor functions as a brake drum for the parking brake assembly.

try to remove them. This means you should just keep replacing lines until you find a connection that comes apart properly. You might just as well plan on doing all the brake lines, except the infamous long one, at the same time.

If you simply replace a single line, you're going to have to bleed the brake system. If you replace all the brake lines, you're still only going to have to bleed the brake system one time. Plan on taking a few nights (a few months?), and do the whole system at one time.

The next problem is with the rubber flex lines. If the rubber flex lines haven't been replaced within the last three years, plan on replacing them when you replace the steel lines. These rubber hoses get soft over the years. Sometimes the inner hose collapses while the outer hose remains intact, which means your brakes won't release properly. If you go through brake pads and rotors on an annual basis, replace these rubber lines; they're probably the problem.

Replacing the flex hoses will do more to improve the feel of your brakes than anything else you do to the brake system. The old hoses swell when you put your foot on the pedal to send the fluid to the calipers. The brake fluid pressure expands the hoses rather than pushing the pads into the brake rotor. Change the hoses and you'll get a much firmer pedal, not to mention a much safer Corvette.

With Project Corvette I went one step further and used stainless braided brake hoses. The advantage with these flex hoses is that the pedal will maintain the firmness for longer than a year.

## The Calipers

All you have to do is read the ads in any of the leading Corvette magazines to know that Corvettes have a caliper problem. Any disc-brake Corvette prior to 1984 is a candidate for new calipers. The only way to take care of caliper problems is to get a new set of four calipers with stainless steel sleeves. To even think about rebuilding the calipers on your car is a waste of time. Rebuilt calipers have now come down to a price where it isn't even worth considering doing it yourself.

If you have a caliper problem, go back and read the article on calipers in the June 1993 issue of

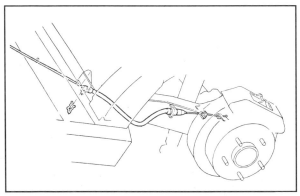

This drawing shows the parking brake cable routing. Make sure the clip is installed in this manner.

Before you install the brake rotor, complete with bearings, you should put a light coating of grease on the spindle.

*Corvette Fever.* There you'll find out how to determine if someone's already replaced the calipers on your car.

I got all new calipers from Vette Brakes & Products. This company started out with brake calipers and simply added new products over the years. The best part is that they warranty the calipers for the life of your car.

The only thing you have to know about Corvette calipers is the number on your Visa card and the size of the wrench it takes to remove the caliper from the bracket. Most professional shops today won't even consider rebuilding a caliper given the price of factory-remanufactured parts. Why should you be any different?

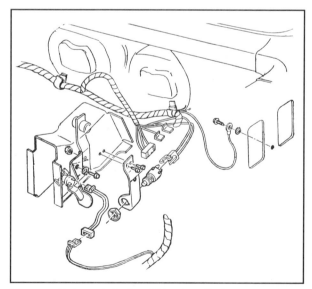

The stop light switch should be installed so that electrical contact is made when the brake pedal is depressed 1/4in.

It's a good idea to put a little silicone lube on the bleeder screw when you install it. This keeps the screw from rusting into place.

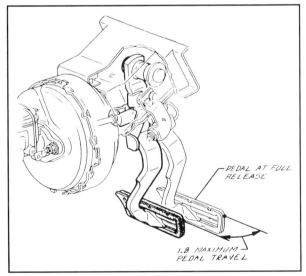

You should have the motor turned off when you set the pedal play for vacuum-assisted brakes. Also, vacuum assist should not be present. Pump the brake pedal five times with the motor off to remove all the vacuum assist.

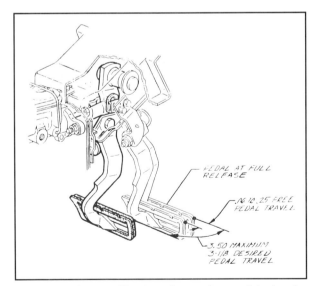

These are the specifications for setting pedal play for non-assisted brakes. If you get more than 3.5in of pedal travel, bleed the brake system one more time.

# Chapter 11

# Body

There was a time when taking the paint off your Corvette involved some fairly serious chemicals. These were chemicals that burned your hands, stained your clothes, and probably did significant damage to your body.

Repairing the fiberglass body of your Corvette is the most time-consuming task of the whole project. It can also be the most expensive. For body work, you really have two choices: pay in time, or pay in money.

Painting a Corvette takes about 140 hours. If you multiply this with the average shop rate, you're very close to five numbers behind the dollar sign. This includes everything though. You drive the car into the shop, and several weeks later you drive away with a perfect Corvette.

The other way is to put your Corvette in your own garage and spend several months doing your own work. Anything you do on your own car is going to save money. The cost will be in the time spent. You have to figure out the value of your time and what else you could do with several months of leisure time. Just remember that the 140-hour estimate is for a professional shop. You could easily double that number.

The good part is that, except for spraying the color coat, your work can be as outstanding as a professional shop. Even better is that all the mistakes you make can be corrected by doing it over again.

When you blow up an engine a lot of money is involved. When you mess up a panel on your Corvette, the only cost involved is time. The actual amount of money you spend on fiberglass repairs and body filler is insignificant. You just spend a couple more days correcting your mistake.

I can remember stripping paint while wearing rubber gloves and big goggles. I especially remember that when the paint remover touched your skin it burned like fire. Those days are gone. Modern tech-

The first step in stripping the paint is to tape off all the areas you don't want stripped. The major problem with this type of paint stripping is that the little plastic particles find their way into every nook and cranny.

The pellets are shot onto the Corvette's surface. A skilled operator can actually remove one layer of paint at a time.

The rear corners were just as bad as the front corners. The only way to repair a mess such as this is to use fiberglass matte on the inside of the panel. The fiberglass matte holds everything together while you properly repair the part your neighbors will see.

nology has now made it possible to do without all of the vulgar chemicals. Instead, we just get a lot of dust.

Today we use a big booth, lots of compressed air, and a whole lot of little plastic beads to remove

Project Corvette was in much worse shape than anyone imagined. Once all the paint was removed, the only thing to be seen was plastic filler from previous repairs. If the previous repairs had been done properly, this pic-

ture might not have been so depressing. Instead the car body was a giant mess. The only thing holding this front corner together was the paint—which we removed.

Where the fender splits you'll need to cut directly through the old fiberglass. This will make it easier to line up the panels.

Corvette paint. For Corvette repair, we're now using technology developed by the aircraft industry.

There are two good reasons for not using chemicals for paint removal. First, most of them don't work any longer, as the newest paints are impervious to paint removers. For the last several years I thought the paint removers were just suffering from poor quality control, until DuPont explained that paints are just getting better. Whatever, the latest paint removers don't remove paint.

Secondly, chemical strippers cause major problems with your finished Corvette. The problem isn't from acid rain or sun; the problem begins when the chemical strippers start to migrate out of the fiberglass and into that beautiful top coat you so carefully applied. It's virtually impossible to scrub all the stripper out of the fiberglass. Someday, several years after you've painted your prized Corvette, this old paint remover will finally work its way into the sunlight, right through your wonderful top coat.

General Motors is adamant that you should never use a chemical stripper on your Corvette. DuPont feels the same way. Both of these companies, which have decades of Corvette experience, feel that everyone should use plastic media blasting for Corvette paint removal.

Plastic media blasting was developed by the Department of Defense in the early eighties for stripping aircraft paint. You should think of plastic media stripping as sand blasting with recyclable pieces of plastic. The whole system operates with twenty to forty pounds of air pressure.

Everybody is skeptical of plastic media blasting until they've seen the results. What finally sold me was the time I saw a body shop owner drag his half-stripped Corvette into the shop at Blast-It.

He figured that after twenty years in the business he knew how to strip the paint from his 1962 Corvette. After several months of frustration, he simply gave up and asked Blast-It to finish the job. That

Once you've made the proper cuts, you can use matte on the backside of the panel.

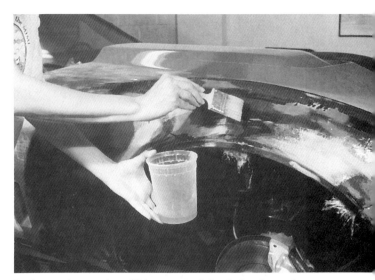

Resin can be used to fill in some of the holes from the topside. The new L88 hood came from Eckler's.

told me all I needed to know about plastic media blasting.

How far should you go? Should you stop at the primer, or the gel coat? Even better do you go right beyond the gel coat into the fiberglass itself? Everybody who's ever painted a Corvette has an opinion on this subject. Most of these opinions are based on Corvette folklore and tribal ritual.

We decided to listen to the experts at DuPont on this point. They see no reason to go beyond the gel coat. In fact, they've found that when people expose the actual fiberglass they create a lot of problems for themselves.

Remember how the old-fashioned paint remover would soak into the fiberglass? Just keep in mind that fiberglass is porous and can absorb all sorts of contaminants. No matter how thin the gel coat might be, it's still a protective layer over the fiberglass. This thin layer not only keeps the fibers in place, it keeps everything else out of the fibers. You should do everything possible to save the gel coat. In our effort to retain the gel coat we were conservative, leaving spots of old paint on the surface.

As wonderful as plastic media blasting might be, it's still not a miracle. When your Corvette comes back from the media blasters you're still going to have to do some sanding.

Just because we're using the latest technology doesn't mean you can go ahead and throw out your orbital sander. You still have lots of time to get very friendly with your sander, not to mention create a lot of dust in your garage. As you spend more time with your sander, you'll notice that the family structure starts to show as many stress cracks as the surface of your Corvette. It seems that most family members don't like dust.

Another problem with Project Corvette was that once we got all the paint off, we could see every botched repair ever made to this Corvette. This was not good. Why is it that everybody always talks about perfect Corvettes, but I never get to work on one of them?

If Project Corvette were my teeth, we would be talking about root canals and porcelain crowns. Yet it got even worse. When I had one of the top fiberglass experts in the country examine the car, all he could say was, "Do you have any idea how much work is necessary here?"

I knew Project Corvette wasn't in the greatest of shape. I fully realized there was going to be some work involved to get one of those NCRS/Bloomington Gold paint jobs. I was not prepared to find that major surgery would have to be performed on the car. This was no minor cleaning procedure, this was orthodontal work.

## Cracked Fiberglass and Other Indignities

If you have any memory of the first chapters, you'll remember that Project Corvette had some minor breaks in the fiberglass. Once we got all the old paint off the car, I found out just how serious these problems were. I'm talking about big problems here; the kind of problems that make you want to start working on Mustangs.

Somewhere along the line, Project Corvette had been hit in the front, both sides, and the rear. It appeared as though Project Corvette had been used as a dodge-em car fifteen to twenty years ago and that whoever repaired the car used old boat technology for the repairs.

A whole new Center-Wheelwell-Forward section was bonded into the original body using fiber-

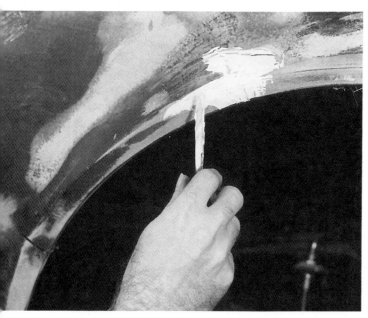

Once everything is in reasonable shape you can use epoxy filler.

glass cloth—strictly old marine technology. The weave of this fiberglass cloth surfaces through any new paint job. Within a year the texture of the cloth becomes obvious.

Basically, then, the front of Project Corvette was a mess. Every single panel, except for the left door, needed serious work. It was time to call the specialists in for consultation.

Legendary Corvette is just down the street from my home. Larry, the owner, has been working with fiberglass longer than I've owned Corvettes. I've used their products on several old race cars, and everything worked. I like products that work, so I went back to Larry for more assistance. I knew that Project Corvette would need major help. This project was beyond the scope of the general practitioner, I needed a specialist.

Larry's first comment was that I had a lot of work ahead of me. I really needed to hear that. After several hours of probing into body filler, crawling around on the ground, and generally making comments about what previous owners had done to the car, Larry laid out a plan in four basic steps:

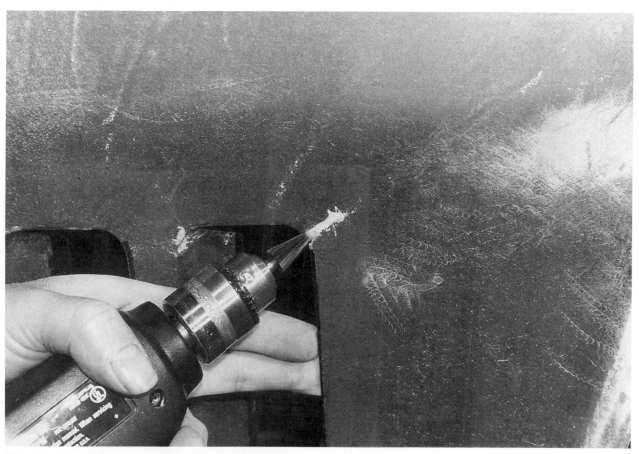

If you have small hairline cracks or stress cracks, you'll need to grind them out. Once the crack is totally removed you can use the epoxy filler.

Step 1: Reinforce all the damaged areas on the back side of the panel, using fiberglass matt and resin.

Step 2: Grind away the upper surface of the panels, making sure you remove all of the previous repair work.

Step 3: Fill the ground-out area with fiberglass matt and resin. Make the final surface slightly higher than the surrounding surface.

Step 4: Blend the repaired area into the surrounding area, using your orbital sander. There should not be a step, of any kind, when you finish this blending.

Backing up the old repair cloth and body filler provides a solid foundation for the new improved repair. Without this solid base there could be serious stress crack problems in the next couple of years. The secret to building this new base is to get a clean surface to which the new fiberglass matt adheres.

The best procedure is to use fifty-grit sandpaper to rough the surface. This ensures the new fiberglass resin and matt will have enough surface to grab. I don't want any problems with this paint job next year, or the next decade for that matter.

The essential word here is fiberglass matt. Never use fiberglass cloth around your Corvette. When you use cloth on Corvettes, the weave will eventually pop through the surface and instantly remind your friends and neighbors that this Corvette has been repaired, and repaired poorly. Project Corvette was living proof of what happens.

After having created a solid foundation for the surface repairs, we ground away all the old fiberglass cloth. More dust.

The second step made a total mess out of the garage, my body, and my lungs. Fiberglass dust will get into the smallest of cracks. I know that two years from now I'll still be finding fiberglass dust in the corners of my toolbox. Hopefully, for the sake of my family life, very little of it will get into the house. Sure.

Before you even think about doing all this fiberglass repair work, you should get two videotapes. The first tape is from Eckler's. I've read dozens of books on the mysteries of fiberglass repairs, but Eckler's two-hour videotape made it comprehensible.

The other videotape is from the GM Pro Tech video series and is entitled "Corvette Refinishing Techniques." This outstanding tape is designed for the professional body shop. However, you might try to order it from your local Chevrolet dealer, as it doesn't seem to be the easiest tape to acquire.

If these videotapes don't work, try living down the road from Legendary Corvette . What they don't know about fiberglass isn't worth knowing. When a new question comes up, I simply get in my car and go see Larry. I usually make up some excuse that I

The trick at this point is to blend everything together in one smooth flowing fender so that it looks the same as when the car left St. Louis.

was just driving by and thought I would say hello. After about five minutes I work my latest problem into the conversation. The best part is that he always has a solution.

## Body Filler

At this point, we have a lot of imperfections, low spots, and general problem areas that just need attention. The purpose of body filler is to fill in any low spots up to the level of the surrounding area.

Then you get to sand again, blending the filled area with the surrounding area. When you're done, everything should be at the same level.

With your Corvette, the area you just filled in should be at the same height as the fiberglass in the surrounding area. When you're all done sanding there shouldn't be any high spots, or low spots. Everything should be smoother than the day when the car left St. Louis. You're going to spend a good deal of time blending the filler. The trick is to remove most of the body filler you just put on the car.

The single most important item you have to remember at this stage of the process is that you're seeking perfection. Nothing else will be good enough. Paint will not hide blemishes. In fact, paint will only make these imperfections more obvious.

You cannot stop at any point in the body filler process and jump to primer hoping for the best. If you can't make it perfect now, take a break and come back to the job later. Remember, we're talking over 200 hours here. The half-hour you think you're saving now will result in an extra several hours of work later, correcting the repair you thought was "good enough."

# Chapter 12

# Paint

The most important point to remember when you paint your Corvette is that there is no need to rush. In fact, you can't rush. Typically, all the steps leading up to the application of paint on your Corvette have taken about twice as long as you originally planned. Forget the original schedule. Recovering at this point is impossible.

Since you've missed all the early Corvette shows, let's concentrate on doing a good job of painting your Corvette and not worry about the time schedule. The worst thing you can do is rush the job with the idea that you can go back next year and fix all your mistakes. This will never happen. What will happen is that the total project will actually take twice as long as you planned. Remember, this is a hobby, not a project at work. Deadlines are for work, not your leisure time.

Painting your Corvette takes a lot of time—more time than you ever imagined. If you start to rush through the next few steps, you'll simply defeat

This was Project Corvette after we finished stripping the paint. The left door was the only panel on the car that hadn't been repaired. The fiberglass repairs were completed, and it was time to start thinking about paint. The secret to a quality paint job is to make certain that every stage reaches perfection.

After the first coat of primer surfacer is applied, sanding begins. Wherever you see a dark or white spot, there is a high spot. Your goal is to reduce the Corvette's surface to one single level.

the purpose of creating the perfect paint platform. Probably the best thing you can do at this point is to go out and look at some perfect paint jobs. They'll help motivate you in the right direction.

## Gel coat

Real frustration arrives when you start asking for advice about gel coat. Repairing fiberglass is easy when you compare it to the advice you receive regarding gel coat. Everybody has a different opinion. Your task is to sort out the informed opinions from old Corvette folk wisdom.

The arguments for using gel coat are impressive. The idea is that this coating of epoxy will act as a sealer between the fiberglass and your paint. This coating, which you apply prior to spraying the primer coat, will prevent all the little strands of fiberglass from surfacing into the paint.

One argument against using gel-coat is that it's very labor intensive. Most shops will add at least a thousand dollars to your painting bill for spraying gel coat. In addition to the extra cost of the gel coat, the entire car must be sanded one extra time.

This gel-coat is also very hard to sand. If everything doesn't happen quite right you might have yet another problem with gel coat. Mix it wrong and it will never harden. This can be a very big problem.

Still another downside of using gel coat is that it's very thick. The new High Volume Low Pressure (HVLP) spray guns won't push this old-fashioned gel out of the nozzle. You have to use a big nozzle on the gun. This is the only way that you can get decent flow through the nozzle. Another exciting thing that can happen is that the gun's nozzle gets clogged and the gel coat spits out in little clumps. This will definitely ruin your afternoon.

The final result of all these possibilities was that I decided not to use gel coat. The sanding issue, not to mention the spraying problems, helped make my decision. I hope that in a few years the fiberglass is still hidden from view and I won't have to completely redo the Corvette Project

The final factor that helped me make my decision to skip the gel coat was that the use of modern catalyzed epoxy primers have made gel coating largely unnecessary. This new catalyzed paint tech-

**Power tools speed up the process considerably.**

nology can do exactly what the old gel coats did—permanently seal the fiberglass under a plastic layer.

One thing I quickly began to understand is that most people listen to all the old tales, and then use the oldest possible technology. When they have problems with these outdated techniques, they simply blame it all on the stupid Corvette fiberglass. By using modern techniques and consulting with experts, you can get good results.

## Sanding Tricks

Now, let's get started. The first step involves sanding the whole car with eighty grit paper. Remember, all the plastic media blasting did was remove the old paint, it did nothing to prepare the surface for the new paint.

The secret of sanding is to use any number of devices that will allow you to knock down the high spots without making the low spots any lower. Think of it as landscaping your Corvette.

The best way is to purchase two power sanders. The first is what people in body shops call a long board. This air driven sander is twelve inches long and two inches wide.

The second type of sander to use is an orbital DA sander. These are small lightweight circular sanders that do a wonderful job of getting into all the smaller spaces where you can't use the long board. Or, with the C3 Corvette, all the curved surfaces where a long board simply wouldn't work.

A third device is the basic old-fashioned sanding block. My personal favorite too for sanding is a sponge. The third generation Corvette is all curves. A sanding block is just too rigid for sanding Corvettes.

A sponge does the same thing as a stiff block but it lets the sandpaper adhere to the curves a little better.

After making sure that all the Corvette's fiberglass is smooth, and as perfect as possible, we can start cleaning -again. There are times when I think this whole painting process is about making a lot of dust, and then cleaning up all the dust from the shop.

Once you've cleaned all the dust from the eighty grit paper you can start sanding all over again, but with 180 paper. The idea is that the surface should be rough enough to give the primer something to adhere to. At the same time you need a surface as smooth as possible. You work up to the flawless surface in a series of steps.

Remember, the top coat is going to look like glass. We're going to work up to that final coat in a series of small increments. At each stage we're going to develop a finer, and smoother, surface. That is really what all this effort is about. You could theoretically begin with 400 grit sandpaper and use it for the total process. The only problem might be that it would take three years and thousands of pieces of sandpaper.

The rough sanding, eighty grit for instance, is used simply to save time. A rough paper cuts quickly, doesn't clog as rapidly, and speeds the whole process along. The only drawback is that the rough paper leaves some pretty horrendous scratches in the surface of the car. This isn't a problem though since you're going to remove these scratches with the finer 180 paper.

After the garage is clean, once again, you can start the next step, which is to finally spray the primer coat, making sure that you get even coverage. After a week, or two, go over the whole car with 220 sandpaper. See, it's time to get dust all over the shop once again.

There's a reason for all of this waiting between coats. All the modern materials are guaranteed not to shrink. The only problem is that the guarantee doesn't come in writing. The best way to deal with this is to let the car set for a week in between steps. This gives each stage a chance to thoroughly dry. This is something that a professional shop cannot afford to do. Since you have no production schedule to meet, and no weekly payroll obligation, take your time.

I know of one restoration shop that likes to let everything set for about two or three months before they apply the final coats of paint. They admit that this is not always possible, but at least that's their goal. They feel the longer they wait the better the chances of having a perfect paint surface.

When you finish sanding the primer coat you should be able to see any low spots. These can be filled with the normal body filler. After feather-edging this filler into the rest of the surface, simply spray another application of primer around the repair. When

Items such as the door jams take considerable time.

This is the goal. While you're in the middle of the painting process, attend as many Corvette shows as possible. You need the inspiration.

you're all done with this process the entire car should be sanded with 220 paper one final time.

The key to this whole process is to make sure you have a perfect surface at every point in the operation. Paint will not hide mistakes. If you can find a flaw, or crack, at this point fix it, do not go to the next step until you've reached perfection.

Once again, the purpose of sanding is to level the surface of the car. Corvette owners don't need to be told about wavy bodies. We know all too well that the sides of our cars wave in and out. We've even come to accept this fact. The National Corvette Restoration Society goes so far as to take judging points away if you don't have the right amount of waves in the side of your car.

Since Project Corvette is certainly not going to be an NCRS car why should I live with the wave problems? When I sand the car I'm actually removing the tops of these body waves. This is what people mean when they discuss block sanding.

The idea is that the sandpaper only hits the peaks of the waves, leaving the low sections alone. In a perfect paint job there's no difference in the levels

of paint, or surface. The final coat of paint is at one perfect level. Primer-surfacer is used to get the final waves out of the car. Several coats of primer-surfacer should be enough to give the Corvette an almost sheet metal appearance.

### Choosing Paint

Paint technology is moving faster than people can keep up with. If you haven't worked with paint in the last couple of years, you're way behind the curve. John Pfanstiehl is one guy who stays current will all the latest technology. Before you even look at your spray gun, go back and read the articles John wrote for the August and September 1993 issues of *Corvette Fever*. Next, go out and buy John's book on painting, *Automotive Paint Handbook*. This is the best single book about painting on the market.

Before you even put the first drop of paint on your Corvette, you must decide on the type of paint system you'll use. Yes, that's right, paint system. We no longer have plain paint; modern technology has brought us painting *systems*. This means you never

High-volume low-pressure painting systems are the only way to apply paint today. The single biggest advantage of the HVLP system is that most of the paint actually goes on the car. Consequently, you need less paint than before, and secondly, you have less paint flying around inside your garage.

mix materials from several manufacturers, instead you need to pick one paint company and stick with them until the final glossy finish is applied. I chose the DuPont system, basically because I used to work for them, and I trust their products. Everything between the gel coat and the sky on Project Corvette was manufactured by DuPont.

You will need to ask a lot of questions, look at a lot of cars, and then make your decision. Remember, once you select a primer, you've chosen the company that will make your color coat.

Primers are the workhorses of the paint world. Shiny high-tech surfaces may get all the credit, but the primer does most of the work.

The basic *purpose* of primer hasn't changed in the last several decades. Primer is simply a heavy paint that fills all the minor imperfections in the surface of your Corvette. We basically discussed it in the last section on sanding: For the primer coat process, you spray a certain amount of paint on the surface of your Corvette and then sand it off.

A second purpose of primer is to provide a surface that the colored paint will stick to. We've all seen new paint jobs in which the top coat peels away from the primer after about six months. This is something we don't want to happen. Peeling is caused by improper surface preparation. In short, somebody made a mistake.

The quality of the final coat of paint doesn't result simply from the amount of primer you put on the car. Rather, it is the result of the surface perfection before you put the color paint on. Remember, primer fills in the voids and low spots. That's why removing it is just as important as putting it on. Color paint will do absolutely nothing to cover up any mistakes you make in fiberglass repair. In fact a high-gloss show quality paint job will just dramatize any mistakes you made in repairing the fiberglass.

Creating a perfect surface is nothing more than taking a series of liquids and then turning it all into dust. Remember, creating dust is very important to getting a perfect surface—so is your vacuum cleaner.

The final sanding for the color coat should be done with a 400-grit sandpaper. This is where you can get really fussy. *Any* imperfection will absolutely jump out at the color-coat stage. All your shortcuts and frustration will jump out and bite you.

The best way to handle the color coat is to find a friendly body shop. They have the capability to shoot the color in a clean environment, which is the body shop's biggest advantage over your home garage. That, and ten years experience in using a spray gun.

The best paint to use at this point is a two-part system. The first part consists of the color coat, covered by a second coat of clear paint. Done properly, this looks wonderful. The final clear coat is designed to protect the color coat from oxidizing. Your Corvette needs protection from acid rain, airborne pollution, and industrial fallout.

The downside of a clear-coat paint system is that the NCRS and Bloomington judges will not approve. In my world, this is no big deal. Project Corvette was for driving, not judging. In your Corvette world, this could easily be a big deal.

If I can improve upon the paint installed in St. Louis three decades ago, I will. I'll keep the same Corvette color, but I want a better quality paint on the car. This goal is in line with the "Ten-Foot Rule" from the beginning of the project. There's no need to create a Corvette that is perfect at the one-foot range. Neither is there any need to create an exact duplicate of the Corvette that left St. Louis in August of 1967.

# Chapter 13

# Trim and Bumpers

## Trim

What little trim you find on the third-generation Corvette is used only to identify the model years. If you have to bring forth a new Corvette every single year, and have very little money in the budget, changing trim is the simplest route. Sometimes I think Chevrolet put the side vents on the Corvette front fenders simply so they would have something to change every year.

Corvette trim packages can be grouped by model years. The 1968 to 1972 Corvettes were all the same cars, with chrome bumpers on both the front and rear. Even the grille opening remained the same during this period. Only the parking lights and the grille itself would change during this period.

In 1968 the backup lights were located in the valance panel below the bumper. By 1969 they moved to the taillight area, where they stayed until the end of C3 production in 1982.

In 1971 the parking light lenses were changed to an amber color, although the early cars got all the leftover clear lenses from the previous years.

These are two of the earliest trim items. In 1968 there were no Stingray badges, and the vents were plain. In 1969 you got the Stingray badge for free, but you had to pay for the trim in the side vent. Less than one-third of all buyers opted for the TJ2 option, which retailed for $21.10 in 1969. One great advantage of this option today is that these four trim pieces can save you a lot of effort sanding and filling to get the fender vents perfect. However, today these vents will cost you about $20.00 for each and every vent.

The front spoilers were standard on the 1978 Indy Pace Cars. They became a regular option the following year. If you drive your Corvette a lot, these spoilers are simply one more item to pick up stone chips.

This fender vent was first used in 1970 and continued until 1972. Three years with the same fender vent is a Corvette record.

Details separate the best cars from the merely nice cars. You have to remember that very little time and money was involved in making this gas filler opening correct. On the other hand, it's details such as this that make your Corvette stand out from the pack.

The year 1971 was also, thankfully, the last for fiber optics, which did nothing for the Corvette. Fiber optics have been a hassle for every owner since the car left St. Louis. If you get yours to work, you're a miracle worker.

When the fender vents are this perfect, all the surrounding items have to be equally nice. This restorer made the nearby rocker panel perfect, right down to the brand-new screws.

Beginning in 1973 all the vent trim disappeared. The "Stingray" emblem remained.

The L88 hood is a very popular addition. Originally, the open cowl area was to be used for ram induction. Today, the L88 hood is often more for show rather than go. "If the hood is there, what's under this hood?"

In 1968, Chevrolet offered three different hoods. Can you imagine the latest Corvette coming with three different hoods today? There was the small-block hood for your average going-to-the-grocery-store Corvette, the special 427ci hood with a couple bits of chrome, and finally, the L88 hood, which drew air from the base of the windshield. The only hood with any trim were the two big-block hoods.

In 1980 the vent trim returned. The big difference was the "Stingray" emblem was now missing. Notice the vent trim is a lot less substantial than it was during the early seventies.

This has to one of the dumbest ideas in the world. Corvette was the first to feature hidden windshield wipers. The vacuum-operated panel should raise up and then the wiper arms will ascend the windshield to perform their duty. That was the way it was supposed to work, but not even NCRS members can make the system work. Chevrolet finally gave up after several years of trying.

The rear spoiler was carried over from the 1978 Indy Pace Car as an option for all 1979 Corvettes. After a few years, however, the fit of the piece deteriorates.

In 1982 Chevrolet wanted to tell the world about the new twin TBI injection system. Unfortunately this system rapidly became known as the Miss-Fire Injection system. The only downside to owning a 1982 Corvette is that you have to deal with this early attempt at fuel injection.

In 1973 the Corvette's bumper would change. While this can hardly be considered a trim change, it did change the grille opening and the general appearance of the Corvette.

As the third-generation Corvette evolved over the years, it actually went from very little trim to virtually none at all. Chevrolet had far more important concerns than changing the trim. Most of the Corvette's changes came as a result of federal safety and environmental restrictions.

Essentially, the Corvette evolved from a sports car to a personal luxury car. The interior changed more than the exterior, mainly to make the Corvette more appealing to a new group of customers who equated less trim with better design. Chevrolet met their expectations.

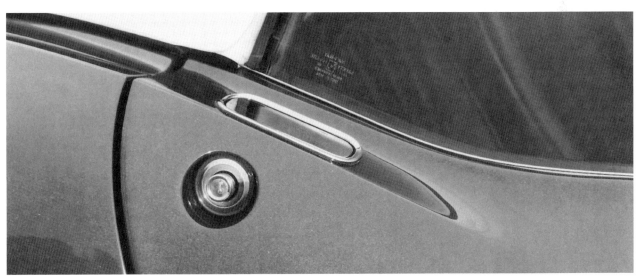

1968 was the only year when this system was used for the door. In 1969 Chevrolet switched to using the top handle to open the door. There was no latch button on the cars after 1968. A proliferation of details like this make the 1968 Corvette easy to identify.

Should you let your Chevrolet dealer advertise for free on your Corvette? They all do it. Think of it as a non-standard trim item. These stickers can be easily removed with a hair dryer and sharp fingernails. Use the hair dry-er to soften the glue and simply scrape the lettering off with your fingernails. You'll probably need to polish the area to remove all the traces of the label.

Every single piece of trim on this 1974 Corvette is perfect. As older Corvettes age, restorations become more detailed and splendid.

This is what the Corvette body and trim are all about. Notice how all the small trim items add to the total picture. An aftermarket radio antenna or a rusted original one would detract from the total car. Attention to these little details results in a finished Corvette picture.

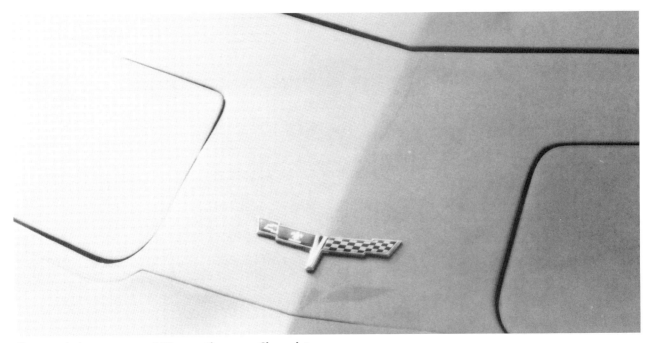

*Above and photos on page 110,* over the years Chevrolet tried a number of different hood badges. All of them are currently available.

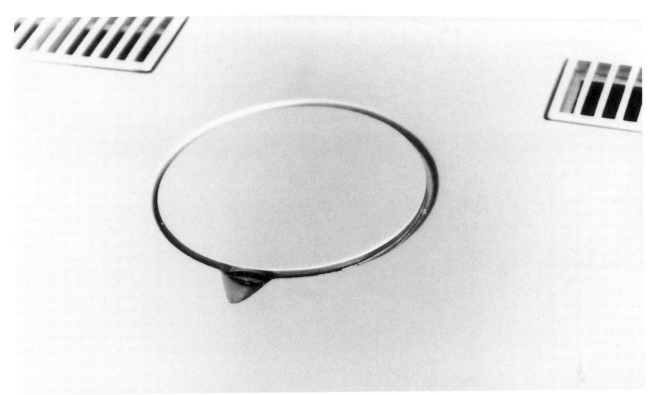

*Above and below,* when the front hood emblem was changed, the gas lid had to follow. In 1974 though, Chevrolet didn't bother and simply left the gas filler lid blank. This was the only year the filler lid had no markings. After the 1975 model year, the rear ventilation grilles were removed.

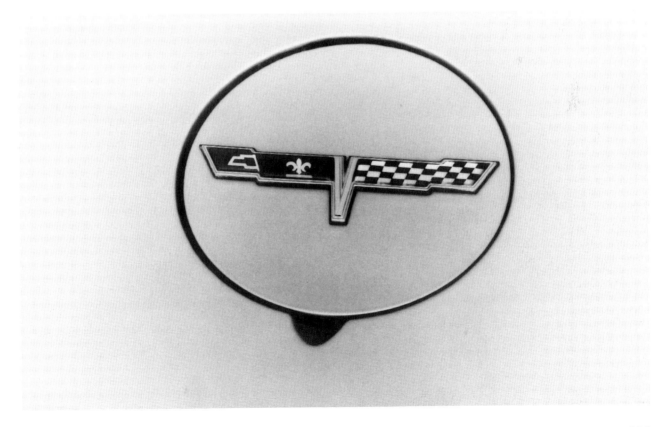

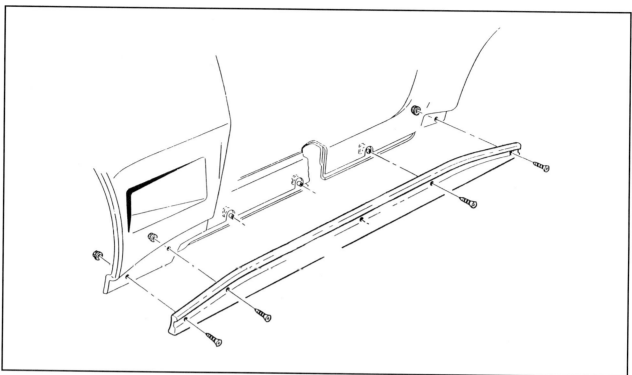

The rocker panel is very easy to replace. This panel takes a lot of abuse and is a simple Saturday morning project.

If you are the compulsive type, you'll line up all the screw heads.

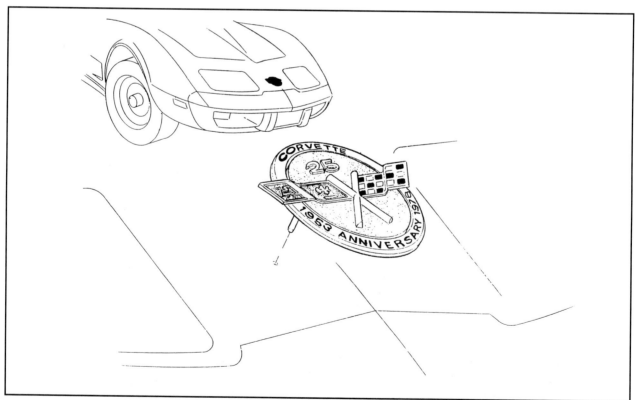

This 25th anniversary front emblem was used only in 1978. I'm always amazed by the number of people who go to great effort with their paint jobs but neglect all these little trim items.

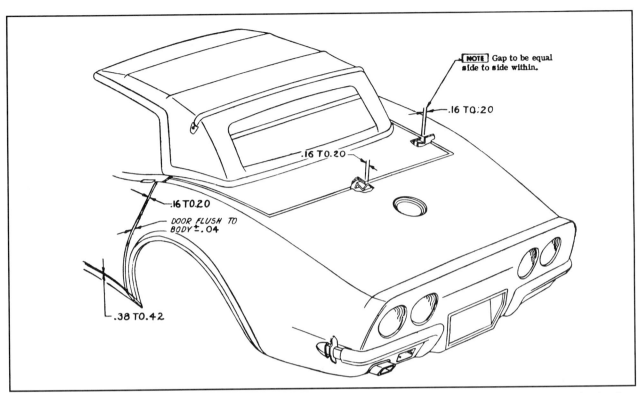

NOTE Gap to be equal side to side within.

.16 TO .20

.16 TO .20

.16 TO .20

DOOR FLUSH TO BODY ±.04

.38 TO .42

*Above and below,* a handy trick for checking body panel gaps is to get some balsa wood strips from your local hobby shop. Remember that 1/16in equals just about .060in. Another point to keep in mind is that Chevrolet considered anything within 1/16in to be good enough. Today that size of tolerance would be considered unac-

ceptable. In fact, today very few award-winning Corvettes are that far out of uniformity. We sometimes forget that all of our attention to the fit and finish of a Corvette is a reflection of more discriminating standards. In the early seventies it was enough if the clutch stayed intact.

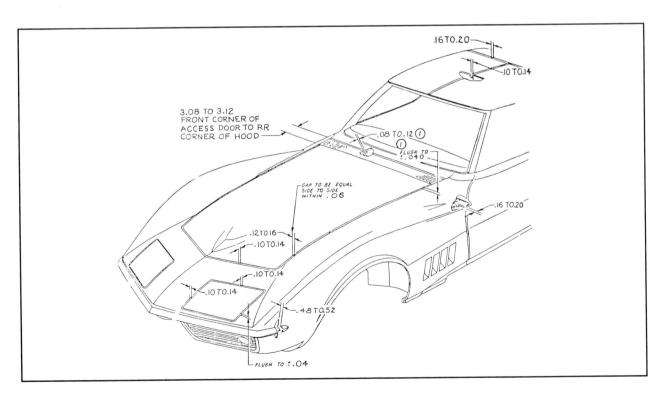

.16 TO .20

.10 TO .14

3.08 TO 3.12 FRONT CORNER OF ACCESS DOOR TO RR CORNER OF HOOD

.08 TO .12 ①

① FLUSH TO ±.040

GAP TO BE EQUAL SIDE TO SIDE WITHIN .06

.16 TO .20

.12 TO .16

.10 TO .14

.10 TO .14

.10 TO .14

.48 TO .52

FLUSH TO ±.04

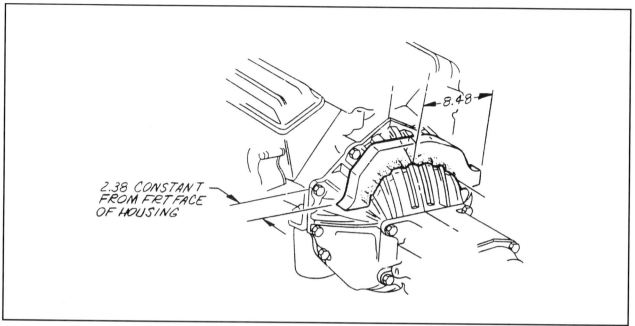

2.38 CONSTANT FROM FRT FACE OF HOUSING

8.48

This little trim item, a foam collar, is something very few people will ever see, but it sure can make life inside your Corvette more comfortable. It keeps the engine heat from migrating into your seating area. Corvette didn't bother installing this feature until 1978, but there's no reason you can't use it on any of the third-generation Corvettes.

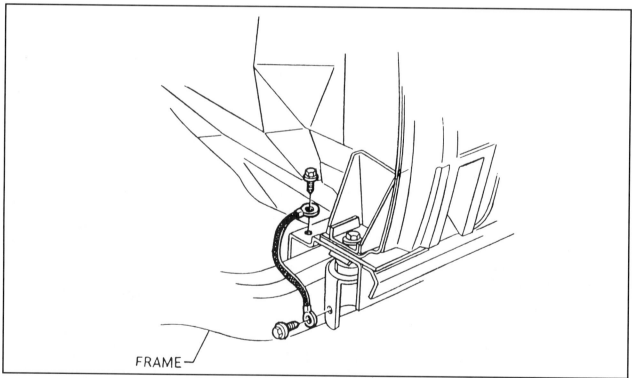

FRAME

This grounding strap is another hidden item that can make a big difference. A fiberglass body can create all sorts of electrical grounding problems. Therefore, make sure all the factory ground straps are still in place and working. Usually a simple cleaning of the bolts and the cable ends is all that's needed. Grounding straps are generally trouble-free, but when they don't work (or aren't installed), they can really complicate your electrical troubleshooting.

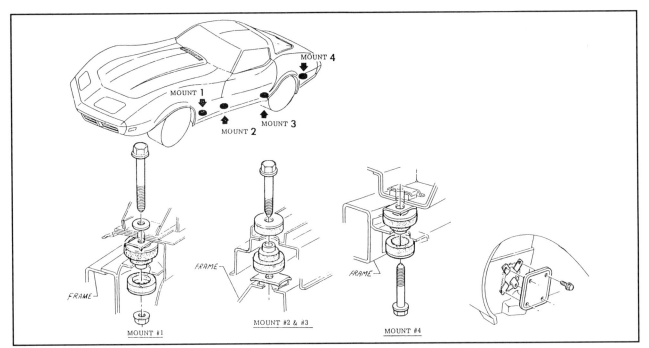

MOUNT 4

MOUNT 1

MOUNT 2    MOUNT 3

FRAME

FRAME

FRAME

MOUNT #1

MOUNT #2 & #3

MOUNT #4

Corvette body mounts were changed to rubber cushions as the car became more of a touring car. Rubber cushions make panel alignment a little more difficult since the body mounts can be over-tightened. This same problem occurs with polyurethane mounts. The single biggest problem with replacing the body mounts is that the nuts and bolts are often rusted together, and the only way to remove them is with a cutting torch. This is guaranteed to make you very nervous.

For some reason a lot of people fail to replace the rubber flap that hangs behind the front grilles. This flap not only keeps the weather out of the headlight assembly, it also gives the car a finished look. Notice the fiber optics system that attaches to the parking light assembly.

In 1970, Chevrolet added these small fender flares. They may not be the total answer to keeping dirt off the side of your Corvette, but they are a big improvement on the 1968 and 1969 Corvettes.

The trim on the big-block hoods are always just a little bit special. Considering what a good job Chevrolet did with marketing the big block, it's a shame they never put a similar hood on the ZR1s in the eighties.

T-tops always leak. For best results, make sure the gaskets are in good condition, and all the adjustments are correct. Before you let a garage elevate your Corvette on a hoist, make sure you loosen the latches. More than one T-top has shattered while the Corvette was being raised on a service lift.

With the L88, Chevrolet really got serious. I suspect there must be a law about hoods like this today. No one has had cowl induction, at least in so obvious a manner, since the L88 hood.

It may not be a factory lighting arrangement, but it sure looks intimidating. Considering how poorly the Corvette's lights work, I'm amazed we haven't seen a lot more Corvettes similar to this.

Luggage racks always look nice on the late-sixties Corvette. They sure make waxing the car a lot harder though.

If you have a hardtop, make sure you check the gap between the top and the door when the door is closed.

Project Corvette had a broken roof where the door had slammed against the hardtop.

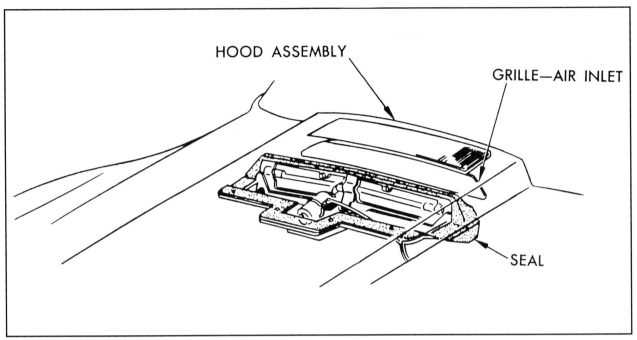

HOOD ASSEMBLY

GRILLE—AIR INLET

SEAL

This type of hood, used from 1973 to 1976, sometimes produces a howl inside the car. Not a real big deal, but Chevrolet dropped this hood for the 1977 model year.

The door is opened by an electrical solenoid when the throttle is near maximum travel.

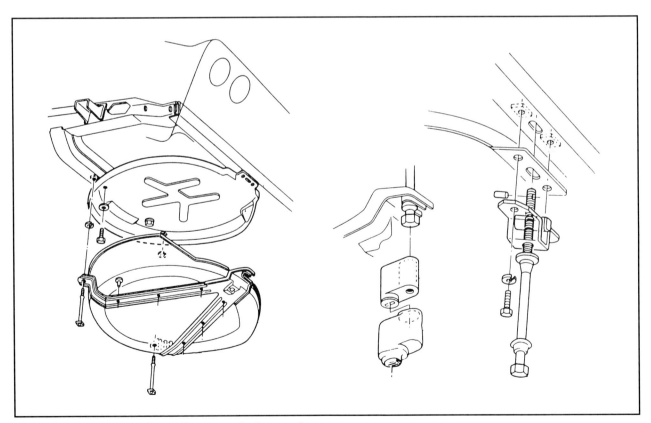

The spare tire carrier can be easily removed when working on the rear end assembly. All of the hardware is currently available, including the lock unit.

Hanging the bumper correctly can pose problems. Notice how the body line is different from the bumper line. At the same time, the bumper itself is not bent. This is one reason the professional restorers check everything very carefully before doing any bodywork.

## Bumpers

Here's the dirty little Corvette secret you never knew: The top-dog Corvettes are actually built around the bumpers. If you've ever been to an NCRS convention or a Bloomington Gold event you've seen the incredible fit of the chrome bumpers. No way will your bumpers ever fit this well; unless, of course, you start with the bumpers and build the rest of your Corvette around them.

Gary, of Caledonia Classic Cars fame, explained how he installs the bumpers in a special jig. Once the bumpers are in the correct location, they rework the Corvette's fiberglass body to meet up with the bumpers ever so perfectly.

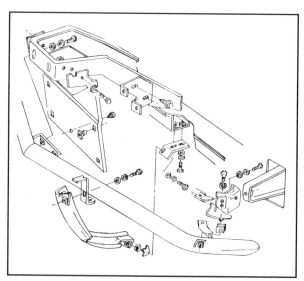

Most Corvette bumpers don't look proper because there are too many adjustments. When you add up all the shims and bolts, it almost seems you could mount a Corvette bumper vertically.

Now I know why Project Corvette will never be a Bloomington Gold car; I did the whole thing backwards. I built a car and then attempted to make the bumpers match the car. Obviously there's no hope.

If you want to see the wrong way to hang bumpers, just examine a few original unrestored Corvettes. I've actually found Corvettes with two different sets of holes in the fiberglass. During the sixties the St. Louis plant seemed to operate on the "bigger-hammer" approach to building Corvettes. No wonder GM built the Bowling Green plant.

When it comes to the pre-1973 Corvettes, you must keep a few points in mind. First, the bumpers really do very little to protect your fiberglass. Second, you can do more damage installing the bumpers than your average parking lot encounter will ever create.

You never want to tighten the bolts on the bumpers until everything is properly shimmed. You have to keep in mind that fiberglass will not bend. The secret is to use washers, or shims, between the bumper brackets and the backside of your fiberglass.

Had you been a little more observant when you took everything apart, you would have noticed the shims are numbered so as to preclude any guesswork. Then again, depending on how much body work you did, none of that may matter.

Basically, you want everything to line up nicely so you can tighten the bumper against the frame braces. There should never be a need to pull things into alignment. More than one Corvette owner has split the fiberglass trying to fit the bumpers. If you actually have to push the bracing ever so slightly against the inside of the fiberglass, you're on the right track.

The other undisclosed secret is to never tighten the bolts on the corner of the fenders. If you try to tighten these bolts, you will ruin your next few

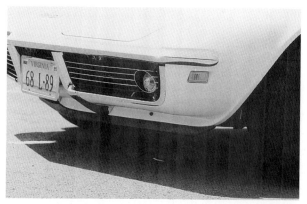

Here's a bumper that's been aligned with care, but is not quite perfect. This bumper is, however, aligned better than it was in 1968. Part of the problem with restoring Corvettes is that we've gotten accustomed to a set of standards that simply didn't apply in 1968.

The original bumpers were made by a small stamping plant in Detroit. All reproductions are made by this same stamping plant, and the quality is virtually the same as it was in the late sixties. Restorers in search of ultimate quality send their bumpers off to private chrome shops that, for a small fortune, will bring the bumpers in line with nineties quality.

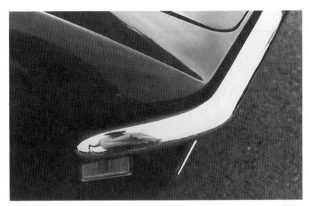

The space between the bumper and the body should be even along the entire length of the bumper. You should use the bumper as a reference point and build the body out in an effort to get the gap perfect.

weeks. In fact, GM never tightened this bolt originally. They were so nervous about broken fiberglass in St. Louis that the assembly-line workers generally just got these bolts finger-tight.

When it comes time to actually bolt the bumper to the inner braces, don't even think about doing it all by yourself. Bumper installation should always be a two-person job, even on the rear of the car.

When you do get around to the back of the Corvette, there's another little secret: The bumpers are installed before the rear valance panel. How many of you have tried to adjust your bumpers only to find that just about everything was impossible to reach? You need to get everything installed, and then, as a last final step, install the valance panel. See how much easier it is when you know all the little secrets? Actually this is how GM did it at the plant in St. Louis.

New bumper bolts are available from Caledonia Classics. After all the money you've just spent to have the bumpers plated, it doesn't make any sense to use the rusted old junk bolts you took off several months (years?) ago.

The new bumper bolts come in two colors. The black phosphate bolts are always used on braces and brackets. Whenever you have a black part being bolted to a black part, you should use a black bolt. The silver cad-plated bolts are used to attach chrome parts. Remember, GM tried to make it as easy as possible.

All of the reproduction bumpers in the country are being made by the same stamping plant that

produced the original. As a former Bloomington Gold winner said, "The same guy is still making the same bumpers with the same old stamping press." We're talking about an authentic reproduction part when we discuss these replica bumpers. In fact you could make a case that these reproduction bumpers are actually New Old Stock. Richard Fortier of Paragon calls these bumpers "Re-Issue" to emphasize the fact that they're not replated, nor are they NOS.

A lot of the top show winners take their original bumpers and send them to their favorite chrome shop. The bumpers that actually go on most Corvette show winners have a finish far beyond the quality ever dreamed of by Chevrolet.

The secret to a quality bumper is in the buffing. Chrome is just like paint. We all know that paint

The rear bumper can draw attention to all kinds of problems. While the bumper is correct, the exhaust pipe is crooked.

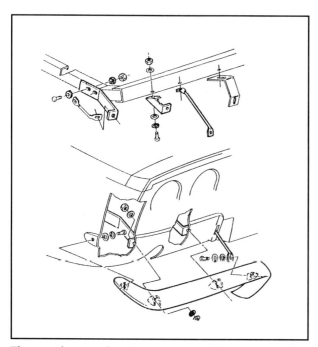

The rear bumper has just as many adjustments as the front bumper. The secret to installing the rear bumpers is to do it exactly the same way the factory did the job. Install the bumpers, and then install the rear panel. If you install the panel prior to the bumper, you'll never be able to reach the bolts. Also, don't over-tighten the bolts. Bumpers can cause a lot of damage to your perfect paint job.

won't hide flaws. In most cases it'll only make the flaws more obvious. Chrome is the same way.

If the raw steel bumper has waves then no amount of copper and nickel will cover up that fact. Your plating shop has to provide a perfect surface for the shine that we call chrome. The reproduction, or re-issued, bumpers actually have a very good plating job. What happened was that no one bothered buffing the bumper to within an inch of its life to get even the smallest waves out of the surface.

This means that you have two choices when you're dealing with the chrome on the ends of your Corvette. You can buy a brand new re-issued bumper that was made exactly the same way your original was formed, or, you can take your old bumper to the plating shop and have it buffed, and plated, to perfection. Just make sure that you walk around several Corvette shows this summer checking out bumpers. When you locate three bumpers that are perfect ask where they were plated.

Project Corvette bumpers were so bent, drilled full of holes, and rusted that no respectable plating shop would even let me bring them inside their business.

I was left with two rusty pieces of junk. This meant that I could scrounge flea markets looking for bumpers suitable for replating, or I could buy a set of re-issue bumpers. I opted for the Paragon solution - new bumpers made on the old presses in Detroit. They work very nicely and are very close to anything

The plastic front bumper arrived in 1973 and created a whole new set of problems. Though we've all gotten used to the look, Corvettes with chrome bumpers will always be worth more money than those with the urethane model.

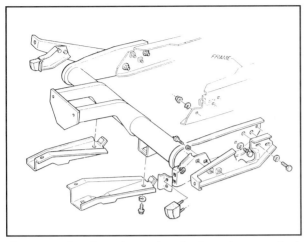

These two drawings show what the front bumpers look like under all that plastic and foam.

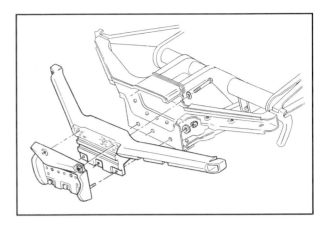

a plating shop could have given me. I think it's even cheaper, although as with some Corvette decisions I'm afraid to check too carefully.

Up to now you probably thought hanging bumpers was simply a matter of getting all the holes to line up properly. At least that's what I always believed. Maybe this Corvette hobby is just getting too hard. It gets worse.

While the third-generation Corvette era began with some very elementary bumpers on the front and rear of the car, the era would end with plastic bumpers attached to both ends of the Corvette. Those neat little chrome bumpers on the early C3 Corvettes were actually more trim than they were bumpers, and the protection they provided was minimal. The government would rectify all that by the end of the 1982 model.

Actually the government passed a law stipulating that beginning in 1973, all cars sold in the U.S. had to have a front bumper that protected the car's lighting or safety equipment from damage during a collision while traveling at 5mph or less.

The new body-color nose piece was made from urethane. The original Chevrolet solution called for an ugly protruding version of the chrome bumper, but this version, which was eventually rejected, would have mounted the chrome bumper on shock absorbers. If you wonder how this might have looked, think about the Fiat X/19 for a minute. Fiat used the system that Chevrolet rejected.

The final solution consisted of a urethane pad on a steel armature. The main support for this pad is placed at the center of the car, with a massive transverse tube bolted to the car's frame. Between the large tube and the Corvette frame, there are two special Omark fasteners. These bolts absorb energy when the forming die, pushed back by the bumper, is forced along the length of the bumper.

In 1973 only the front of the Corvette got this 35lb arrangement. The rear kept the old style chrome bumpers.

In 1974 the rear end of the Corvette changed. The squared-off tail introduced in 1968 was replaced with a tapered urethane plastic cone, and the four

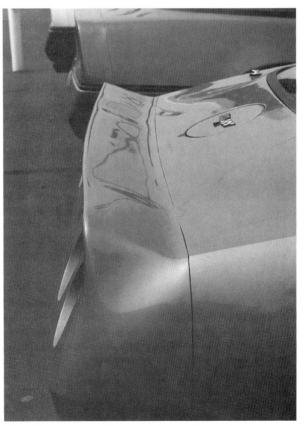

The biggest problem with urethane bumpers is warpage. After several years in the sunshine, the surface gets very wavy. I know of no way to restore this finish, especially since the material was designed to be flexible. One day it got too flexible and never returned to the original shape.

Matching paint is another problem with flexible panels. The paint required for the flexible parts fades differently than the paint used on the hard fiberglass body panels.

lights and the license plate were recessed into this urethane structure.

Under the cover there's a box-section of aluminum impact bar mounted on two slider brackets, each with an energy absorbing Omark bolt. The 1974 Corvette could pass the 5mph impact standard with no problem.

When 1975 rolled around, small black impact pads grew on both the front and rear of the Corvette. This was also a sign that things underneath the system had changed. In 1975, Corvette had to pass both an impact test as well as a pendulum impact test.

The nose was changed to a different type of plastic, and inside the bumper, the interior was constructed of plastic cells that look a whole lot like an ice-cube tray. These small cells are designed to absorb any impact and then return to their original configuration, pushing the face of the front bumper with them.

The Omark bolts were removed from the rear as well, and replaced with Delco's hydraulic Ensorbers.

By now, it's hard to tell whether the chrome bumpers or the urethane bumper suffered most from the ravages of time. The chrome bumpers rust and the urethane bumpers have distorted beyond all belief.

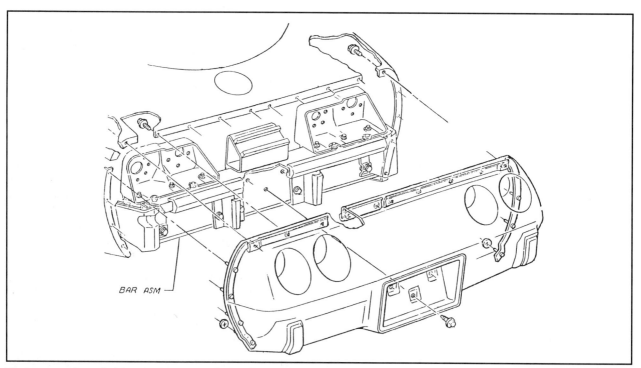

BAR ASM

There are a lot of things going on under the flexible bumpers. It's probably easier to line up chrome bumpers than it is to properly install a urethane cover properly.

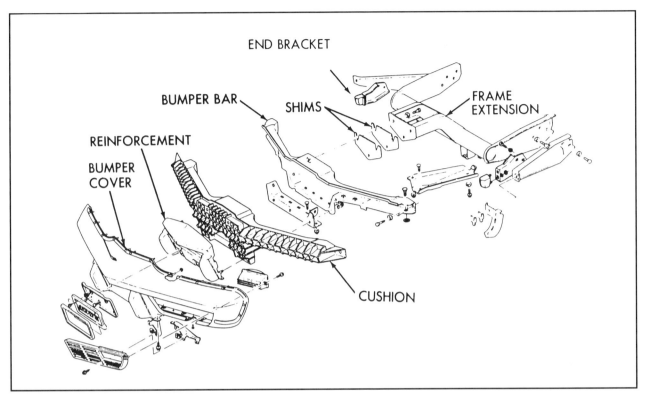

 END BRACKET

BUMPER BAR

SHIMS

FRAME EXTENSION

REINFORCEMENT

BUMPER COVER

CUSHION

The construction of these urethane bumpers gets a little complicated. Here is the parts display from 1975 to 1977.

Even the price for repairs is roughly the same between chrome and urethane bumpers. If you look in the Eckler's catalog rear chrome bumpers cost $300 each, or $600.00 for a pair. A fiberglass replica rear bumper for the 1975 Corvette lists for $374.95. With a paint job, the fiberglass replica will cost about $600.

The one thing that could exceed your Visa limit would be an authentic urethane bumper from GM. The 1974 version is over $1,000 while the 1976 version is almost $900.

This raises another important point. Mainly, the urethane bumpers look like a bit of trash after a short time. Remember this stuff was developed in the late sixties, and no one knew what the sun would do to these bumpers. The fiberglass replica is an alternative, which can be finished to look just like the rest of the body panels. However, with just the slightest bump, you've got a cracked bumper.

On the other hand, do you really intend to bump into things with your freshly painted Corvette? For the average weekend Corvette, the fiberglass replicas work just fine. Actually when they're finished properly, fiberglass replicas look better than the factory bumpers.

The years between 1974 and 1982 were a transition period for bumpers. The early urethane bumpers were terrible. They didn't look all that nice and they didn't hold up very well, but they did move us into an era where you no longer find chrome on either end of a Corvette. I just wish they had perfected the urethane bumper a little sooner.

There's just no way to preserve the shape of these urethane bumpers, which is one reason a lot of people are switching to fiberglass replica bumpers.

# Chapter 14

# Electrical System

Is it really a big deal to drive your Corvette at night? I never drive my toys in the rain, so why do I need windshield wipers? If I keep going down this list, I really wouldn't have needed to rewire Project Corvette, which would have made my life much easier. The less I have to look at wires and the accompanying problems, the happier I am.

I really don't like wiring. When it comes to electricity, I would rather be sanding fiberglass. I really don't like wiring, because typically one of the wires breaks and all the smoke gets out.

Everyone knows that smoke is what makes electricity work. Think about the last wiring problem you had. Everything in your Corvette was working just fine until one of the wires broke and all the smoke escaped from the wire. You've all had this experience. You just never understood electricity enough to make a proper diagnosis.

You should also be aware that I started my life by working on English cars. If you've ever owned an English car, you fully realize how frustrating wiring problems can become. There's something about all

When you get to this point in the process, you're hoping someone will walk by the house and offer you what you've got invested in your Corvette. I found that attending local Corvette shows was a good form of therapy.

The battery is the key to your Corvette's electrical system. Before you begin checking various electrical components, check the battery and make sure it has an adequate charge. If you don't have a fully charged battery, nothing else will matter. Never start out on a troubleshooting expedition with a defective battery.

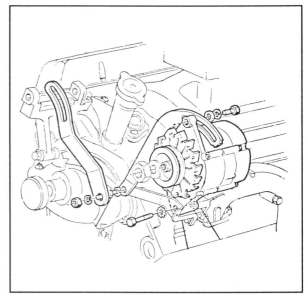

The alternator's only purpose is to keep the battery charged. When you drive your Corvette, it's actually running off the battery. The alternator will replenish the battery and make sure it always has an optimum charge. If your battery keeps going dead, check the tension on the fan belt. To understand the electrical system on your Corvette, check all the simple things first. Don't jump to faulty conclusions and start randomly replacing components. If you suspect the alternator is dead, you can easily remove it and take it to your local rebuilder for checking. It is always best, though, to have the alternator checked while it's in the car, so the shop can check the entire charging circuit.

those different colored wires that can intimidate the best of us.

While working on Project Corvette, I found a book that explains electricity better than anything else on the market. Actually, I started reading Dr. Jacob's *The Doctor's Guide to Optimizing Your Ignition* as

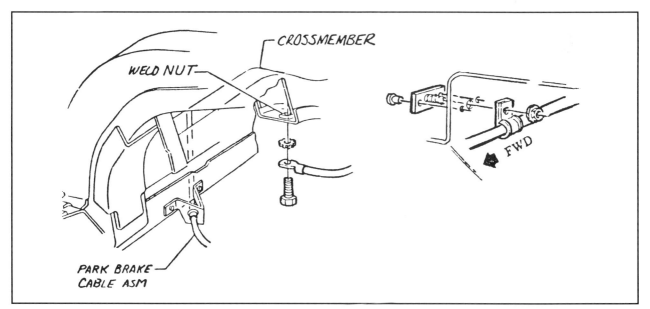

The battery sends electricity out to the various corners of your Corvette, and the power returns through the ground circuit. If the battery voltage cannot make the complete trip around your Corvette, you have a problem. If your battery is fully charged, the second step is to check the ground cable. The cable must make full contact with the frame. Make sure the connection is free of rust and corrosion.

Here's the perfect alternator. At least it looks nice. If it puts out 14.6 volts, then it works as good as it looks.

a way of getting prepared for the engine installation. It was also a good way to avoid installing the wiring harness. I knew *The Doctor's Guide* was my sort of book when I read in it: "Nobody understands elec-

tricity." Armed with this fact, and a few other good hints we'll get to later, I was ready to attack the wiring.

A major problem with wiring is that over the years people modify wiring systems. The previous owner of my Corvette project felt the need to re-arrange all the wiring in the back of the car and a major portion of the wiring behind the dash.

Rather than add more splices, and create more places for the smoke to get out of the wires, I decided to just put a new wiring harness in the car. Do it once, and do it right. At least that was the plan.

The worst part of the electrical system on Project Corvette was that I had no idea if anything even worked when I started. Project Corvette came without a battery. I tried to put off the wiring problems for a long time, but the fateful day finally arrived. The only reason I approached the wiring when I did was that I thought the wiring would be easier to install while the interior and engine were still out of the car (don't confuse "easier" with easy—the process will just be less painful).I even decided to remove the doors and steering wheel. If you've ever done much work on dashboards, you know how uncomfortable it can be to work around the doors and steering wheel . The human body was not designed for installing dash wiring. I decided it would be easier to

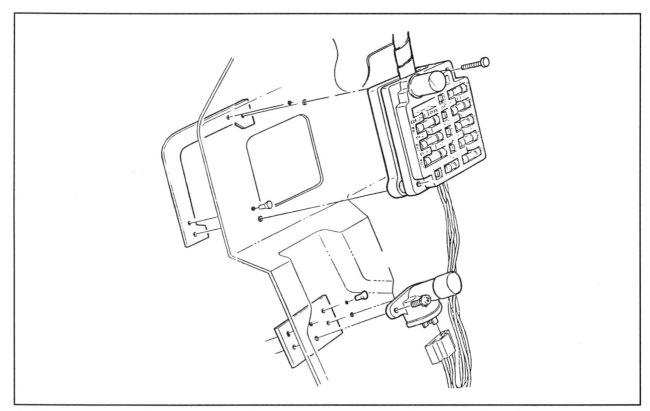

The fuse box is the first place you should look when you start having a problem. A fuse doesn't go bad for no reason at all. When you find a blown fuse, always try to ascertain why it blew.

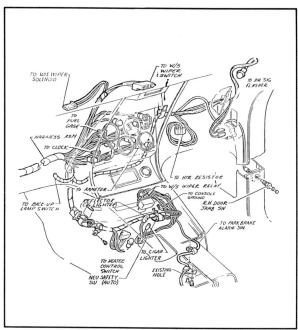

This perfect fuse block is built by M. Parker, a company that makes the best reproduction electrical harnesses in the business. In many cases they've gone back to the original supplier for parts. No judge can tell that this fuse block and the accompanying wiring harness are not original. We're talking about a perfect part at this point.

Wiring the area behind the center dash is the most difficult. With a lot of wires and very little space, this will take a lot time. Forget about deadlines and just spend a couple of hours every night for a week, or month.

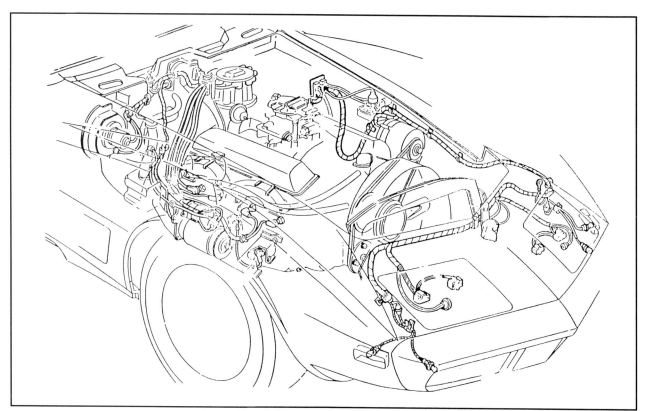

Pictured here is the harness for the front lighting system. All third-generation Corvettes are fairly similar to this 1975 car.

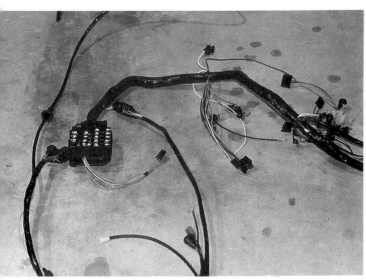

One way to approach the harness installation is to lay out the entire harness on the floor. This way you can identify where all the ends belong. It's a lot easier to identify things if you have some room to move about. The worst part of harness installation is that you're generally working in a tiny cramped space.

just get them out of the way for the duration of this project. Actually, I just didn't bother putting them on after we shot the paint.

The next step was to remove the dash, which wasn't all that hard, except for the panel in front of the driver's seat. One of the previous owners failed to read the manual where it says rather clearly that you should lower the steering column before extricating

the dash panel that houses the speedometer and tachometer. This unknown previous owner simply pulled on the panel until it broke. With the dash folded in two, he was probably able to pull it out rather nicely. The worst part was that he used the same technique to put it back in. None of this was noticeable until we disturbed the panel one last time.

Before you do anything on your Corvette, please purchase the factory manual. If the price of the manual seems a little high, then don't touch anything on your Corvette. The previous owner of Project Corvette destroyed several hundred dollars worth of parts because he was too cheap or lazy to purchase the manual, which would have clearly outlined how to approach dash removal.

There are four basic wiring harnesses in the Corvette. The main harness contains the fuse panel. The rear harness runs along the left side of the interior. A third harness is for the front lighting system. The fourth harness contains all the engine wiring. We're going to skip the fourth harness until engine installation.

The first task is to simply tear out everything that relates to the interior. Installing a wiring harness requires access to every nook and hidden part of the interior, and the job is a lot easier if you don't have to crawl around the steering wheel and the doors, pulling back carpeting as you go along.

The steering wheel is very easy to remove on these early C3 cars. You simply pop the horn button off and then remove the six screws that hold the wheel to the steering column. At that point you'll notice one nut holds the steering wheel hub to the steering column. This nut can be removed with a

This would have been a good stopping point for Project Corvette. The dash area is the worst part of the entire job. The problem is that it's the first harness that gets installed. Everything else comes off this main harness.

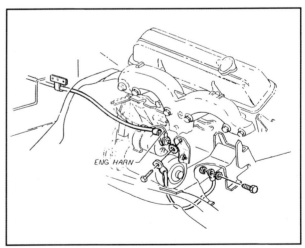

Before you replace your starter, check all the terminal ends, beginning with the starter terminal at the solenoid. Next, check the ground cable, making sure to check both ends. Also, make sure the battery terminal inside the driveshaft tunnel is free from rips and abrasions. Finally, clean the cable ends and tighten the bolts.

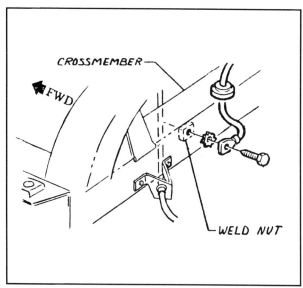

The battery ground cable is another source of problems. You have to remember electricity travels in a circuit. Problems with grounding are a common electrical difficulty.

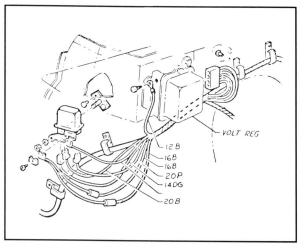

Early cars used a separate voltage regulator. When GM integrated the voltage regulator into the alternator, Corvette followed suit. If you have to replace the alternator, change the voltage regulator at the same time. There's very little sense in taking a chance with these components.

1/2in drive socket, but an impact wrench will usually work a lot better. Besides, you're going to need an impact wrench for the next step.

I've always used air-driven guns, but I'm beginning to think that a little electrical impact gun would be handy around the garage. You wouldn't need to have the air compressor on all the time, and there would certainly be less noise. Just make sure that you get one with a 1/2in drive.

The next step is to beg, borrow, or buy a steering wheel puller. There's probably a way to get the hub off without a puller, but not without a lot of frustration and possible damage to the steering column. A point to remember here is that the only way to operate the puller is with an impact wrench.

A socket and ratchet put too much side tension on the steering wheel puller, giving you all sorts of problems. I know, I tried doing it with a normal 1/2in drive socket. After a half-hour I simply reached for the trusty old impact wrench and the bolt came off in about ten seconds.

It only took me about another half-hour to repair the damage I'd caused to the threads on the end of the steering column. Use an impact gun. Just explain to the family that you need this tool for your sanity. They won't believe that, but try it anyway.

If you have a tilt-steering wheel, forget the whole idea and simply leave the steering wheel in place. Tilt steering wheels have about a zillion different parts, none of which can be easily replaced when you break them. Most shops will not even think of repairing a tilt column. Don't think that you're going to be any better at it. There's a good chance you can

do the job, but on the outside chance that something will go wrong, taking one apart isn't worth the possible problems.

The only question I have is, "How did the blue steering column get in Project Corvette?" There's no question that this Corvette left St. Louis with Cordovan Maroon paint. Later, a green was poorly applied over this color. So where did the blue come from?

The longer I've worked with Project Corvette, the more questions I have about its history. The records are now fairly complete back to 1978, when the car resided in upstate New York. Project Corvette had only 37,000 miles on the odometer at that time, which means the first owner(s) put less than 4,000 miles a year on the car for the first decade.

Sometime before 1978 the whole car was rebuilt. There's no evidence of a roll bar, so it probably wasn't raced. Why was it rebuilt then? Project Corvette probably has less than 45,000 miles, and this is the third time it's been apart. Some of the bodywork has been repaired three and four different times.

The first owners, the Held family, now live someplace in Florida. No one knows exactly where, so our paper chase has come to an end. How in the world did this blue steering column get in the car?

According to one record I located, the speedometer was replaced in 1981—when the dash panel on the driver's side was broken. The problem is that this panel was used only in 1968. In 1969 the ignition switch was moved to the steering column. Rather than attempt to locate another fiberglass panel, I decided to put my newly found fiberglass skills to

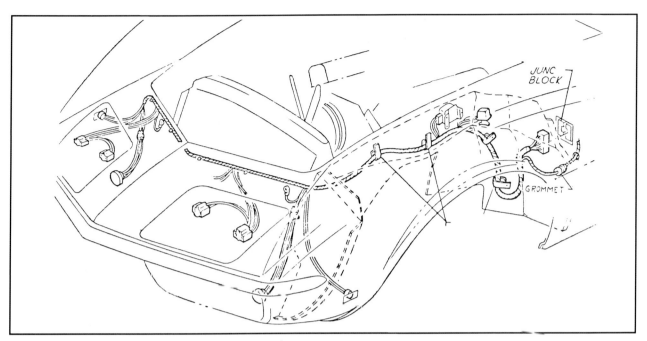

Here is a rough idea of how the front-light wiring harness installs. Notice how the fiber optic system goes through the firewall.

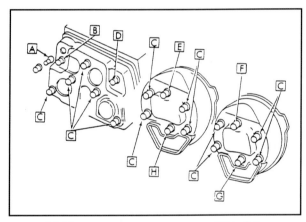

| | Light | Wire Color |
|---|---|---|
| A | Door Open Warning | Light Blue w/ Dark Green Stripe |
| B | Headlamp Door Warning | Light Blue & Pink |
| C | Instrument Cluster Illumination | Gray |
| D | Seat Belt Warning | Black |
| E | Parking Brake Alarm | Pink |
| F | High Beam Indicator | Light Green |
| G | Left-hand Directional Indicator | Light Blue |
| H | Right-hand Directional Indicator | Dark Blue |

the test and repair the original panel. Project Corvette was a veritable training program in fiberglass repairs.

Frank, at M. Parker, created all the new wiring harnesses. I think M. Parker makes just about all the reproduction wiring sets in the world, at least for Chevrolets. After several decades of buying reproduction parts that were a reproduction of nothing that ever saw the St. Louis factory, it was a pleasure to deal with a company that knows what it means to

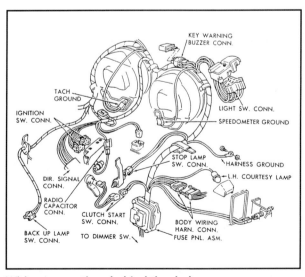

Wiring connections behind the dash.

132

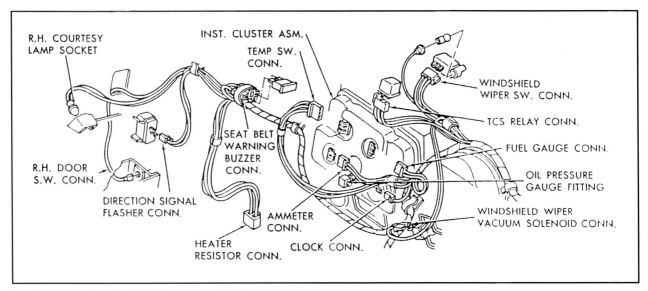

**Wiring connections behind the center of dash.**

create a correct part.

When I put the old wiring harness next to the new ones it was amazing. Every single wire and connector matched perfectly. Even the stupid light mon-

itoring system used in 1968 was exactly the same.

When it comes to installing a wiring harness, you absolutely must get a copy of the *Assembly Instruction Manual* (AIM), as well as the Haynes, or fac-

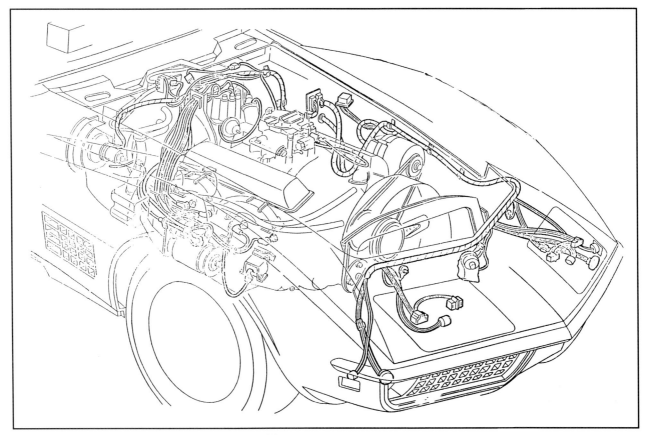

**General arrangement of engine compartment wiring.**

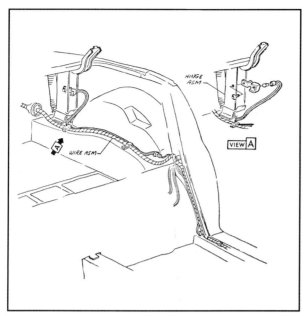

**General arrangement of rear compartment wiring.**

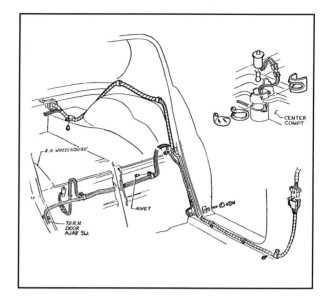

tory, manual. Don't even think about anything else. The beauty of AIM is that it shows you how the wires were routed the first time they were installed.

Wiring harnesses were originally designed to be dummy-proof. The poor guys on the assembly line certainly didn't have time to look up information on a chart. Consequently, the harness is designed so that everything falls right into place. If you stop and think about what you're doing, it should not be problem. The best way is to lay the harness beside the car and make a practice run at identifying all the connections.

With the harness laid out so that everything is in place, use helpful hints from Dr. Jacobs. It seems that General Motors actually used a logical system for wiring colors: Yes, GM and logic do go together.

- Red wires are for + 12 volt delivery
- Black wires are for ground
- Brown wires are used to turn something on and off
- Blue wires are used to power lights and for transmitting electrical signals
- Purple wires are used to make momentary connections, like a starter
- Yellow wires are for signal-type information, like a door switch
- Green is for information associated with contact points, such as coils and tachometer impulse wires.
- White is for a pulse, as well as being common in ignition signal pulsing

If you write this list on a big chart and keep the AIM manual in front of you, wiring is not all that difficult. You should also call Jacobs Electronics and get the Doctor's book. You'll definitely need it when you get to the engine, and it sure is a big help in understanding wiring.

# Chapter 15

# Vacuum System

If you thought the wiring was fun, wait until you get to the vacuum system, everybody's favorite part. Chevrolet decided a vacuum system was the hot setup for the 1968 Corvettes. This created problems, beginning in 1968, which have continued ever since that fateful day over twenty-five years ago.

The electric motors on the second-generation cars worked just fine. Yet, in 1968 we had to learn about vacuum-operated devices; Chevrolet made us do it. To make life more interesting, Chevrolet threw in a vacuum-assisted windshield wiper door for a few years. Eventually though, even Chevrolet gave up on that idea.

The best thing you can own is one of the little vacuum testers from your local supply house. This will allow you to pull a vacuum line and test the operation of the individual components.

The starting point for all this nonsense is the large metal canister behind the left front wheel well. Here's where I finally got smart. When the master

The headlight system worked very well on the earlier cars. For some reason, probably having to do with money, the system was changed to a vacuum-operated system. In about one-third of these cars, this system works fine. In the other two-thirds, it gives people problems. Fortunately we've learned to rectify the problems rather easily.

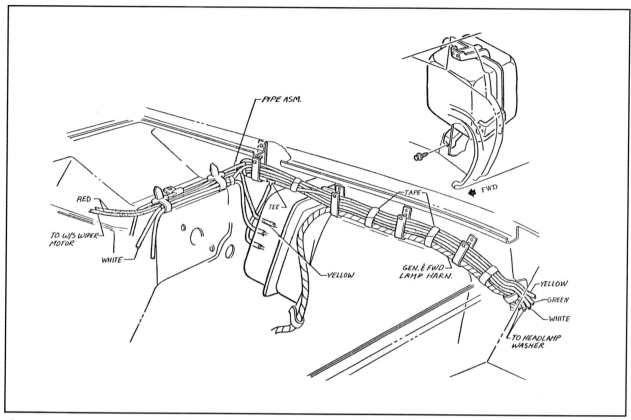

There are a lot of components in the total system. The best place to start is the vacuum reservoir under the left fender. The vacuum, stored in this canister, is produced by the engine at idle. There is a rubber hose that connects to a nipple on the intake manifold behind the carburetor.

This actuator used three different styles of rear tubes over the years, all functionally interchangeable. At this point you may well have two different types, but this only matters if you intend to show at NCRS or Bloomington. The example shown here was rebuilt by Caledonia Classic Cars. They can rebuild your original unit to the original specifications, including date codes. The cannisters can be removed with four bolts.

cylinder was off the car, I removed the canister and restored the outside of it.

Before you even do that, though, you should check the canister with your handy vacuum gauge. If the canister won't hold a vacuum, you've just found a major problem. The good part is that most radiator shops can repair any rust holes in the can.

The next items to check are the headlight actuators, which are usually a real problem. The inner and outer seals usually deteriorate and allow leaks, and consequently, the headlights will not go up and down. There are three solutions to this problem. First, only drive your Corvette during the daylight, which really doesn't solve the problem. Second, buy new actuators, an expensive proposition, complicated by the fact that most of the reproductions on the market are incorrect. There's no reason to replace perfectly correct parts with faulty reproductions unless you can gain performance.

If we bought new reproduction actuators, they would work exactly as rebuilt units, but if anyone in the future wanted to build an NCRS Corvette they would have to locate correct 1968 actuators and then pay to have them rebuilt. Why not just rebuild the actuators at this point and be done with it for the

The round vacuum canister for the 1968 wiper door is shaped differently from all the other years. There's a good chance your unit was replaced sometime in the last quarter century.

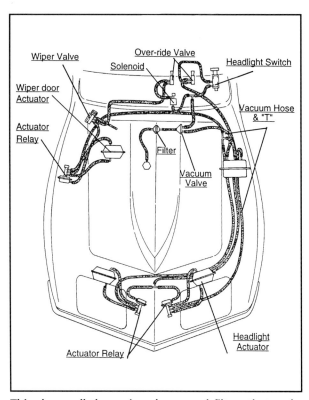

This shows all the various hoses and filters that make your system work. This is not an easy system for the inexperienced person to troubleshoot.

next twenty-five years? The best, and third, solution is to send them to Caledonia Classics for rebuilding.

Caledonia rebuilt units are remarkable because they look just like brand-new units, and Caledonia completes the rebuilding job so quickly it makes a mess of your schedule. I sent the actuators away, assuming they'd be gone the usual couple of weeks (months?), and got them back in just over a week. This worked out so well that I ended up sending Caledonia all the vacuum devices for rebuilding.

I had already decided my next Corvette frame will be shipped to Caledonia for restoration. Now that I've sent them all the vacuum canisters, maybe I'll just send them the whole car. It would be a lot easier. The only problem is what would I do for frustration and fun?

I've come to the conclusion that rebuilding Corvettes may be some form of therapeutic self-abuse. If Caledonia did the complete rebuild of Project Corvette, I would probably have to spend a fortune on therapy. Better that I just send Gary as many parts as possible and use Project Corvette as a substitute for the therapy all of us so desperately need.

Maybe though we could get the Corvette hobby covered under the Federal Health Plan. We are engaged in some form of mental health therapy, why shouldn't the government help us with our recovery programs? What we really need is a twelve-step, government funded, program for Corvette addiction.

Back to work. Once you get all the canisters back from Caledonia Classics, everything can be bolt-

ed in place and you can start to run vacuum lines. And you thought we weren't going to have any fun this week. Once again we run into problems with the reproductions currently on the market.

The original vacuum hoses for the wiper door, the headlight doors, and the heater controls, all have very clear markings. The large vacuum hoses, for instance, have a single white stripe that's painted on the hose. Most of the reproduction hoses on the market come from Dr. Rebuild. A lot more companies are jumping into this area. C Central is one firm reproducing their own hoses and not just shipping Dr. Rebuild hoses under their own address. Just ask a few Corvette owners where they buy their replacement vacuum lines.

Some of the reproduction hoses have thicker walls than the original, which results in an outside diameter that is way too large. It may not be a big deal, but it's still a waste of money. When you buy your parts, ask questions of people who have been down this road before.

I now have real respect for any Corvette that can pass the NCRS Duntov award. A restored car is one thing. A restored Corvette where everything works is something else again. Someday, in this decade, Project Corvette may actually get to that point. After all, we're all allowed our private dreams.

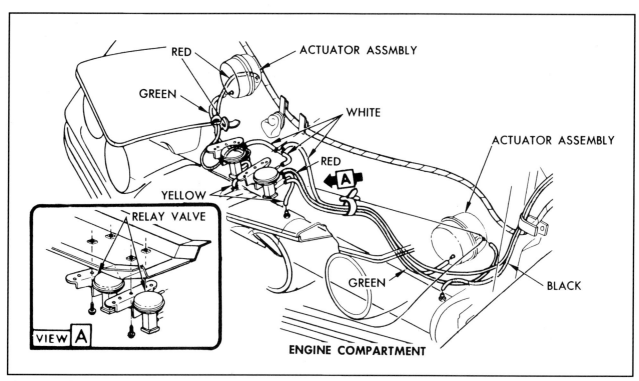

These two drawings should get you started on your vacuum project. Do not take anything apart until you have the replacement handy. If we all followed that advice, we would be a lot better off. On the other hand, if we all followed that advice, we might as well quit working on Corvettes and take up solving jigsaw puzzles.

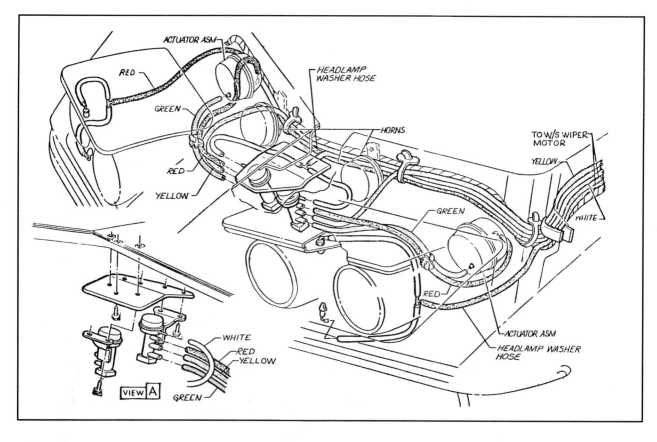

138

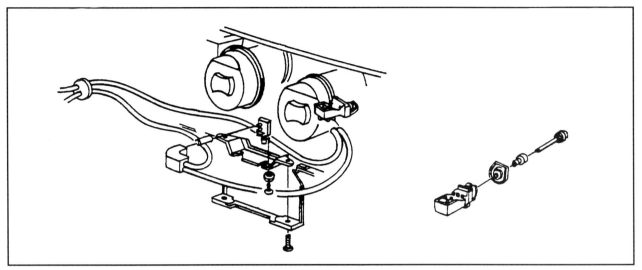

This drawing shows what goes on behind the instrument panel.

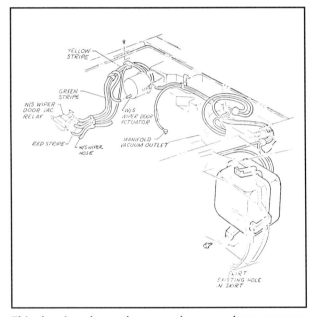

This drawing shows the general vacuum hose arrangement as if you were looking over the right front fender.

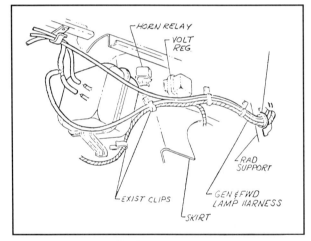

Pretend you're looking up from about the center of the car and you'll get the proper perspective. The vacuum hoses are bundled with the wiring harness where they pass through the radiator support.

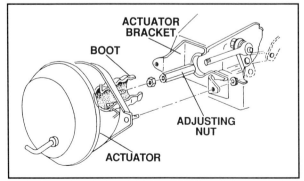

You can adjust the headlight opening height by using the long adjusting nut.

*Chapter 16*

# Transmission

Nothing says more about the third-generation Corvette than the transmission. In 1968, eighty-two percent of the Corvette buyers ordered four-speed transmissions. In 1982, you couldn't even buy a four-speed. Something had changed. Maybe everything had changed. By 1982, the Corvette had come full circle; the outrageous hot rod of the sixties had become the Riviera of the Chevrolet line.

In 1981, the last year for the four-speed Corvette, only fourteen percent of the buyers opted for this gearbox. Thirteen years earlier, Corvette owners had a choice of several different four-speeds. Considering this, one of the rarest Corvettes on the market might be a 1981 four-speed with a radio delete option. We're talking possibly less than 100 cars with this combination.

Seriously though, the change in transmission marked a difference in what Corvette owners thought was important. Just as Chevrolet emphasized ease of entry when they designed the C5 cars, the end of the C3 cars signaled the end of Corvette

buyers who wanted to depress a clutch pedal. The Corvette has constantly evolved with the age of its owners. The move to automatic transmissions says a great deal about the evolution and age of the Corvette owner.

## The Four-Speeds

In the beginning there were three-speeds. The base Corvette came standard with a three-speed transmission, but almost everyone opted for the four-speed gearbox. In 1968, 326 people got their Corvette with the three-speed transmission.

The most common four-speed was the M21 gearbox with the close gear ratios. The four-speed

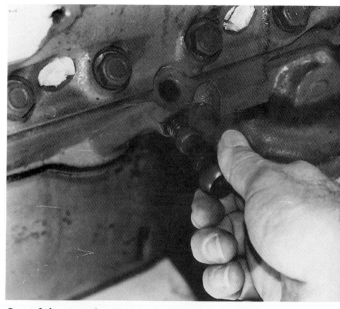

One of the most important items in your Corvette is this little ball that screws into the side of the engine block. It attaches the clutch linkage. If you build a monster motor, like Project Corvette's, make sure you use a block from a stick shift, or have your machine shop drill a hole in the block for this ball. Otherwise you'll have to do like we did, remove the motor and start all over again.

The original pressure plate as it came out of Project Corvette.

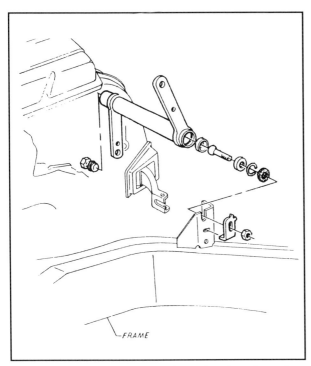

Here is how it all comes together: The threads go into the engine block, and the clutch linkage slides onto the ball.

Hays, a division of Mr. Gasket, supplied the flywheel. I also used a Lakewood bell housing. The plate behind the flywheel means that if the flywheel blows up, I won't lose the engine block. The explosion will be totally contained within the Lakewood housing.

transmission that comes with your prize really makes no difference. The M22 rock crusher gearbox may be a little more desirable, but you pay for it with a lot more gear noise.

This M22 transmission was finally dropped in 1972. This gearbox was really designed for racing purposes, and when only 130 were sold in 1971, the accountants saw a lot of wasted effort.

## Flywheels and Clutches

Chevrolet spent a lot of time designing the flywheel and clutch in your Corvette. You should think twice before you start making radical changes in this area. If all you plan to do is drive your Corvette on the street, then stick to stock replacement parts.

Changing the flywheel is something everyone talks about, but it really isn't necessary. First, as good as an aluminum flywheel is for racing, it's a poor choice for the street. Remember, the flywheel is about mass and inertia. You want as much inertia as possible on the street, where you're always at the bottom of your torque curve.

Unless you totally abuse your clutch, it should never be a problem. Most of the clutches that get replaced are abused. No one wants to admit they don't know how to shift their Corvette, so instead they abuse the manufacturer of the clutch.

The racing clutch discs that you read about in all the magazines are strictly for racing. They're de-

signed to grab at high rpms, and there is no slip in a racing clutch. On the street we want a little bit of slippage. Without slip we couldn't leave most stoplights.

A common mistake is to replace the stock flywheel. This can screw up performance and may require a new bellhousing (again, don't ask me how I know). Think before you change anything in your Corvette's driveline. Chevrolet thought of all the problems and designed what they thought was the best all-around combination. What makes you think you can improve upon their blend?

## The Automatics

The Turbo-Hydramatic (THM) 400 was the standard automatic transmission for the Corvette until 1976. The THM is an example of typical sixties over-engineering, and it was one of the best transmissions GM ever made. It was certainly one of the most robust units they ever developed, even if it lacked all the gee-whiz technology of the nineties.

This is the Lakewood bell housing. It's not stock and it's heavy, but it will protect your body should the clutch decide to blow up.

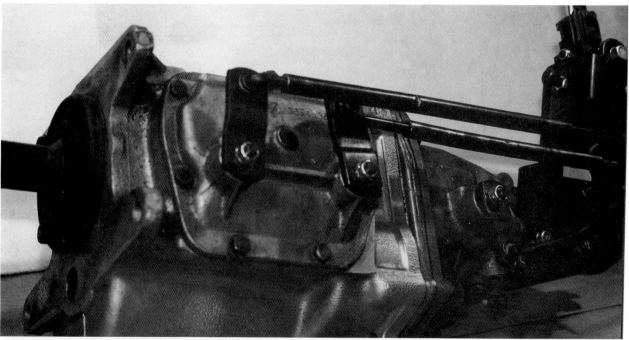

Hurst Shifter, a subsidiary of Mr. Gasket, rebuilt the old shifter, and it's a lot cheaper than buying a new shifter unit. It also works just as well as a new shifter. Great performance, less money.

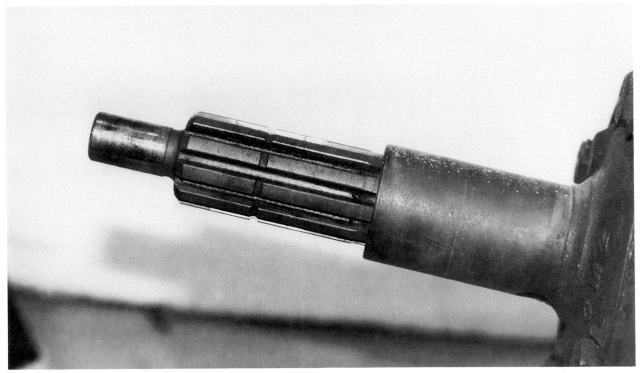

The input shafts are all the same on the manual transmissions.

The best part is that if you buy a Corvette with one of the THM 400 automatic transmissions, any local transmission shop in the country can repair the unit. Every transmission technician over age forty got their start with 350 and 400 transmissions.

The THM 350 was first installed in 1976. There are some people who prefer the THM 350 to the 400

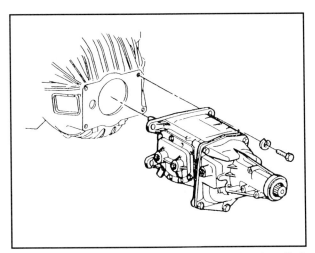

Once the clutch is aligned and the bell housing installed, you can install the transmission. The engine and transmission must be installed as a single unit in the Corvette.

because of the difference in gear ratios. The 350 unit has third and second gears spaced much closer together. Whereas the 400 unit dropped off as it shifted into third gear, the 350 has no such drop. You can almost think of the 350 as a close-ratio automatic gearbox. The optional L82 kept the 400 unit, and the 350 was offered with the base engine in 1976.

The 350 and 400 transmissions are physically quite different, and if you suspect that some switching may have taken place, it's a very simple matter to

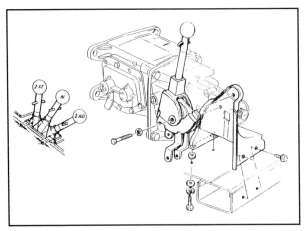

The standard Corvette shifter bolts to a bracket, then to the cross member.

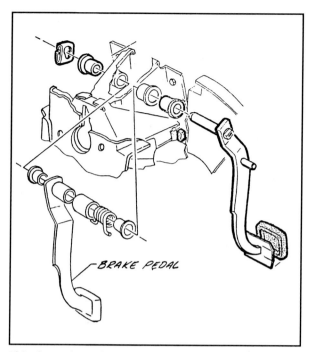

This shows how the brake and clutch pedal attach. The clutch pedal actually provides a place for the brake pedal to pivot.

crawl under the car to check. Just look at the transmission pan on the bottom of the transmission.

The pictures in this chapter should help you identify them with no problems at all.

The next automatic transmission change came in 1981. This time the THM 350C was installed. The THM 350C is basically the same as the THM 350, but electronics were added to the unit. The transmission featured a lock-up torque converter for second and third gears.

This lock-up torque converter eliminates all transmission slippage when the Corvette reaches cruising speed . The economics of gasoline in the seventies meant that torque converter slippage wasn't worthwhile. It's estimated that a lock-up converter is worth 3 mpg.

The 350C transmission has a control system that uses road speed, engine temperature and throttle position for determining when this lockup should occur. In mid-1980 GM began using the Computer Command Control system to monitor all these functions. This meant that the ECM, or Engine Control Module, took over a lot of these functions.

Identifying the 350C is fairly simple. On the left side of the unit, above the transmission pan, there's an electronic plug. If you don't find an electri-

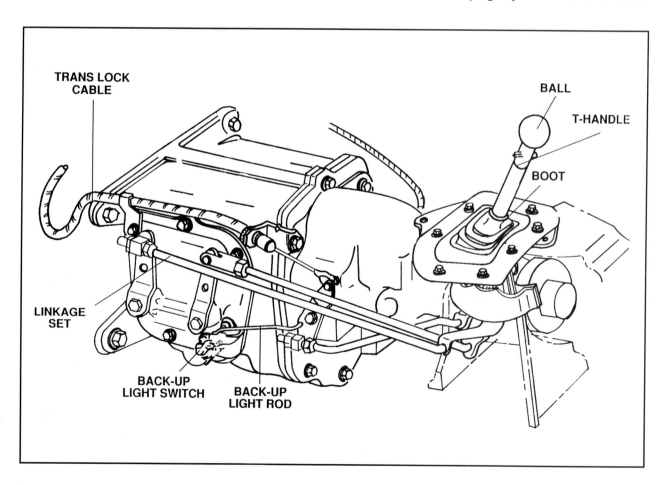

TRANS LOCK CABLE

BALL

T-HANDLE

BOOT

LINKAGE SET

BACK-UP LIGHT SWITCH

BACK-UP LIGHT ROD

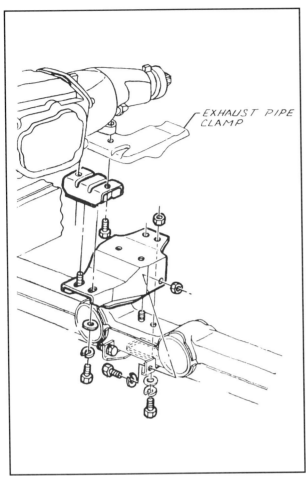

When the Corvette went to a single exhaust, they added an extra bracket to hold the exhaust pipe.

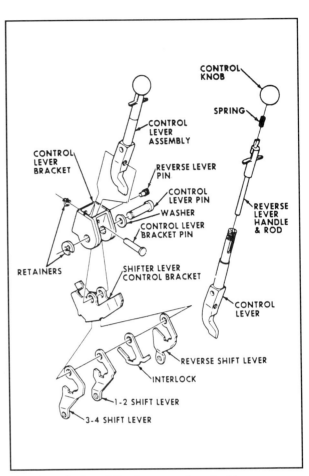

Here is a display of the four-speed control-lever components.

cal connection on the side of the transmission, then you haven't got a 350C.

When you get to about 35mph with the 350C transmissions, you might feel like it's hunting for the proper gear. What's happening is that the lock-up torque converter is engaging and disengaging. This is normal and generally nothing to be concerned about.

There is always the danger that somewhere along the line the original transmission may have been switched to another rebuilt unit. The standard procedure in transmission shops is to remove the original unit from the car and take a rebuilt unit from the shelf, which means your Corvette no longer has a numbers-matching transmission. Remember, just a few years ago, late-seventies Corvettes were just another cheap used car. People may have done all sorts of strange things to them. It pays to crawl under the car to see if the transmission has been changed.

If your Corvette is an automatic, there are only a couple of things you may need or want to do as preventive maintenance. Your primary responsibility

is to always keep a close eye on the transmission fluid. Make sure the level is always correct. More automatic transmissions have been ruined because of neglect than any other reason.

When you check the transmission level, make sure the engine is running. Secondly, when you look at the dipstick, check both sides. More than one person has been fooled by simply looking at one side of the dipstick. The result is a lot of burned clutches.

When you check the transmission fluid, bring the dipstick up to your nose and sniff the fluid. When your clutches are ready to depart, they slip and burn, causing a distinct smell of burned transmission fluid. It's a smell you don't want to find.

You also need to be concerned about changing the transmission fluid. The Dexron II transmission fluid should be changed on a regular basis. If this fluid isn't changed on a regular basis, it shouldn't be touched. As long as the transmission is working, leave it alone. Change the fluid every two years or never.

After a car goes over 50,000 miles, you have gone over the edge. Nasty gunk is what's holding

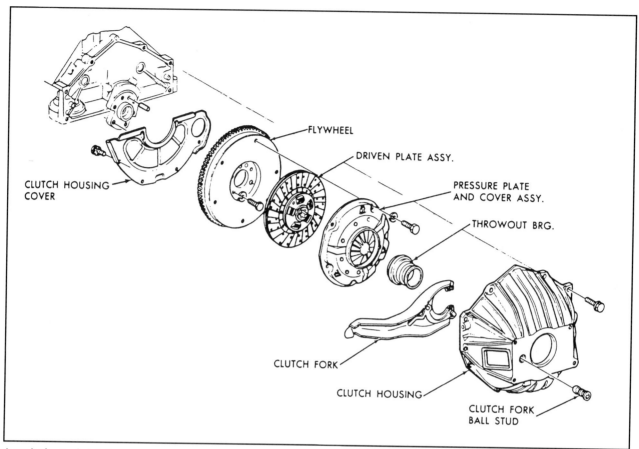

A typical set of clutch components.

The labels in the diagram read:

FLYWHEEL

DRIVEN PLATE ASSY.

PRESSURE PLATE AND COVER ASSY.

THROWOUT BRG.

CLUTCH HOUSING COVER

CLUTCH FORK

CLUTCH HOUSING

CLUTCH FORK BALL STUD

Details of the clutch cross-shaft assembly. The near side bolts to the frame bracket, while the far side bolts to the engine block. If you're using a replacement engine block, make sure you have a hole drilled for this cross-shaft. Automatic engine blocks have no hole.

the transmission together. There will be times when changing the fluid will actually cause the unit to stop functioning. Don't blame your local transmission shop if this happens, blame the last three owners for

Transmission maintenance consists of cleaning the pan and changing this filter. This is important to the longevity of the transmission.

not being responsible enough to change the transmission fluid every twenty-four months.

The year 1982 was a landmark in Corvette history; it was the first time since 1953 when the Corvette could only be purchased with an automatic transmission. It was also a test year for the 700-R4 from the Hydromatic Division, and the first time a true four-speed automatic transmission was installed in the Corvette.

This new transmission caused a lot of problems in the early years, none of which should concern you at this point in history. Every transmission shop has accumulated a great deal of experience with this unit, and repairs, not to mention design faults, have long since been corrected. Besides, if you want a 1982 Corvette, you have no choice but to live with the 700-R4.

## Playing With Fluid

One lesser known thing you can do to your Corvette transmission is to change the fluid to a Ford Type F transmission fluid. GM has always liked a smooth shift. The Hydra-matic Division has always felt that a transmission was perfect when the customer could barely feel the automatic transmission shift from second gear to third. One of the most important characteristics of Dexron II transmission fluid is that it allows this soft gentle shift.

The transmission has an outlet and a return line for the transmission fluid cooler. This cooler is usually the bottom portion of the radiator. In some rare cases an auxiliary cooler may have been bolted to the front of the radiator. These are not from the factory.

The valve body of the transmission resides above the filter. The valve body is a very delicate item, and the car must be driven if you do any work on the valve body.

The THM 400 pan is far from a rectangular shape. You should be able to spot this pan quite easily.

The THM 350 pan is basically a rectangle with a corner removed.

Ford, on the other hand, has always liked a crisper tighter shift. The main characteristic of Type F transmission fluid is that it allows the shift to be a little harsh. Ford calls it crisp.

Most Corvette owners prefer the same sort of shift that Ford likes. The quick way to get this harder shift is to replace the Dexron II transmission fluid in your Corvette Hydra-matic with Ford Type F fluid.

The change to Type F transmission fluid will require one additional modification. In order for it to work properly you'll have to get all the Dexron II out of the transmission. The two fluids are not totally compatible.

When you normally change the transmission fluid you're only changing the fluid in the filter pan. Several quarts remain in the torque converter. In order to change to Type F you're going to have to remove all the fluid in the torque converter.

You'll need to drill a small hole in the edge of the torque converter to let all the fluid drain out. You can then plug the hole with an 1/8in pipe plug. From there you can refill the unit with Type F.

## Are Shift Kits Any Good?

You've read about them in every single magazine. Shift kits are supposed to be simple to install. You've also asked the question: "If these kits are miracle workers, why didn't GM install them in the first place?"

First, these kits may not be the answer to all your problems. For one thing, they increase pressure inside the transmission, which can increase leaks. If the seals in your transmission are marginal, you stand a good chance of creating some new leaks.

The added pressure in the transmission may also cause more wear on the hard parts in the transmission, which means the steel plates will absorb a little more heat. It isn't a big problem or anything to

The 350C unit was the first transmission to use electronics. It can easily be identified by the electrical plug on the side of the unit.

be concerned about, until you take the unit out of your car for rebuilding.

Regardless of the type of transmission in your Corvette, you should have very few problems. If you do start having problems, chances are they're going to be beyond your weekend-warrior capabilities. Every town in America has at least one good transmission shop. You should ask a lot of questions and find this shop. When you think it's time for some serious transmission chores, leave the Corvette with them and ask them to preform their magic. Just make sure you tell them you want *your* unit rebuilt, not replaced with a unit off the shelf.

*Chapter 17*

# Small-Block Engines

Chevrolet engines have won more races than any other engine in the world. We're talking about real world-class power when we deal with the small-block engine that's powering your Corvette.

The marvelous thing is all the variations of this engine Chevrolet produced. The engine diversity in the Corvette line is amazing, not to mention the varieties sold in the Chevelles and Camaros. Between 1968 and 1982 the Corvette engine was totally transformed from a noisy gas-guzzling, fun-to-drive V8 to a low-horsepower, responsible citizen. It wasn't until the LT-1, in the fourth-generation Corvettes, that the horsepower would return.

In 1968 the small-block engine was available in two variations. In 1982 there was only one engine in the whole Corvette line—you had no choices. The horsepower ratings ranged from 350hp to 200hp. Of course, horsepower was calculated differently then, but that's still a tremendous divergence.

Rebuilding the engine in your Corvette is a significant project. This is not a one-weekend activity. Before you even touch the first bolt, you'll need to make some major decisions.

If you decide to pull the motor out of your Corvette, you should consider a major rebuild. You don't want to rebuild the engine in your Corvette

The original base engine in 1968 was a 327ci small-block engine with 300hp. Notice the air pump is already in place. The quest for a cleaner world had begun.

This is what the unrestored Corvette engine looks like. There's nothing wrong with this engine compartment that a little effort and orange paint can't repair.

more than once a decade. This is especially true for cars from the late seventies, in which modern electronic engine controls make engine removal and installation a lot more difficult. In these cars, simply making sure all the wires and vacuum lines are properly connected is a time consuming project, not to mention attaching the emissions controls.

Why do you want to rebuild the motor? Anybody who races a Corvette does not need to read this discussion—you repair engines on a regular basis. The rest of us are usually just embarrassed by the amount of smoke coming out of the tailpipes.

Excess oil consumption and too little power are the only justifications for a new motor in your Corvette. Having some spare time in the winter is not a good enough excuse. The reality is that most of us put less than 3,000 miles a year on our Corvettes. Since we change the oil twice a year, adding a quart every thousand miles is no big deal.

Excess oil consumption means the parts inside the motor are starting to wear out. When the parts begin wearing out, the oil starts getting into the combustion chambers and ends up coming out the tailpipes. Don't let oil *leaks* confuse the issue. When oil leaks out of the motor, it simply means a seal or

gasket is worn out, not the mechanical parts of the motor. Replacing gaskets is usually a lot easier than rebuilding a motor.

The casting number on Project Corvette's original engine block identifies it as an engine block for a 327ci, 350bhp motor. The casting number is the first step to determining the originality of your Corvette's motor.

Here's the original motor coming out. You'll notice the rocker arm covers are definitely not original. This was only the beginning of my problems.

In order to get a handle on the problems of oil consumption, you first need to seal all these leaks. Only then can you figure out if the car is actually burning oil. On the other hand, if big blue clouds of smoke follow your Corvette around, start saving for a new motor. Likewise, if your oil pressure is below 10lb on the gauge, start keeping track of your bank balance. In fact, if the oil pressure gets this low just driving down the road, get ready for a connecting rod that might try to jump out of your prized numbers-matching block.

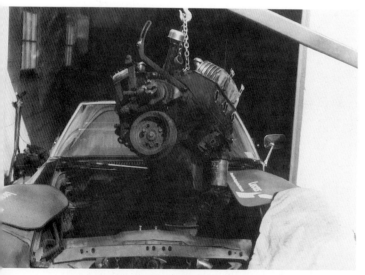

Notice the bracket on the engine block for the air pump. Obviously, no air pump came with the car.

As you work on your Corvette, take a lot of pictures. Most importantly, make sure all the details are obvious. In this picture you can see the location of the brackets in relation to the water pump.

Another picture of the original motor as it was coming out of Project Corvette. This one shows the last of the original ignition shielding.

The key to a strong Corvette motor is careful preparation. Honing plates have become standard equipment in the quality engine shops, such as RHS. This guarantees the piston bores will be perfectly round.

One way to check for general engine performance and lack of power is to have your car checked by an emissions station. This will tell you a lot about how well the car is actually running. You'll want to know how well the engine is burning the gasoline dispensed by the carburetor.

This Offenhauser manifold is an old aftermarket fuel-injection arrangement from the sixties. I'm not sure exactly how it works, but it's an example of what you can find at flea markets. This would be sort of neat to have on your street Corvette, if you could ever get the thing to work properly.

When you have perfectly round piston bores, it becomes critical that the piston-ring end gap be correct.

The last thing you need is for the ends of the piston rings to start banging into each other.

Power is all relative. If you have a 1976 Corvette, it's hard to tell when the motor's down on power. It left St. Louis that way. Nothing you do is going to fix that problem, short of replacing the entire motor.

## Save the Original Motor?

If you have a numbers-matching car, the best approach is to rebuild the original motor. If you want a banzai motor, you shouldn't destroy all the original parts. Simply pull the original motor out of your Corvette and put it in a corner of your garage. There's no shortage of small blocks in the world, just a lack of numbers-matching engines for your Corvette.

## The RHS Motor

When I asked Racing Head Service (RHS) to build a street motor with a big flat torque curve, I had no idea what they were capable of constructing. The result of the RHS effort was a small-block 383ci engine with more power than the ZR1 and the Callaway Super Natural. This is power.

It is also the kind of power that can destroy driveshafts, not to mention tires. I'm talking about 418lb-ft of torque at 4000rpm. I'm living with more than 400lb-ft of torque from 2500rpm to 4500rpm. This is serious street power.

I've always believed certain things about Chevrolet engines. First, Chevrolet makes the finest racing engines in the world. Secondly, there are a lot of people in the world who can make a Chevrolet engine run a lot better than I can. RHS simply proved that fact.

In the old days all of us used to bolt our own engines together. Today, even most of the racing teams around the world have someone else do it for them. If all these big-time racing teams buy their motors, then I have no business attempting to build a real Chevrolet motor in my two-car suburban garage.

The folks at RHS in Memphis, Tennessee, know about motors. They understand motors the way Tammy Wynette understands sad songs. I think half the people in the South were raised with Chevy small blocks for cradles. If you get your motors built by somebody with a Yankee accent you're probably down on power.

There are far too many Chevy engines and way too many small machine shops that try to put these motors together. For every Chevy engine block ever cast there is a self-proclaimed expert on these

Four-bolt main caps really aren't necessary for street engines. Two-bolt blocks are more than enough, especially if you use ARP hardware.

Careful crankshaft preparation is essential to making horsepower. RHS takes special care with the radius of the crank journals.

This is the camshaft from Competition Cams that gave us the high torque numbers. The trick was high lift with almost no duration.

This is the best way to insure your timing gears are installed properly.

engines. Every teenager who ever went through an auto shop course pretends to know all about building high-performance engines. The key word here is "pretends."

Every day of the week, serious engine builders all over the country have to dispel myths about Chevy powerplants. In an effort to give Project Corvette the latest high-tech power, I worked with RHS and Edelbrock to find out the real facts.

Keep in mind, RHS builds a couple of high-performance Chevy engines every day. They have millions of dollars worth of machining equipment, two dyno cells, and a flow bench for the cylinder heads. If it can be done to a Chevy engine, RHS has probably tried it. An engine shop of this size has already tried all the combinations that don't work, plus the few that do work.

Most importantly, RHS has both the ability and the equipment to separate fact from fiction. When you build more engines in a week than the average machine shop does in a year, you learn a lot about how to make power. When you purchase an RHS engine, you're buying all this knowledge.

Another advantage of RHS is that, Ivars, the owner, is a Corvette guy. Somehow I feel better

These are the Keith Black hypereutectic pistons, one of the best values on the market.

There's a lot of quality hardware in this picture, not to mention a lot of hard work.

The block has to be modified in this area for a 383ci, long connecting-rod combination. This is one reason why you need to have an experienced engine builder for your Corvette.

when the owner of the company has driven Corvettes for several decades. There's an understanding here. You know the man speaks Chevrolet—call it Corvette bonding.

## Torque Is Power

The first question Ivars asked me was what I intended to do with Project Corvette. Now that's a novel approach. Different motors for different purposes. I felt Project Corvette needed a high-torque street motor.

Even though I intend to use the car at high-speed track events, most of Project Corvette's life will be spent on the street, running below 4,000rpm. Horsepower just isn't a relevant question for this type of street engine. Too many people get carried away with big horsepower numbers and find out that Geo Storms blow them away when leaving a stoplight. Street driving requires torque. Torque is what pushes you back in your Corvette's seat. Torque is why people love big blocks. I asked RHS to give me big torque numbers, even if it meant cutting back on the horsepower. Ivars agreed that this was a smart move and went on to point out that, "Torque is for driving, horsepower numbers are for bragging."

Horsepower is really a mathematical function of torque and rpm. The following formula clearly shows

$$\text{Horsepower} = \frac{\text{Torque} \times \text{rpm}}{5,250}$$

As horsepower and rpms increase, torque decreases. That's why the maximum torque figure is always at a lower rpm than the horsepower number. Therefore, when you build a motor for the street, you should be mainly concerned with torque numbers. Build yourself a motor with as much torque as possible and then lie about the horsepower figures—just like everybody else does.

Project Corvette has enough torque to pull down small buildings. The following dyno runs proved that.

| RPM | Torque |
|-----|--------|
| 2500 | 402lb-ft |
| 3000 | 411lb-ft |
| 3500 | 408lb-ft |
| 4000 | 418lb-ft |
| 4500 | 408lb-ft |
| 5000 | 379lb-ft |

| Original 327/350 | 1994 LT1 | 1994 LT5 | Callaway Super Natural | Project Corvette |
|---|---|---|---|---|
| 360@3600 | 340@3600 | 385@5200 | 412@4500 | 418@4000 |

Now compare these numbers to the claims of some of the Corvette legends.

Project Corvette is about serious power. Don't forget I'm doing this with cast-iron cylinder heads, a 9.0:1 compression ratio, and a 750cfm carburetor. I'm also doing it for about half the price of a Callaway or LT1. Yes, life is good at RHS.

## Four-Bolt Mains

People spend a lot time exclaiming they own motors that have four bolts for every main bearing cap. These people shouldn't be so smug. There's no reason to use a four-bolt main engine on the street. First, you'll probably never put out enough horsepower to need all the added strength. A two-bolt block, with top-quality ARP studs, can easily handle 500lb-ft of torque. How many street-driven Corvettes put out those numbers? Some Corvette people need to get in touch with reality and quit spending unnecessary money.

More importantly, a four-bolt block won't give you even one additional horsepower. Four-bolt engines were designed with long-distance endurance racing in mind. If you have under 500lb-ft of torque and drive on the street, then a four-bolt block is simply a luxury you really don't need.

Even if you do have 500lb-ft of torque, or horsepower, you won't be able to use this mega-power for any extended period of time on the street. Just tell all your friends you have a four-bolt block. They'll never know the difference. Project Corvette does quite nicely with the two-bolt main bearing

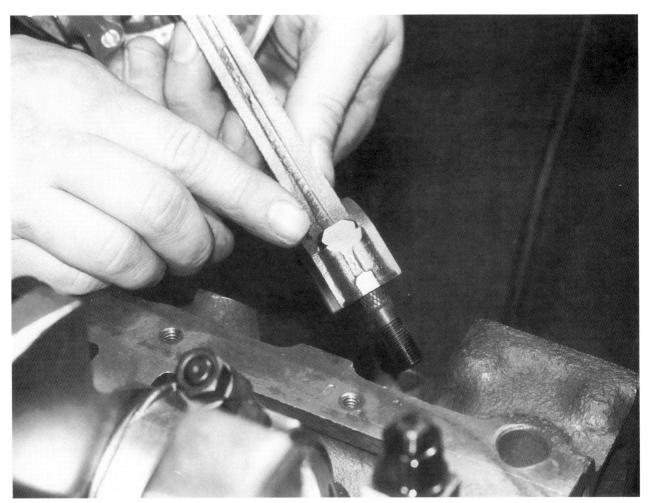

The connecting rods also have to be modified slightly. This engine combination puts out a lot of horsepower but is a very tight fit.

The power comes from these World Products heads
with 2.02 intake valves.

RHS matches all the intake ports to the manifold.

If your engine shop is still porting cylinder heads without a flow bench, start looking for a new shop.

All the valve guides are checked with a dial indicator for the proper clearance.

caps and ARP hardware. I'm quite happy with only two ARP studs on each main bearing cap.

## Forging vs. Casting

Here's another place where you can save money. You really don't need forged pistons unless you're going well over 400bhp. Be realistic about your horsepower numbers, and save the money you would spend for forged pistons. Cast pistons work quite nicely for most street engines.

Just because racers use forged pistons doesn't mean these are the ideal solution for your street Corvette. Most factory high-performance cars of the sixties ran quite well with cast pistons. In fact, under most conditions, cast pistons run better since they can be installed with closer piston-to-cylinder-wall tolerances. This means cast pistons are a lot quieter when you start your car in the morning.

If you're driving on the street and running below 5,000rpm, you don't need eight expensive forged pistons. Only when you run over 400hp and above 6,000rpm do you really need the fancy forged pistons.

I took a unique way out of this forged vs. cast piston debate with a new high-tech solution. I used Keith Black hypereutectic pistons. These are cast pistons, but the alloy used in the piston contains a much higher level of silicon than a conventional cast piston, which means the higher the engine temperature gets, the harder the piston alloy becomes. This hardness reduces piston wear. Less money, longer wearing—this piston sounded like a winner to me.

Forged crankshafts are another case in which people do something just because all the racers do it. As long as your horsepower is below 400hp you don't need a fancy crankshaft. Remember, the idea is to spend your money where you can feel it, not where you can just talk about it. Besides, I wonder how many people who claim to have all these fancy parts actually have them?

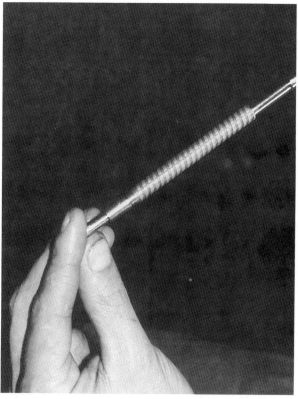

The next step is to use the proper diamond hone to make sure the valve guide-to-valve stem clearance is perfect.

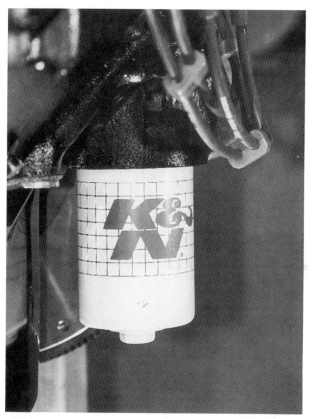

RHS uses K & N oil filters. That convinced me to start using them as well.

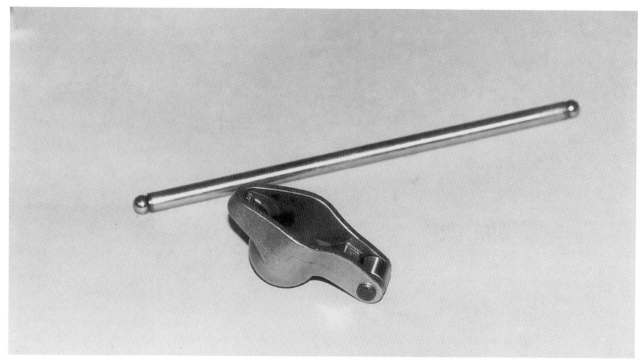

Competition Cams supplied the proper roller-tipped rocker arms, as well as the pushrods. You should keep the stock Chevrolet rocker-arm ratio unless you want to get involved in a big hassle with rocker-arm geometry.

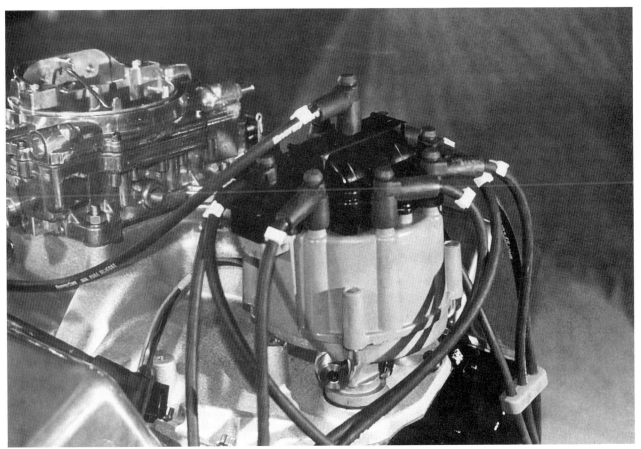

Jacobs supplied the ignition system. Though I wanted a high-tech ignition system, I still wanted to use the cable-drive tachometer. Jacobs developed this distributor for our application, and it's now available for the rest of the world. This distributor is the answer for all of us who want a stock dash on the inside and modern technology under the hood.

## LT1 Camshafts

I hate to break your heart, but the LT1, and especially the old .030/.030 camshaft, is not a very good choice for your average street car. In fact, I once had a conversation with the man who designed this camshaft, and his personal opinion was that it was a lousy camshaft for street driving.

The only reason he designed this camshaft was to keep Duntov happy at the proving grounds. Zora always liked high rpm engines. He was willing to sacrifice everything to run over 6000rpm. With the LT1 he gave up all the power under 3000rpm. This is not something you really want to do.

I've been able to spend some time with the people at Competition Cams, which is directly across the parking lot from RHS. Competition Cams create a lot of the camshafts for the NASCAR folks. Their suggestion was that the average person should look at all the numbers in the catalogues, make a choice, and then pick the next mildest camshaft. "Always choose a camshaft a little less radical than what you think you really need."

With the Project Corvette motor, I wanted a solid motor at low rpms and good mid-range torque. In order to get monster torque numbers, Competition Cams suggested a very high lift with very little duration. This is the secret to big torque on the street. Competition Cams and RHS certainly made the right decisions; I ended up with more power than the ZR1 and the Super Natural.

Nothing is free, however, because with this camshaft selection, I probably gave up well over 20hp at the top end of the rpm curve. The only time I might notice this lack of power, though, will be on the front stretch of Pocono—once a year. For the reality of driving on the street, RHS and Competition Cams put the power where I actually drive the car and sacrificed power at a point in the rpm range, which I might see only twice a year.

Since I don't see myself running much over 6000rpm for extended periods of time, I also used hydraulic lifters. Life is easier if you don't have to adjust valves and get oil all over the engine compartment. You should make use of modern technology

This is the completed engine. From this point, it's on to the dyno cell.

every chance you can. Just because this Chevrolet motor was originally designed in the early fifties is no reason to keep using fifties technology.

### Jacobs Electronics To the Rescue

The stock HEI distributor is a wonderful unit that works just fine for most applications. The only problem with Project Corvette is that it has a tach drive cable. The 1968 Corvette not only used a tach cable, it also used an old point-style distributor. This 1968 system really isn't up to current standards.

I was faced with a couple of choices, which were complicated because of the Corvette cable tach drive. Something had to give. While I could have used a stock GM HEI ignition system and installed a new tachometer in the car, that would have meant cutting up the interior and installing a non-stock tachometer. Not exactly what I had in mind.

My other choice was to install a Jacobs ignition system and have a non-stock engine compartment. This was the better choice. We could improve the ignition system with the Jacobs unit and still keep the

interior looking the way Chevrolet designed it. If you're really fanatical about a stock-looking engine compartment, you can always cover the Jacobs distributor with ignition shielding, and very few people would know what you did.

### What Makes an RHS Engine Special?

It's really not that hard to bolt a Chevy engine together. Thousands of machine shops build these engines everyday, so what makes RHS special? As I followed the Project Corvette engine around the RHS shop, I began to understand why RHS is the largest performance engine builder in the U.S. It's called quality—the type of quality that's built into the design process—not something added onto a finished product.

RHS doesn't just bolt the engine together and hope it works; they include quality checks at every interval along the way. Of particular interest to me was the cylinder-head vacuum test that checks for valve leakage. Every single valve in every head from the RHS shops is checked with a vacuum instrument to

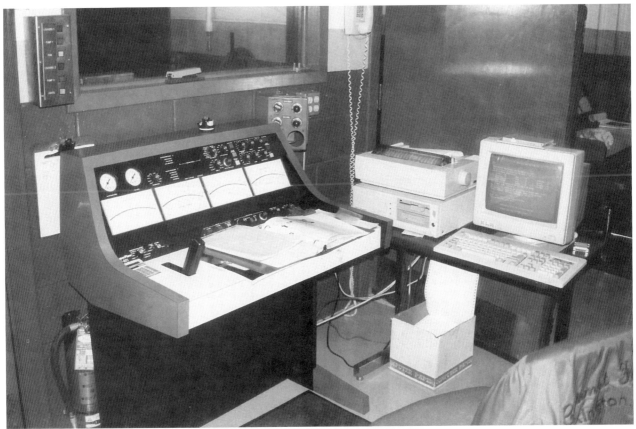

Here we have modern technology at it's best. Even with all the years of experience that Competition Cams has with small-block engines, it still took eight dyno runs to get the maximum torque out of Project Corvette.

make sure the valve is properly seated. I know of no other manufacturer goes to all this trouble to ensure a quality product.

Since RHS uses cylinder heads from all the major manufacturers, I brought them a couple heads from several major manufacturers to test. Sure enough, all the big-name cylinder heads showed at least one leaking valve. No matter what brand of cylinder head RHS installs on your engine, it gets checked and repaired before it goes on your engine. This is an example of the quality you get with an RHS engine.

When the engine is completely assembled, it's placed on a special machine called a SIM-TEX machine. The engine is driven with an electric motor, and the oil pressure, as well as flow, is checked and monitored on a fancy digital readout. While all this is going on, the operator runs a compression check on all eight cylinders.

Thus, before the manifolds and oil pan are installed, RHS has checked the oil circulation and ring seating. Incidently, Project Corvette had 190lb of pressure at all eight cylinders. Very few shops have this sort of equipment, not to mention the proper attitude that requires it.

Hooked up to the dyno, this engine is ready to be tuned to its full potential.

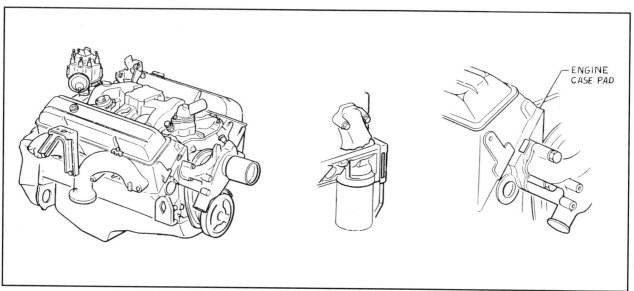

Specific information about your Corvette's engine is found on the engine stamp pad (also known as the engine case pad). This machined surface is found just in front of the right cylinder head. The engine suffix code identification indicates horsepower and transmission type.

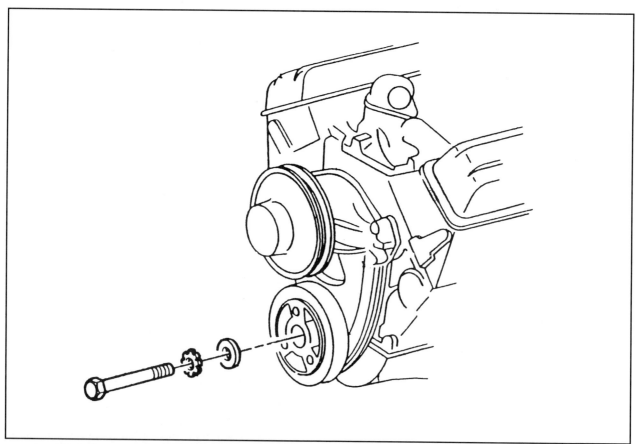

You should install and remove the front damper pulley with a special tool. These damper installation tools are so cheap that it would be foolish to use anything else.

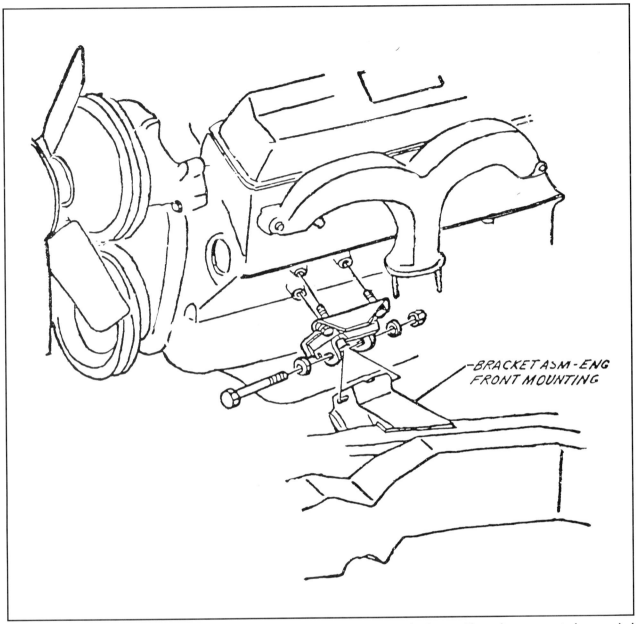

BRACKET ASM - ENG
FRONT MOUNTING

The best way to remove the engine mount is to slightly raise the engine and then extract the single long bolt. The engine can then be removed with the mount still attached to the frame. Chevrolet appears to have varied the direction the bolt was installed. Simply determine which direction, front or rear, works best for you.

### I Need, or Want, the Original Engine In My Corvette

There are several ways to deal with the almighty Corvette serial-number question. With Project Corvette I simply set the original engine aside. When I finally sell the car, the original engine will be part of the deal, along with several hundred pounds of springs and shocks.

Without the original engine installed, I can never show Project Corvette at Bloomington or NCRS events. If you're building an NCRS car, you must have all the orignal components, or at least parts with numbers that approximate the original piece. However, too often these old parts are worn out. During the past twenty years all the power went into retirement, just like the workers that made them.

The standard approach up to now has been to have your local machinist rebuild the engine. That way you can keep all original numbers intact. However, the local machine shop simply can't afford all the latest equipment, and very few local machine

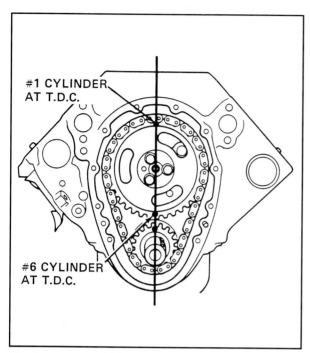

#1 CYLINDER
AT T.D.C.

#6 CYLINDER
AT T.D.C.

It's always a good idea to triple-check items like this if you're building your own small-block. It's a lot easier to be extremely careful than it is to do the job over.

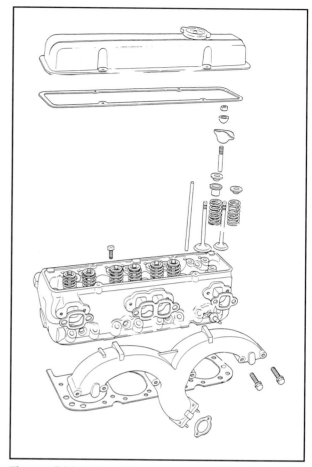

The small-block head has been around for almost fifty years. There's still only a handful of people who know how to extract the maximum horsepower from this casting.

shops have $8,000 worth of diamond hones for matching valve guide to valve stem clearance. RHS has all this and much more.

While I was visiting RHS, the machinists discussed putting an oil cooler on the connecting-rod honing machine because the temperature of the honing oil was changing the dimension of the big end on the rod. Most machine shops couldn't even measure this difference, let alone care about it. This type of precision equipment is what separates RHS from the rest of the world. Because RHS cares about Corvettes, they will rebuild your Corvette engine with all the latest high-tech equipment while making sure that all the correct stamping and casting numbers are properly returned to their original home.

If I were doing Project Corvette over again, I might send them the original engine and have all the internals replaced. This way I could have an NCRS 327 motor with over 400lb-ft of torque at about 3500rpm. This is less than our RHS 383ci engine has, but at the same time, Project Corvette could be an NCRS car.

Having your original motor rebuilt by RHS means you could still use the Keith Black pistons and the Competition Cams valve train. Best of all, you could use gasoline from the local gas station, something that wasn't possible with the stock engine.

Keep in mind that Project Corvette is now putting out 418lb-ft of torque and I can still buy gas at the local service station. The original 327/350 en-

gine only put out 360lb-ft of torque and needs special racing gas that costs over $3.50 a gallon.

Fewer and fewer people are driving their old Corvettes today because the old high-performance cars need a very high octane of fuel. RHS solves that problem by putting together a high-tech motor that uses all your original casting numbers. Wouldn't it be nice to own a matching-numbers Corvette that could be driven at NCCC events?

The only problem I had with Project Corvette was the betting pool. My friends have a very disturbed sense of humor and started a pool on which part of the drivetrain I would destroy first. It was my own fault—I insisted on showing the dyno sheets to anyone I even remotely considered a friend.

My recommendation is that if you have RHS build you a motor, study the dyno sheets in privacy and don't let anyone see what real power looks like. It's easier that way. At any rate you won't have to listen to a lot of sick humor about broken parts and your ability to handle all that power.

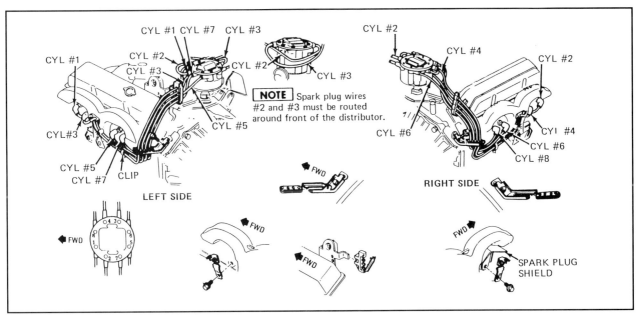

LEFT SIDE

RIGHT SIDE

NOTE Spark plug wires #2 and #3 must be routed around front of the distributor.

SPARK PLUG SHIELD

Spark-plug wire routing is a little complicated for the Corvette. It's one of the few Chevrolet engines in which the wires are routed down the back of the cylinder heads and under the exhaust manifolds.

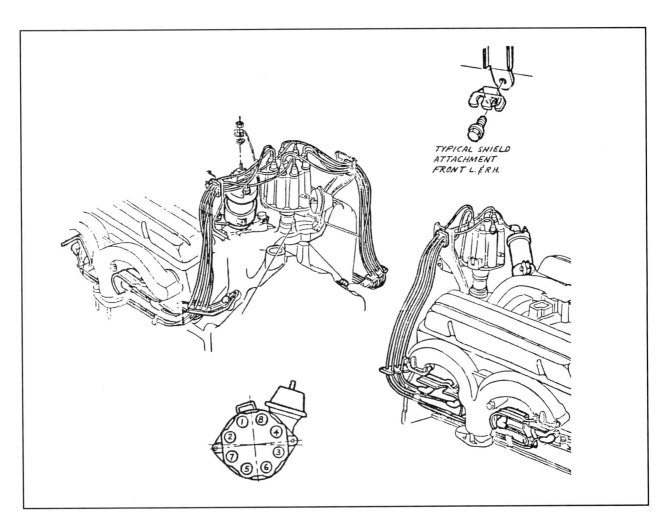

TYPICAL SHIELD ATTACHMENT FRONT L. & R.H.

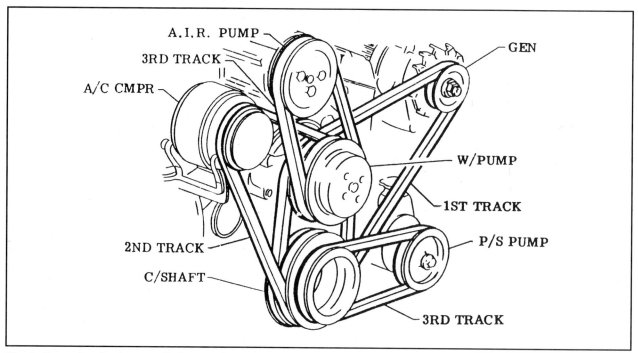

The belt routing is always a little complicated. These drawings explain why Chevrolet went to a serpentine belt in 1984.

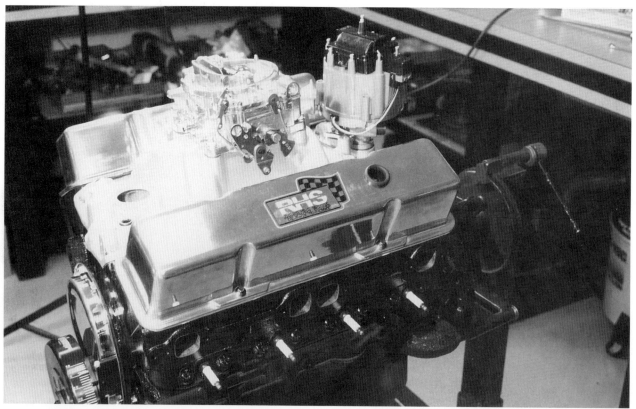

This is the Project Corvette motor just before it went to the dyno. Note the Vibratech front damper—the industry standard, and the damper everyone else tries to copy.

Notice how all the emissions hoses have been left in place on this restored Corvette. When you're working with the late-model C3 Corvettes you should make sure your car is emissions legal.

# Chapter 18

# Big-Block Engines

The big-block engines weren't around for all that long. The only thing we know for sure is that the legend of the big-block Chevy will outlast all its parts. Sometimes this fable of big-block power towers over the actual facts. Then again, isn't that true of most heroic epics?

In 1968, Chevrolet was letting the Corvette customer choose between four different 427ci engines. By the end of the C3 Corvette era in 1982, there were none left. The final big block was offered in 1974. By that time it was a 454ci block, merely a shadow of the powerplant that started the legend. It was almost a mercy killing.

The only two engines to be concerned about here are the 427 and the 454.

| Cubic Inches | Bore | Stroke |
|---|---|---|
| 427 | 4.250 | 3.76 |
| 454 | 4.250 | 4.00 |

Before you get carried away by the magic of the big block, make sure you fully understand how much engine you're working on. These engines get very heavy and very bulky. The cylinder heads alone weigh as much as a complete Honda engine. Remember, the average big-block engine is close to 700lb, which is a problem for the average home garage.

This is the monster, the big-block engine that created the myth. Actually, the ultimate-horsepower big blocks all used a single four-barrel carburetor, but the three two-barrel carburetors are still mighty impressive. They weren't so much a fuel-management system as they were a fuel-dumping system.

The 454ci engines were big, but they never attained the legendary power of the 427 engines. The 454 was more of an answer to the impending emissions standards than they were for brute power.

Th L88 engine is the stuff of real legend. Even today, people can't totally agree on exactly how much horsepower this engine produced. All we know was that it was a bunch. This Corvette monster was created when it was still legal to release a genuine racing motor to the general public, in the hope that no one would actually purchase the motor. Actually very few people purchased these motors, which is why you're going to pay extra money to put one in your garage today.

Then again, when you bought a big-block Corvette, you knew it wouldn't be easy. Before you begin this project, take a walk through the history of big-block engines offered in the third-generation Corvette. It always pays to reflect on a national treasure.

There were four versions of the 427 when Chevrolet introduced the 1968 Corvette. You could get everything from a basic four-barrel carburetor with hydraulic lifters to the outrageous L88, a motor built strictly for racing.

Chevrolet fudged the L88 numbers a little bit. One of the engineers who worked on the project pointed out that they never actually lied about the 430bhp number. They said it put out 430bhp at 5800rpm, which was true, but they neglected to tell GM that it put out even more horsepower above 5800rpm. As this engineer pointed out, "You do not build a career at GM by lying about horsepower numbers."

This big-block lineup was carried over into the 1969 Corvettes, and almost 3,000 more big blocks were sold. In fact, in 1969 over half the Corvettes that left St Louis had big blocks installed. So much for all the stories about rare big-blocks.

In 1970 the 427ci was gone, replaced by the 454ci engine, which was never quite the same. Actually, the engineering staff had designed a 430ci en-

## Horsepower By Model

|  | L36 | L68 | L71 | L88 |
|---|---|---|---|---|
| BHP | 390@5400 | 400@5400 | 435@5800 | 430@5800 |
| Torque | 460@3600 | 460@3600 | 460@4000 | N.A. |
| C.R. | 10.25 | 11.0 | 10.25 | 11.0 |
| Camshaft | Hydraulic | Hydraulic | Mechanical | Mechanical |
| Ports | Oval | Oval | Rectangular | Rectangular |
| Carb. | 1x4-bbl | 3x2-bbl | 3x2-bbl | 1x4-bbl |

The air cleaner on the L88 was special. The actual filter element resided in the hood. What you see here is the foam sealing ring and the flame arrestor. It would not be good if the engine backfired and burned your racing car to the ground. Chevrolet understood that street-legal race cars were one thing, and fires were a totally different subject.

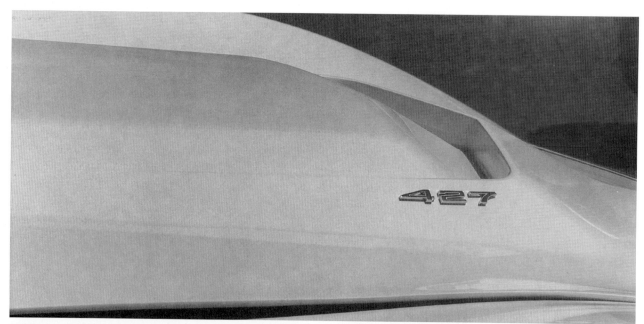

Notice the L88 hood. Air for the engine is drawn from the cowl intake, and the area above the air filter is several inches higher than the hood for Corvettes with mere mortal engines. Today there are probably ten times the number of L88 hoods than there are L88 engines.

The exhaust manifolds are bigger than the engine in the new Chevrolet Geo. The cylinder heads are the size of a small house. We're talking major torque with these motors.

This is the L88 once again. Notice that it came complete with all the requisite emissions equipment. The AIR equipment is probably the hardest part of a correct restoration. Many of the reproduction parts are not quite the same as the original parts.

gine developed from Can-Am racing experience. This was a monster bore with a very small stroke.

| ENGINE | BORE | STROKE |
|---|---|---|
| 427 | 4.25 | 3.76 |
| Mystery 430 | 4.44 | 3.47 |
| 454 | 4.25 | 4.00 |

The 430 never became a real engine. Chevrolet could get some truly tremendous power from this motor, but they could never get it clean enough to pass the required emissions tests. Besides, production of the motor would have required casting a whole new engine block, something GM wasn't willing to do.

The introduction of the 454ci engine was actually the end of big-block performance. In the beginning, the 454 engines mirrored their 1969 427 counterparts, but over the next few years, GM installed a program to eliminate costly, low-volume options from the production line. Also, the market for these monster motors was getting smaller. In 1970 just over a quarter of the Corvettes had big-block engines. In each of the following years, the percentage continued to decline. By 1974 not even fifteen percent of Corvette buyers asked for the 454 engine. The customers had voted.

One other item contributed to the decline of the ogre motors. In 1971 the executives at GM decreed that all GM engines would be able to run on regular pump gas of 91 octane. The LS6 needed at least 103 octane. This ruling actually makes it easier for us to own big blocks today since we can't easily buy any gasoline approaching 103 octane. In fact, if you're building a big-block Corvette for the street, you should try to keep the compression below 9.0:1.

The final blow for the big engine was the use of catalytic converters. Chevrolet designed a system that used twin converters. The federal government decreed that these converters had to function for 50,000 miles. The 454ci engines could barely make it to the half-way point in the test. Rather than completing the test, Chevrolet decided to abandon the program. A declining market and "integral phosphorous contamination" in the catalytic converters spelled the end of the era.

In 1974 only 3,494 big-block Corvettes were built, less than ten percent of the total market. Don't look for the big block to return either. Believe me, the Corvette group has tried. GM has laid down a policy that states no GM car shall ever require a gas-guzzler tax. Without an exemption from this policy, you'll never see a monster motor in a Corvette again.

By the end of the big-block era, over 50,000 big-block engines had been installed in Corvettes. Contrary to popular opinion, the big block is hardly a rare motor; 50,000 of anything is a lot. If Chevrolet

This is the "small" horsepower 427 engine. These motors were dead reliable. They had so much torque that they were seldom stressed. Usually the driver's courage gave out before the motor expired.

This 427ci big block was the big horsepower motor that Chevrolet wanted you to use on the street. As long as you kept your foot out of the two end carburetors, you could get 13 to 15mpg. Once you started jumping on the gas pedal, the mileage went to the single digits. Even though the new Corvette engines can flow more air, it just isn't the same.

Noise is what made it all so much fun. Hearing one of the unmuffled monsters at 145mph is something we'll all remember. I don't care how much horsepower the newest Corvette wonders put forth, they still don't shake the earth.

The 454ci engine was really a step backwards. These new motors were designed to pass the new federal emissions standards, not win races. Actually, by this time

Chevrolet racing was working with 510ci all-aluminum engines with a totally different bore and stroke.

put a big-block engine in every new Corvette built today, it would take over three years for the numbers to reach over 50,000. The idea that they're rare is just another part of the Corvette legend.

Big-block Corvettes demand a high price today because for every big-block motor installed in a Corvette, there are eager buyers standing in line. It's simply a matter of supply and demand. If only 40,000 people wanted a big-block Corvette, the prices would drop through the floor, just like they did in the middle of the mid-eighties gas crisis.

As long as there are more buyers for big motors than there are big-block cars in the marketplace, the price will remain high. However, the market can change. Nonetheless, I still want a big block in my garage someday.

## The Block

With a big-block Corvette you don't need the four-bolt main bearing block. In fact, it's impossible to tell, without dropping the oil pan, what sort of block you really have. There are blocks with identical casting numbers with both two-bolt and four-bolt main bearing caps. And the difference doesn't really matter, unless you're building a mountain motor racer. These engine blocks can absorb the stress of 400hp with only two bolts on the main caps. Only

In 1973 the LS4 only put forth 275bhp. Notice the air pump is now down under the alternator. These are still nice motors: There's enough torque to scare you, and enough reliability to keep your Corvette budget under control. A lot of people expect the 454 engines to be similar to the 427, just bigger. This wasn't the case back in the late sixties, and it still isn't the case today. This LS4 engine turned the same quarter-mile numbers as the LT1 Corvette. The old 427ci engine in 1968 was faster than both of them.

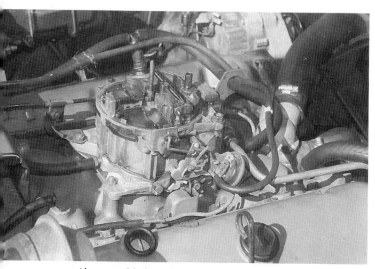

*Above and below,* this is your basic 454 today, in original condition with all the vacuum lines intact. Don't let the non-stock hose clamps bother you, this is the sort of car you should be shopping for. An original, unmodified Corvette is always the best purchase. This engine compartment could be turned into a prize winner for less than $500.00.

when you go over 500hp and 7000rpm do you really need the four-bolt blocks.

The secret to getting a long life out of your engine is to use ARP studs in place of the bolts that Chevrolet originally installed. Chevrolet even pointed out in their power book that there was no need to use four-bolt main bearing caps on the street.

## Crankshaft

The crankshafts for big-block motors are just as tough as the engine blocks. Two forged crankshafts and one cast crankshaft are available. The forgings can be used for all practical purposes identically. Only one forging, #3963523, is still available from Chevrolet.

The big difference among cranks is that if the crank was originally installed in an LS6 engine, it's been nitrated and cross-drilled. The cranks installed in Chevy trucks didn't get all this special treatment.

Special cranks are hard to find, so for the most part you simply have to worry about the crank being straight and free of cracks. If it turns out you have a good crank, then you can have the main bearings cross-drilled.

You can easily take .020 off the main journals. Make sure the machine shop machines a generous fillet radius when they do this. The bearings should fit with a .002in to .0025in clearance.

## Balancing

In normal Chevrolet practice, all 427 cranks are balanced internally, while the 454 engines are balanced externally. Crankshaft counterweights aren't

large enough to balance the weight of the pistons and connecting rods, and so the extra weight was added to the flywheel and front damper. Consequently, the 454 engines must have the proper front damper and flywheel attached. These engines can be internally balanced by a competent shop, but be prepared to spend some more money. Check to see that the proper damper and flywheel are installed before you make any sudden moves.

With the 427 engines the crankshaft counterweights are large enough that internal balancing is no problem. Actually, you have very little choice, unless you're having Racing Head Services build a custom motor for your Corvette.

## Induction Systems

There's really little point in the three-two barrel carburetors at this point. They only have historical interest, other than providing a topic for conversation at work. People seem to forget that even Chevrolet went to one giant four barrel when they wanted maximum performance. The three-by-two system was really just a way to pretend you were getting good fuel mileage and a modicum of power.

This is the sort of engine compartment that makes you want to start asking questions, and maybe taking a compression test. All the money's been spent on chrome. The air filter is the wrong size, and the emissions equipment has been removed. Basically add up all the money spent on the chrome and deduct it from what you're willing to pay.

M.F. Dobbins did all the detail work on this outstanding example of a 1968 427ci engine. Most importantly, he made sure all the emissions equipment was in place and operating.

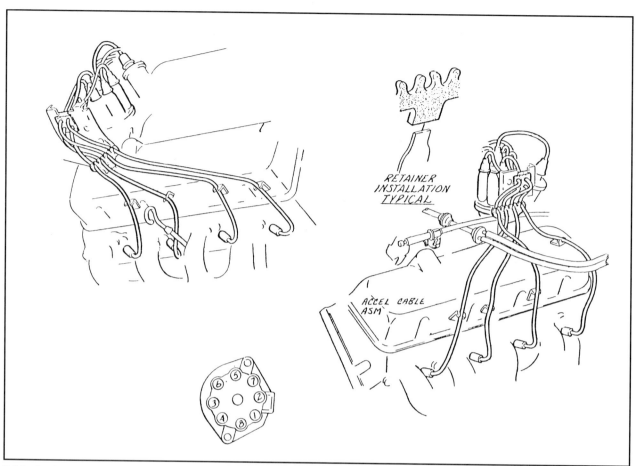

With the big block, the spark plug wires come over the top of the motor.

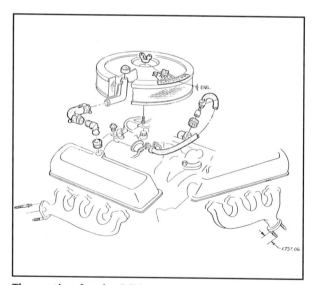

The routing for the PCV system on the 454ci motor. If the crankcase ventilation becomes clogged, you might start to have major oil leaks. If the ventilation system fails to operate, the pressure inside the engine block forces the oil past all the gaskets.

No one owns a big-block Corvette today for fuel mileage. The only reason to own these cars today is for the way they shake the earth. The only way to get maximum power is to use one big carburetor. The multiple carburetor set-up is just too much trouble. I doubt if even half of the units still in existence today are working properly. One big Edelbrock, or Holley, would speed up most of these big-block Corvettes.

When it's all said and done, the big block is not so much about speed as it is about noise. There is nothing that shakes the earth like one of these motors running through side pipes. Hey, if it weren't for Hooker side pipes, I doubt many people would use these engines in vintage racing.

The main reason for running these motors today is for the nostalgic thrill. They came from a wild era that will never come again. Modern cars are just as fast, but they do it with high technology and make real funny noises. What I really want is a Corvette capable of scaring women and small children. Someday I shall own a Chevy engine that truly shakes the earth.

# Chapter 19

# Fuel System

Two huge milestones passed during the life of the third-generation Corvette. Leaded gas disappeared in 1974, and the carburetor was finally laid to rest in 1981. . Who would have believed in 1968 that the Holley and 11.0:1 compression ratios would no longer be a part of the Corvette legend? Even worse, who would have believed that premium gas would cost more than thirty-five cents a gallon?

Now let's deal with some basic assumptions about the Corvette fuel system. The stock Corvette fuel system is more than adequate for any driving you might do on public roads. Chevrolet has spent millions of dollars to develop the fuel system on your Corvette. They have huge laboratories devoted to fuel systems. Are you actually going to improve on this system?

To imagine someone working in a small two-car garage can improve upon this system is largely a myth. Granted, certain modifications will result in increased performance for certain narrow applications, but the fact remains that the stock system remains the best all-around compromise for normal driving.

The fuel system must also be well maintained. You have to make sure every part of the system is in top operating condition to deliver the performance that Chevrolet intended. Instead of spending a lot of time and money on modifying the fuel system, you'd be better off making sure everything is operating properly.

Let's start at the back of the car. The gas tank is more than simply a place to stick the build sheet. It

The fuel mileage might not be what you're looking for, but can you imagine driving this car down the backstretch at Watkins Glen? This is a serious Corvette fuel-injection system. The system is found on one of the Greenwood customer cars from the seventies.

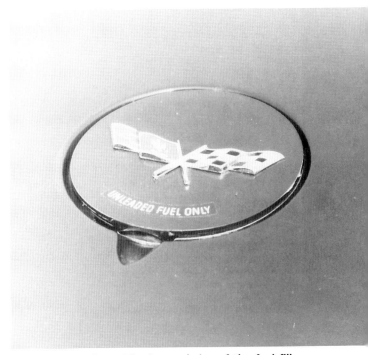

The fuel starts here. The internal size of the fuel filler neck changed when the Corvette started to use unleaded gas. Any number of people took a chisel and attacked the filler neck so they could continue using leaded gasoline.

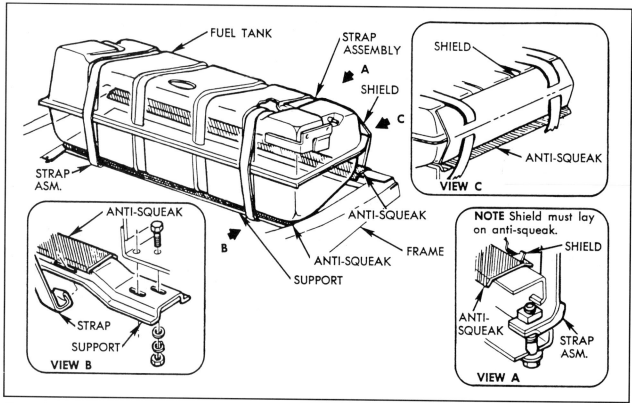

FUEL TANK · STRAP ASSEMBLY · A · SHIELD · C · SHIELD · ANTI-SQUEAK · VIEW C

STRAP ASM. · B · ANTI-SQUEAK · FRAME · ANTI-SQUEAK · SUPPORT

ANTI-SQUEAK · STRAP · SUPPORT · VIEW B

NOTE Shield must lay on anti-squeak. · SHIELD · ANTI-SQUEAK · STRAP ASM. · VIEW A

The early C3 Corvettes used this type of gas tank. The legendary build sheet, which told assembly-line workers which parts to install on your Corvette, was usually placed on top of the gas tank. Once the spare tire carrier and the exhaust are removed, it's no big deal to drop the gas tank. The secret to performing this job is to have little or no gasoline in the tank. Remember, gasoline weighs about 6lb per gallon. A full gas tank could easily exceed 100lb.

The gas line starts at the bottom of the tank. The fuel pickup and the tank sending unit are all one assembly. In order to remove them you'll need to spin the collar until the openings line up with the tabs. Make sure you use a brass punch for this operation. One spark in this area and you could end up having to put a new garage on the house. Old gasoline vapors are extremely dangerous, far more dangerous than the actual gasoline.

is also a place to store your gasoline before it's burned. I found out that if you leave gasoline stored in your Corvette's tank for ten years it turns into some strange sort of chemical. It smells bad, looks bad, and certainly won't explode in a combustion chamber. What it does very well is form a thick nasty film over everything it touches.

The bad gas and the chemical film are no major problem—both can be removed. What can't be eliminated is the fine rust that's formed on the inside of the tank. Just like when your non-Corvette starts to rust away, there's not much you can do to stop the rusting, you can only slow it down.

I had the gas tank professionally cleaned and the interior rust removed to the best extent possible. To prevent a second occurrence of the problem, I used a gas tank sealer from The Eastwood Company. After pouring the sealer in the tank, you should rotate the tank, making sure you get a nice even covering over the whole inside. Think of this as painting the inside of your Corvette's gas tank. That's what the tank sealer from Eastwood does.

Sealer will stop any further rust in the gas tank. This coating will chemically imbed any of the fine

I had the old gas tank cleaned and then sealed with tank sealer from Eastwood. Gas-tank cleaning is so expensive these days that it would have been cheaper to simply purchase a new reproduction gas tank.

rust that couldn't be removed. Consequently, the new RHS motor will burn pure gasoline, not some gas/rust mixture.

Unfortunately it now costs over a $100 to have a gas tank cleaned. By the time I was finished with the whole process, I could have purchased a reproduction gas tank. It would have looked better from the outside and would have been perfect on the inside. On the other hand, I keep telling myself that I should have some original parts on this car. Maybe this way they'll let me keep my NCRS membership.

## Fuel Lines

The most common fuel line problems are the rubber hoses on top of the tank. These deteriorate to the point where fuel starts running out on the ground. The good part is that the fuel tank is easy to drop out of the Corvette, once you remove the spare tire carrier.

Pardon me if I'm stating the obvious, but before you drop a gas tank, it should be as close to empty as possible. This may seem obvious, but I've seen too many people struggle with 200lb gas tanks over the years.

Furthermore, don't remove the complete fuel line on the right frame rail. Chevrolet placed this line on the frame prior to dropping the body. There are some beautiful reproduction fuel lines on the market, and all of them require you to remove the body of your Corvette for proper installation.

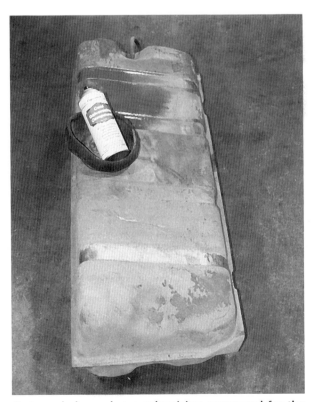

Eastwood also makes a galvanizing compound for the outside of the tank. This is not really a paint, but rather an actual galvanizing finish. It's tricky to properly apply, and it always looks as if you just painted your gas tank.

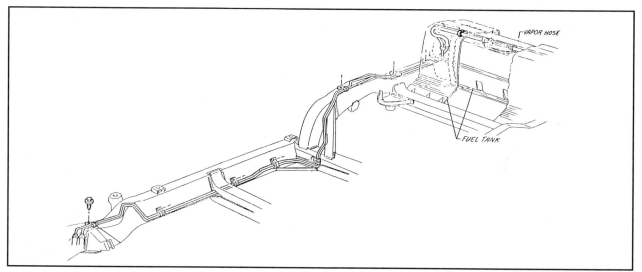

Don't remove any fuel lines unless you intend to separate the body from the frame. It is impossible to install these lines unless the body is removed.

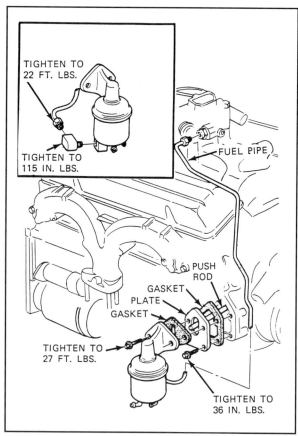

The real secret to fuel-pump installation is to put the pushrod, covered with cold grease, in the freezer. When you install the pump, put the frozen pushrod in place and bolt the fuel pump in place. A frozen pushrod will stay in place; whereas, a room-temperature rod will keep sliding out as you try to bolt the pump into place.

## Fuel Pumps

The stock Chevrolet fuel pump works quite well. The two things you want from your pump are pressure and volume. The pressure should be low, and the volume should be high. Remember this and you're on your way to solving most of your fuel pump questions.

The stock Corvette pump should be able to fill a one-gallon can in not much more than thirty seconds. It should be able to do this at about 5lb of pressure.

Typically, when the fuel pump goes bad, your Corvette idles fine but simply will not drive. The other symptom of a bad fuel pump is that the pump starts to leak fuel in a rather impressive manner. What happens is that the rubber diaphragm inside the pump ruptures.

One little-known trick for installing the fuel pump is to take the pushrod that runs off your camshaft and place it in your freezer for an hour prior to installation. Then put a light coating of chassis grease on the rod and install the rod in the block. The combination of being cold and thick will cause the grease to hold the pushrod in place while you install the fuel pump.

## Fuel Filters

You can't change your fuel filter often enough. This task should be on your annual checklist. Since none of the third-generation Corvette fuel filters are expensive, we're not talking about a lot of money here.

If you live in a place where you can still purchase the old-fashioned gas, count yourself lucky. The rest of us are stuck with an ethanol, low-octane

Edelbrock is the best choice for a street replacement carburetor. A variation of the old Carter carburetor, the Edelbrock is now legal to use in all fifty states.

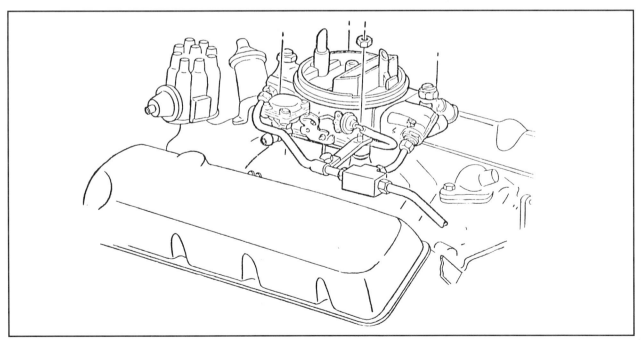

The original fuel systems used a variety of lines and distribution blocks. Over the years a lot of these have been lost and damaged. Paragon has the best selection of fittings for the pre-1984 Corvettes.

The air filter is an essential part of your Corvette's fuel system. A well-running Corvette burns a fuel-and-air mixture. The ratio of fuel to air is carefully calibrated. A clogged air filter, or even one that is poorly constructed, will not let your Corvette burn the gasoline properly.

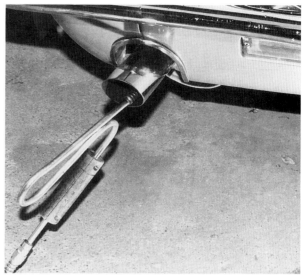

The government is very interested in what comes out of your Corvette's tailpipe. There was a time when you were the only one really interested in the operation of the fuel system. With all the various emissions inspection programs going on around the country it seems that the government is more involved in your Corvette's fuel system than you are.

swill that the enviro-Nazis claim will help the rain forest. We know that it doesn't do our Corvettes any good.

## Single-Plane Manifolds

I thought everybody knew about intake manifolds until I talked to Jim Losse at Edelbrock. Edelbrock still gets a lot people ordering single-plane manifolds for their street cars. This just doesn't work. You *never* want one of these manifolds on your street car.

The single-plane manifold only produces horsepower at high rpms. Do you really want to turn 6000rpm on the way to work every morning? Before you do anything to your induction system, pay attention to your tachometer. You'll notice that on the average day you seldom get above 4000rpm. This is the way you drive.

Big horsepower numbers are the result of taking power away from the bottom end. Dale Ernhardt doesn't really care if his engine won't idle. In fact, he really doesn't care if his engine doesn't even run below 4000rpm. You care about things like idle and power below 3000rpm. At least you should care.

Your Corvette needs power in the rpm range in which you drive every day. With Project Corvette I made the decision to ignore the top of the rpm range in the interest of being able to drive out of the

parking lot. Besides, it wouldn't be too impressive if Subarus kept beating us to 30mph.

If you really want something to think about, remember that the stock four-barrel manifold from Chevrolet is as good as any performance manifold up until 4500rpm. Only after that point will you really notice a difference with an aftermarket manifold. Since I plan to occasionally use Project Corvette on the racetrack, its new Edelbrock manifold will be worth the effort. The important point, though, is that I stuck with a dual-plane manifold that's designed to give power, and more importantly torque, under 4500rpm. Also note that we used an Edelbrock 750cfm. When I've let people look at the dyno sheets they simply refuse to believe Project Corvette has such a "small" carburetor.

Edelbrock made the carburetor choice for me. and all I can say is that it worked out quite nicely. If you would rather believe the guy sitting next to you at the bar, that's your business. The fact remains that Edelbrock knows a little more about induction systems than the people at the last Corvette club meeting.

# Chapter 20

# Exhaust System

Now that you've got the gas burning properly, you'll need to get all these burned gases out of the engine and into the atmosphere. Emissions controls are a part of modern life. For too many years we paid absolutely no regard to what came out of our tail pipes. Now, not only are we concerned, but so is everyone else, especially the government.

When it comes to your exhaust system, make sure you do everything legally. In the old days the exhaust system was a matter of personal preference.

Now, the federal government dictates what you do with the burned exhaust gas. With the earlier cars there is still room for creativity, but for those of you who own the later model cars, the federal government makes all the decisions for you.

The exhaust system on your Corvette falls under EPA federal guidelines. Forget what you've done in the past. Forget what your friends are doing. The Feds are serious about the exhaust system on your Corvette.

This is a real exhaust pipe, on one of the old Greenwood Corvettes. I suspect Greenwood made these pipes in his own shop since I've never seen another exhaust pipe quite this large. Imagine the sound these pipes could make pulling into your driveway. Imagine the sound your neighbors would make if you left for work in this car every morning.

In the early sixties, the Corvette group decided to solve the ground-clearance problem by running the exhaust pipes directly through the frame cross-member. They retained this cross-member until 1982, even when the Corvette went to a single exhaust pipe.

Chevrolet went to the federal government when your car was new and guaranteed that your Corvette would not pollute the environment. Chevrolet declared that if all the emissions devices were in place and operating, the Corvette would be a good citizen. They even guaranteed this would continue to be the case for the first five years of the car's life, or 50,000 miles.

Emissions control devices installed at St. Louis must be present and in operating condition. The government has declared that Corvette owners cannot remove that which Chevrolet installed. That is the law. If you make any of the emissions control devices inoperable or remove them, you can be denied the right to register and drive your Corvette. Isn't it great we actually have to get permission from the federal government to drive our Corvettes?

Section 202 of the Clean Air Act of 1977 specifically states that it is illegal "for any person to remove or render inoperative any device or element of design installed on or in a motor vehicle or motor vehicle engine in compliance with regulation under this title prior to its sale and delivery to the ultimate purchaser." The law goes on to state that it is also il-

Hooker is the industry standard for aftermarket exhaust pipes. If your Corvette doesn't have the factory exhaust pipes, it most likely has Hooker pipes running down the side of the car. The original factory off-road pipes were made by Kustom Equipment, a small speed shop that was located in Flint, Michigan. Their bundle of pipes was slightly different from the Hooker pipes shown here. Most people have never seen the original pipes, and never will.

These have always been the outlaw Corvette pipes. If you own a 1975 or newer Corvette, you truly have outlaw pipes since you are not allowed to remove the catalytic converter from your Corvette. If a shop gets caught putting these pipes on the later third-generation Corvette, the EPA can levy some fairly severe fines on the shop. That's one reason you're seeing fewer of these cars.

Here's another Corvette that never left St. Louis with a set of side exhausts. Very few people would ever guess this is a modified Corvette. You have to ask yourself whether you want to build the Corvette you always wanted, or the Corvette someone else ordered in the late sixties.

This is a set of factory side pipes installed on a 1968 Corvette. This was an option for only the 1969 cars and was not available until January of 1969. Nonetheless, it looks nice.

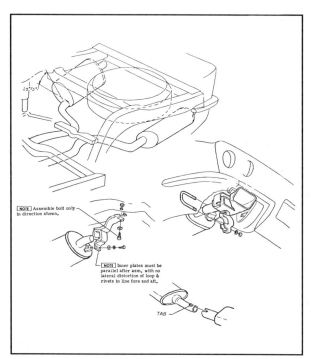

This series of drawings shows the correct way to hang the dual exhaust pipes. The exhaust system should always float on the hangers. You have to leave enough clearance around each part to allow the pipes to move. The trick is to put all the clamps on finger-tight. This will allow you to move each part around, as you attempt to get the total system in the proper location. Then, and only then, should you tighten the clamps so the pipes are crushed together.

sional should be knowledgeable about the original equipment. If a shop does any exhaust work on a Corvette that has been tampered with, without replacing the converter, they are engaged in criminal activity. Currently, no reputable shop will touch a car that has been tampered with, unless they're allowed to replace the converter.

Shops are very careful because the EPA has an undercover sting operation constantly at work. They take cars around to various exhaust shops and ask for illegal work to be performed. The shops that oblige the "customer" do not pass GO. They do not even get a "Get Out of Jail Free" card.

There are still companies that sell exhaust systems for late model Corvettes without the converter. The federal government has simply looked the other way up to now. The real crack-down is on the installation of dual-pipe systems. While it's okay to own these exhaust systems, you can't install them on your Corvette.

Now in the nineties we finally notice the elephant resting in the Corvette hospitality tent. It's called the "Enhanced Emissions Test," brought to you by the same folks that consider taxes "investments."

In order to register your Corvette for the highway, you're required to certify that your prize possession does not pollute. If your Corvette is missing the catalytic converter, you must have one installed before you can legally put your Corvette on the road.

At least with the older Corvettes you can return them to stock condition. With the 1994

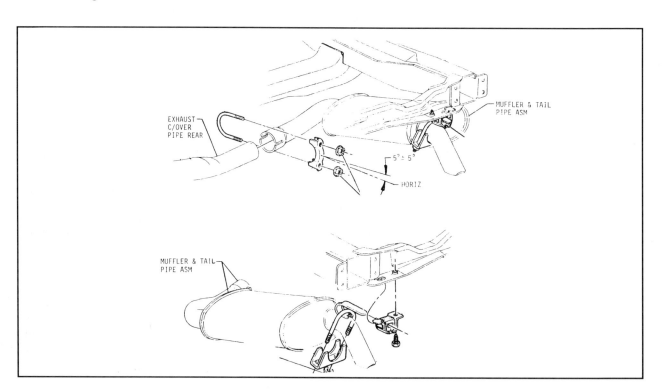

192

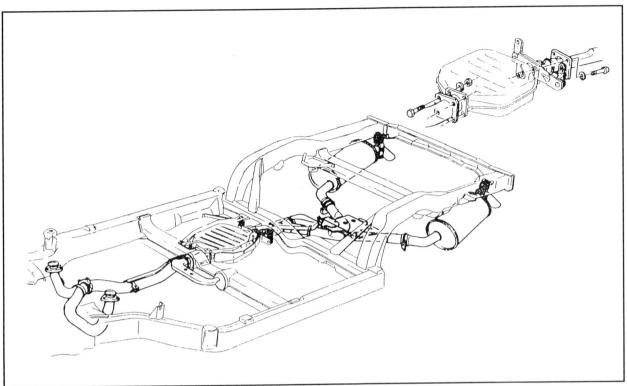

The 1975 Corvette took a major step backwards in performance, or a major step forward if you're pro-environment. The Corvette got a single exhaust pipe. Chevrolet tried to cover this up by hanging two mufflers out on the back of the frame, hoping no one would notice. The federal law for this system states you can do anything you want to the rear of the converter, but you are not allowed to reconfigure the system from the converter forward. Doing so is a violation of federal law. In some states you may not be allowed to register your Corvette until you have returned the car to the single exhaust system.

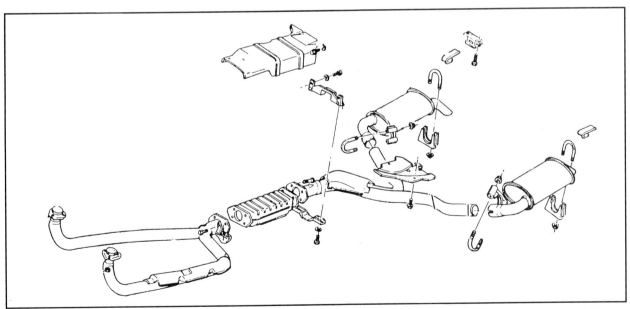

C Central can supply all your exhaust needs. They manufacture an aluminized system that looks just like the original Chevrolet system. It's a lot easier to replace an entire exhaust system rather than piecemeal parts. You can save money by not buying all the parts, but the extra time will more than consume the difference. I guess it all depends on how much you value your time.

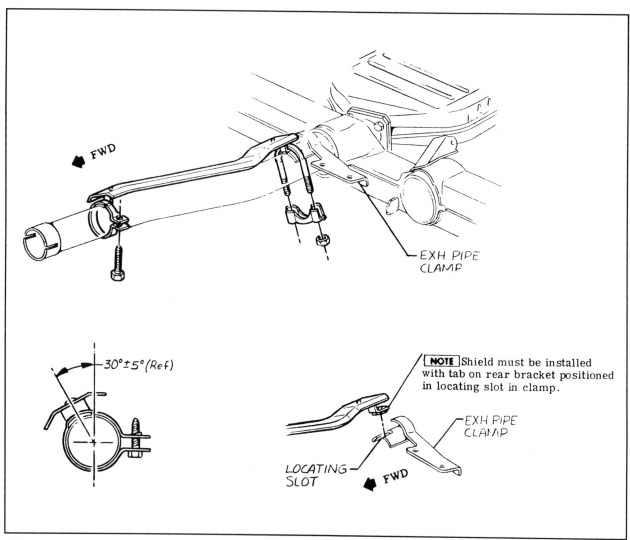

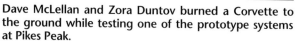

NOTE Shield must be installed with tab on rear bracket positioned in locating slot in clamp.

The catalytic-converter Corvettes use a lot of shielding in order to protect all your fiberglass from exhaust heat. Chevrolet was especially sensitive to the heat issue since

Dave McLellan and Zora Duntov burned a Corvette to the ground while testing one of the prototype systems at Pikes Peak.

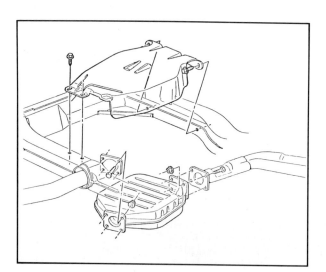

Corvettes, a few too many aftermarket PROMS, or chips, were sold. Chevrolet, as will all other manufacturers, now embeds the chips in plastic, in an effort to prevent installation of the aftermarket chips. Remember, Chevrolet didn't do this to you, your congressional representative did this for you.

Even if you live in a remote area, don't get excited. Emissions tests are coming to your area, very soon. No one is exempt. The day is coming when every Corvette in the U.S. will have to be periodically certified to make sure all the factory-installed emissions equipment is present and operating.

There are presently some loopholes in the law that might let you slide through the process. In Pennsylvania, for instance, you don't have to pass an emissions test if your car is registered as a classic or historic vehicle. Don't look for this exemption to last

*Above and below,* it seems everyone has a different idea about what to do with the tailpipes on the post-1975 cars. The original tailpipe was turned downward, with a slash cut.

Since Project Corvette is a 1968, I didn't need to be overly concerned about EPA restrictions. This meant I could return to my childhood and use Hooker pipes.

*Above and below,* one of the biggest problems with headers is that the bolts holding them to the engine block keep coming loose. Stage 8, a bolt company in California, sells a locking header bolt. They take a little longer to properly install, but they never need the weekly tightening.

very long though. Remember, the government has a way of catching its oversights.

Some people have even gone to the extreme of registering cars in states where no vehicle inspection of any sort is required. However, that strategy is illegal. If you get caught, the wrath of the tax folks will come down on you since this strategy could be interpreted as an attempt to avoid taxes.

The easiest approach is to simply restore your car to the way it was when it left the Corvette plant. Emissions equipment is now being reproduced by Paragon, and they are doing their best to make the proper exhaust manifolds and AIR manifolds available.

Most of the original exhaust pipes are also being reproduced. The government doesn't care what you install behind the catalytic convertor; just make sure everything between the engine and rear flange of the converter is factory correct.

The new side pipes for the late model Corvettes are a great example of what is possible while staying within legal boundaries. Project Corvette is such an old car that I'm allowed the freedom to do whatever I want. Life is fair.

The problem for most owners of older Corvettes is the AIR pump. Ten or more years ago, everyone took this pump off, believing their Corvette would perform better without this little item. If you have to ask how much a correct AIR pump costs at

C Central makes exact reproduction exhaust systems for the Corvette. This muffler belongs on the 1968 Corvette. You can't buy a closer reproduction.

*Above, right and page 198,* these are all examples of emission control devices. If you're going to legally drive your Corvette in most states you're going to become very familiar with these mechanisms. The federal government has ruled that you have to maintain your emissions systems in the same configuration as when the car left St. Louis. Some of the late-sixties cars are exempt from this legislation, but that may have been just an accident.

this fall's flea markets, you can't afford it. Correct AIR pumps are among the most expensive items available.

Until now, only the NCRS people have been buying these pumps. Just think what will happen to

these prices when every owner of a seventies Corvette is on the market looking for the correct AIR pump.

You can avoid a lot of these problems if you make sure the emissions control devices are still present and operating on your car. Just a few years ago these items were of concern only to NCRS members. Today everyone has to follow NCRS standards.

Replacing the complete emissions system could easily cost several thousand dollars. The cost of this work is something you have to calculate into the purchase price. Remember, the government is not interested in how nice your car looks or how great it runs. They won't even bother checking the actual exhaust gases until they can put their hands on the factory-installed emissions equipment. Equipment that won't be cheap if you have buy it. Just remember you bought your Corvette to drive, and that now the government gets to decide whether you can exercise that right.

Now that I've convinced you to simply replace the exhaust system on your Corvette with a stock system, the next step is to consider the best material for the exhaust system. For the last decade everyone has been touting the use of stainless steel. Then along came the aluminized systems. Of course we still have our plain old carbon steel systems that most of us have been using for decades.

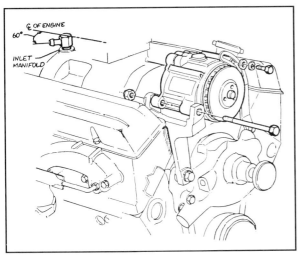

Here is how the AIR pump mounts to your small block. Your Corvette did come with an AIR pump, didn't it?

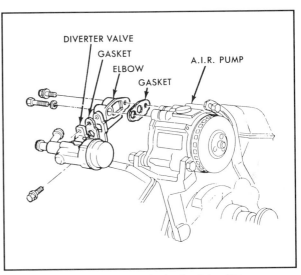

The diverter valve bolts on the back of the AIR pump.

C Central makes most of the exhaust systems found in the Corvette replacement market. Scott, one of the owners of C Central, feels that the aluminized exhaust systems are the best all around pipes. C Central has had a lot of problems with stainless steel pipes because they simply run too hot. What happens is that stainless pipes hold the heat, which then radiates up to the floor of your Corvette. This heat is so fierce that it even turns the steel blue. If you have a show car blue exhaust pipes aren't exactly original equipment

Indeed one of the reasons that we find a lot of stainless steel pipes on all the modern cars is for the very reason that they hold the heat so nicely. The more heat we can get into an exhaust system the cleaner the emissions will be coming out of the tailpipe. This doesn't make it any better for normal use on our old Corvettes.

This same exhaust heat also causes stainless steel pipes to expand at a tremendous rate. Sometimes the overall expansion can amount to over an inch in the total system. This in turn gives you some pretty impressive clamping problems.

Clamping stainless pipes is a very basic problem since some of the stainless steel pipes are so hard that the clamps simply can't squeeze the pipes together. Remember, the original carbon steel exhaust system is a very soft metal. When we clamp two pipes together we're actually crushing the outer pipe over the inner pipe. Crushing is how we get our most effective seal. This quality of seal is very difficult to get with most of the stainless steel pipes.

C Central coats their carbon steel pipes with an aluminum spray on both the inside and the outside. This helps to keep the rust and corrosion to a minimum and gives you a long lasting system that maintains the stock appearance.

This brings up one of the worst things you can do to your exhaust system, whatever the material. Don't start your Corvette once a week in your garage, even with the door open. There are any number of Corvette owners who like to go out to the garage on a weekly basis and start their Corvettes while there's still snow on the ground. This does a lot more harm than good because the hot exhaust gases hit the steel in the exhaust system and form condensation. In some cases you can even see this moisture run right out of the tailpipe.

If you run your car for only ten or fifteen minutes, this moisture will settle in the bottom of your muffler, and rust will begin to form. I can't remember ever seeing a muffler that rusted from the outside. Every single muffler I've replaced has rusted from the inside out.

If you can't start your Corvette and drive it at least twenty miles, leave it alone. A twenty-mile test drive ensures the complete car is up to operating temperature. It also ensures that enough heat is generated to boil away any condensation that developed as a result of starting your Corvette.

### Sound By Hooker

When it came time for Project Corvette to get an exhaust system, I decided to go back and live out my teenage fantasy. Ever since I saw the James Garner racing Corvettes, not to mention the Delorenzo/Thompson Corvettes of the late sixties, I knew I would have side pipes on my late sixties Corvette. The original racing pipes for these Corvettes were made by a small shop in Flint, Michigan, called Kustom Equipment. Now the only place you can get the old-fashioned side pipes are from Hooker.

These aren't the prissy little side pipes Chevrolet used on the street cars. Those delicate little

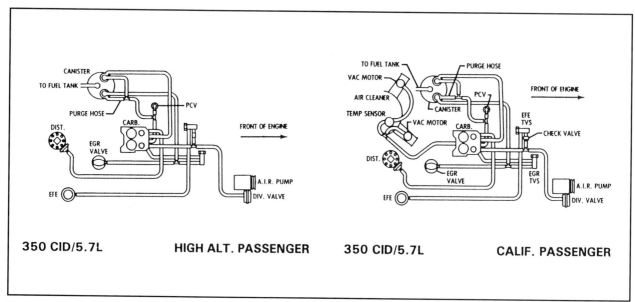

350 CID/5.7L      **HIGH ALT. PASSENGER**      350 CID/5.7L      **CALIF. PASSENGER**

The exact routing of vacuum lines will vary, but an arrangement similar to these is fairly typical.

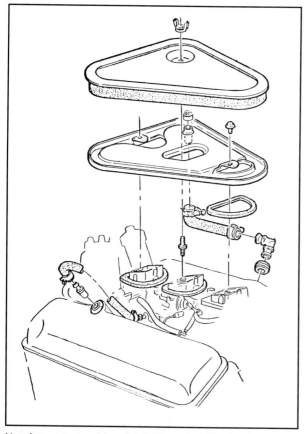

You have to consider the PCV system a part of your exhaust system. The Federal government certainly checks it when they verify that your exhaust system is in compliance with the federal code.

Chevrolet pipes, with all the chrome shielding, went through the GM committee structure. The Chevrolet side pipes were engineered so you wouldn't burn your leg getting out of your Corvette.

Gulstrand used pipes that could cause third-degree burns. They looked and sounded nasty and mean. These pipes had no chrome to clean; you simply painted them every weekend.

Project Corvette was too good of a car for just plain old painted headers. We needed the latest technology—Jet-Hot exhaust coating, a metallic-ceramic combination developed to protect military parts from corrosion, abrasion, and thermal fatigue.

Ford uses Jet-Hot coatings for the Mustang, and Chrysler uses it for the exhaust tips on the Viper. Even though it comes in a variety of colors, we stuck with the flat-black look. In other words, I used the newest technology in the exhaust system and nobody will even notice it was done—stealth technology at it's best. Let the Viper have the ten-cylinder engine; we've got our whole exhaust system coated with space-age materials, not just the exhaust tips.

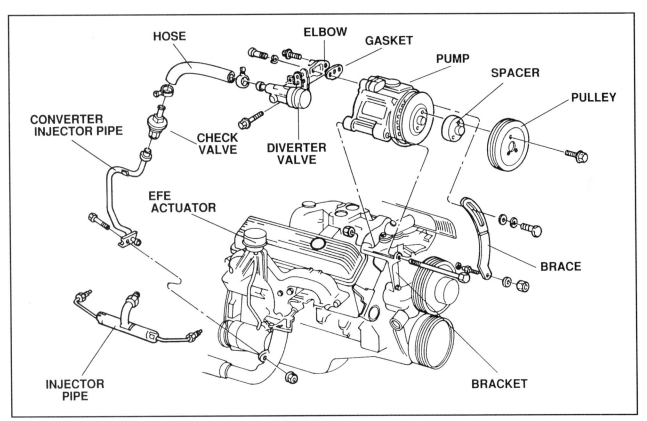

This is the general arrangement for the AIR system. The purpose of this entire system is to inject extra fresh air into the exhaust manifold. The extra charge of air caus-es the unburned hydrocarbons and carbon monoxide to burn more completely, reducing emissions.

If your Corvette came with side pipes, this cutout didn't exist. This picture also shows how a 1968 Corvette looks when it reaches the end of the line. One of two things will happen to this car. Some kind soul could adopt and restore the car, or it could continue to decline until it's only valued for its parts.

Delorenzo raced this car at Daytona. The pipes are an original set of racing headers that shake the earth.

# Chapter 21

# Axle and Differential

The rear axle is one of the strongest items on the Corvette. Very few things ever go wrong with the rear axle on the third-generation Corvette. The only two problems that do happen have occurred on such a regular basis that the technology for repairs is very common.

When I talk about the rear axle I'm going to be talking about everything from the right brake rotor to the left rear brake rotor, including the wheel bearings in the rear control arms.

The first problem with the rear axle occurs where the driveshaft ends and the differential starts. A universal joint is used to connect the driveshaft and the pinion gear in the rear axle. Universal joints, or U-joints, are fairly robust items. Seldom does anything go wrong with them. When something does go wrong, you notice it by a clunking sound on acceleration. Universal joint problems aren't the easiest to diagnose. Only when they are in horrible condition do they exhibit any real play. Sometimes the prob-

lem is that they actually bind up, in which case you'll find no play in the joint. Most of the time the only way to check them is to remove the driveshaft and check the movement on the workbench.

By the time you've gone to the trouble of removing the driveshaft or axle shafts, you might as well replace the universal joints on general principle. U-joints are so inexpensive that it's foolish not to replace both of them once you have the axle on the floor.

The old axle universal joints can be a real hassle to remove. I know this from my experience with Project Corvette. The easiest method is to take the shaft to your local machine shop and have the U-joints pressed out with a hydraulic press.

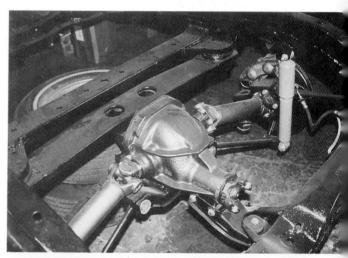

The differential unit is bolted to a cross-member, which is bolted to the frame at either side. The axle, or half-shafts, not only transmit the power to the wheels but also serve as locating devices. A lower control arm, or strut rod, is then used to locate the lower edge of the trailing arm. The trailing arm, or control arm, bolts into a frame pocket. The unit allows you to readily adjust the suspension camber and toe. However, designed in the very early sixties, the unit is heavy. Technology has pushed the modern chassis far beyond this design.

The Corvette rear axle maintained the same basic design from 1963 until 1982. There were a series of changes during that period, but the basic idea remained the same.

Here's the suspension on Project Corvette. The stock spring has been replaced with a modern fiberglass spring, and the lower control rods have been replaced with stronger units. These Herb Adams control rods are also easier to adjust than the stock eccentrics.

Pictured here is the stock unit with the eccentric in the inner side of the control arms. These rust rather readily, forcing you to use a torch to loosen them when performing an alignment. An air impact gun also works quite nicely if you're having difficulty. The differential cover is not a stock unit. This is a stronger unit available from any number of Corvette suppliers.

When replacing U-joints, it's best to replace them with assemblies that have grease fittings. There's one school of thought that feels the drilled hole for the zerk fitting is a possible stress point. On the other hand, if you grease the joints on a regular basis, you shouldn't have any problems again in your lifetime. Remember, your Corvette is a street car, not a race car. Grease fittings for street cars win the contest in my experience.

The next problem occurs directly behind this universal joint. Where the pinion gear exits the case there's a grease seal. This oil seal wears out and axle lube begins to exit the case and spread itself on your garage floor.

Don't assume that all the gear oil on your garage floor is coming just from the front pinion seal. The seals for the axles, on the side of the case, leak just as often, if not more often.

The oil seals on the side of the differential case don't wear out so much as it is as they actually carve grooves in the axle shafts. After ten or twenty years the groove is so deep that even a new axle seal can't stop the flood.

The solution here is to have very thin bushings installed over the axle shafts. It's best to let your local machine shop perform this task. What they do is install a bushing, or a thin covering, only a few thousandths of an inch thick, over the axle shafts.

The parts are only about twenty dollars a side but if you don't have the correct tools you might as well start ripping $20 bills in little pieces. Just explain to your machine shop that you want the same service they perform on front damper pulleys. This is exactly the same problem that you see with front

Here's a totally stock rear cover with the spring attached. Too often the ears that accept the bolts on the differential cover break. With the spare tire cover in place you may not notice this damage. It pays to check on this cover occasionally.

Here's the Vette Brakes & Products rear spring again. The bushings are from Energy Suspension. These long bolts can be used to adjust the rear suspension height. One old Corvette trick is to use a longer than stock bolt to lower the rear of the car. This whole picture is a plethora of Corvette aftermarket parts. The rear sway bar and lower control arm are Herb Adams pieces available from Moroso.

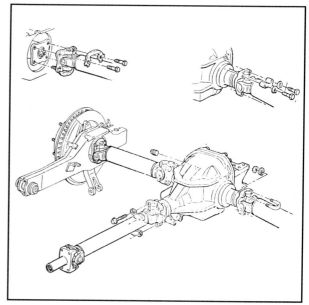

There are a lot of universal joints in the Corvette. Always replace them in pairs. If you suspect a U-joint is bad, remove the offending shaft and replace the joints on either end of the shaft. While you're at it you might as well have the shaft bead-blasted and painted the correct color. This is also known as compulsive Corvette behavior, which will allow you to meet a lot of new, and similarly disturbed, friends.

damper seals on the motor, and the new parts work the same way.

The real problem is that the differential case is not very easy to access. First, the spare tire carrier is in the way. Second, it's dark up there.

The is the trailing arm with the shock absorber removed. Chevrolet upgraded the diameter of the half-shafts during the seventies. Since they left the universal joint size the same, the benefit of the larger shafts is questionable.

The little circlips can be a pain in your posterior. Needle-nose pliers are the best solution. Spray a lot of penetrating oil around the clips, or let some brake fluid soak into the joint. Brake fluid is a wonderful penetrating oil, and sometimes cheaper.

This chassis is from an early-sixties race car. Notice the vintage adjustable Koni racing shocks. An interesting aspect of this car is the way the shoulder harness was mounted to the chassis. This is quite possibly the only truly secure system.

The easiest technique seems to be keep the rear axle as clean as possible (mainly so you can tell when the leaks get really bad) and fill it as often as necessary. The rear differential is one of those items that you try to ignore as long as possible.

When your Corvette differential starts dropping oil all over your garage floor you'll clearly need

This picture shows the cross-member as well as the rubber suspension bump stop.

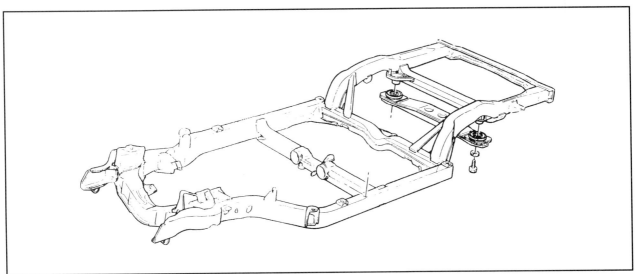

The cross-member that holds the rear differential to the frame is held on by two bolts. The easiest way to remove the differential unit is to drop the whole cross-member. However, after you remove the two bolts, nothing happens. I finally used a little heat from the oxy-acetylene torch around the rubber bushings, and the whole unit came loose. Make sure everything is well-supported when you try this trick, and only do one side at a time.

The nose of the differential is bolted to a frame cross-member through the use of a bracket. Make sure you remove this bracket before you attempt to drop the differential unit. The biggest problem here will be that the head of the bolt is not only rusted but hard to reach.

to keep a closer check on the gear oil level. Next, you're going have to decide when you want to remove the unit for a total rebuild. This means taking your Corvette off the road for a while. Rebuilding is a

The differential is held to the cross-member by four bolts, an area prime for rust, so you may have to clean the area before attempting to loosen the bolts. With patience you'll find the bolt heads and be able to remove the bolts.

winter project, not to mention being out of the realm of the home mechanic.

## Rear Cover Problems

Most rear differential covers never fail. When they do fail they all have the same problem. One of the ears for the spring mounting bolts breaks. This means your spring is now only held on by three bolts. Since the differential cover functions as an attachment point for the rear spring this is a rather important part to have broken.

The aftermarket has come up with a different design for the rear cover that seems to work quite well. This replacement cover can be installed while everything remains in the car. Just don't expect it to be easy, or clean. It's a matter of working around a lot of parts covered with smelly gear oil.

While changing the differential cover it's worth getting a bright light and checking the gears for wear. You probably won't find any problems because if the gears are bad you would have heard a howling noise long before this point. Nonetheless it's worth taking a look.

If you have a broken cover, and serious oil leaks, then you should be considering dropping the whole unit out of the car and having everything done at one time. There comes a point when patching things up is futile.

A number of companies make stronger covers and the price is more than reasonable. You can replace the cover with the unit still in the car, but it's not the easiest task. On the other hand if all you have is a broken cover it might be best to drop the spare tire cover and begin work.

## Gear Ratios

While we're still considering the rear axle let's consider what the differential actually does. Its primary purpose is to force the power coming out of the transmission to make a ninety degree turn. Simultaneously, it also changes the number of turns necessary for the axle shafts to go around. A 3.70:1 axle ratio means is that for every 3.7 turns that the driveshaft turns the axle will only make one turn. Changing rear end ratios can lead to one of the single biggest performance modifications you can make.

A change in the rear axle ratio will make your Corvette feel more powerful than all the engine work you can possibly afford. If you change your gear ratio from a 3.55 to a 4.11 ratio your Corvette will feel like someone hit the nitrous button when you leave the stoplight.

If you have your axle housing out of the car to replace the leaking seals, a gear ratio change is something you really should consider. Comparing the cost of changing gears with that of increasing engine performance, the gear work is a real bargain. People

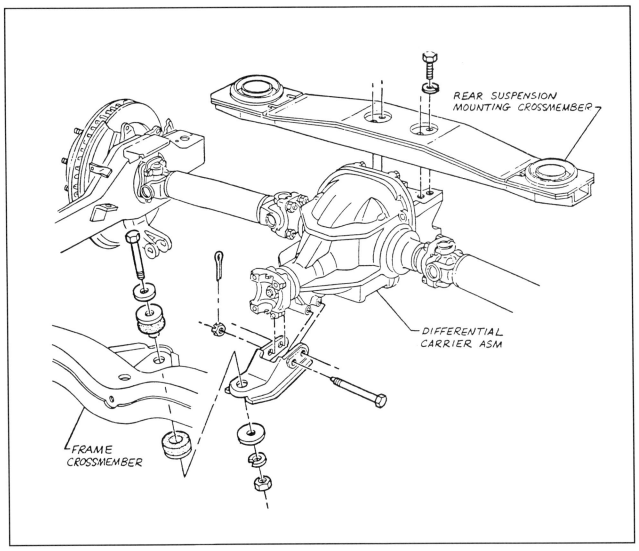

A good drawing of the attachment points for the differential.

consistently spend thousands of dollars on engine enhancements when for mere hundreds of dollars they could have a much quicker car through a simple change of gear ratio.

The 3.70:1 rear axle ratio is usually the best all-around gear ratio. This is a compromise between turnpike cruising and acceleration, but the acceleration will be respectable and you'll still be able to drive seventy miles an hour without turning 7,000 rpm.

If you seldom venture on the major highways then you could consider a 4.11:1 ratio. This ratio will give your Corvette tremendous acceleration, but top speed will drop off considerably. More importantly at seventy miles an hour your motor will be turning about 3,800 rpm. Your Corvette motor will easily do this but things may get a little noisy. Also, your fuel mileage will go directly over the edge.

The nose of the differential is bolted to the frame cross-member. Chevrolet used rubber bushings, but Energy Suspension makes an improved polyurethane bushing for this application that presents no problems.

In order to remove the control arm, you'll have to remove the shock. Remove the top shock bolt and let the shock absorber come down with the whole unit.

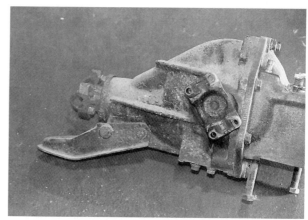

A sideview of the differential. The seals and shafts both go bad and result in oil leaks. Once you have the unit out of the car, decide whether you want to send it out for refurbishing or tackle the internal rebuilding yourself. Notice the little plastic breather on the rear cover. Sometimes this vent can get plugged and cause leaks. It's not a bad idea to crawl under your car and see if the breather is clear.

This is what the differential looks like when it finally comes out of the car. The unit is heavy, so the task is best handled by two people. Removing the differential is not something you want to begin by yourself some late night.

Here's the strengthened aftermarket cover. Unless you're doing an NCRS restoration, these are well worth the extra money. Remember, do it once and do it right.

When you remove the rear cover, this is what you're going to find. It's a good idea to get a professional Corvette shop to make any repairs beyond this point.

## Gear Ratio Chart

| Gear Ratio | Mph/1,000rpm | Rpm@70mph |
|------------|--------------|-----------|
| 4.11:1 | 18.0 | 3,800 |
| 3.70:1 | 21.4 | 3,200 |
| 3.55:1 | 22.3 | 3,100 |
| 3.08:1 | 25.7 | 2,500 |

The overall diameter of your rear tires will change these calculations slightly but you should be able to see what happens when you revise the rear axle ratio. I know every Corvette owner claims to drive really fast but in reality very few of us exceed seventy miles an hour for more than an hour at a time. Unless you traverse Texas on a regular basis the 3.70:1 gear ratio is the best compromise.

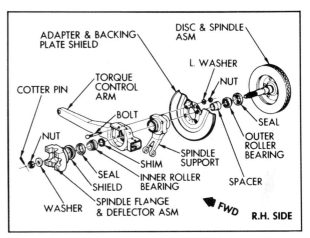

Pictured here is the rear control arm and the bearing assembly. Having rebuilt several bearing assemblies, I suggest you send them out to be professionally rebuilt so the unit is properly shimmed and assembled. Once you get your Corvette together, you don't want to go back and correct your mistakes.

As was just pointed out, if you rarely travel the major highways of the United States then the 4.11:1 ratio might be something to consider. This ratio will give your tremendous acceleration at the price of reduced cruising speed.

Given the current state of American highways, and the proliferation of the uniformed tax collectors, a 3.08:1, even a 3.36:1, is really not all that desirable. Corvettes are about acceleration and a gear ratio change is the best, and least expensive, way to maximize that acceleration.

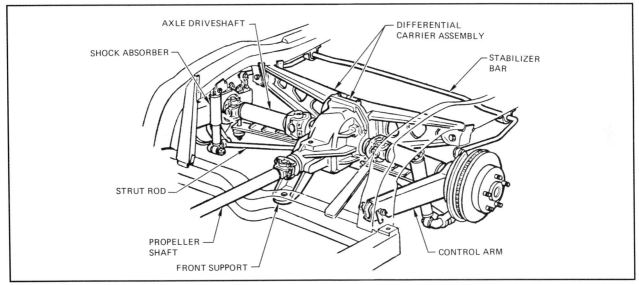

The control arm is critical to a quality rear suspension. The rear part of the control arm holds the bearing, and the front part fits into the frame pocket, along with the alignment shims. Make sure to check your control arms for rust before you start the rest of your project.

A lot of people have experience in rebuilding Corvette rear bearing assemblies. Caledonia Classics, Mid-America, and Van Steel all rebuild these units.

If all you do is trailer your Corvette from car show to car show, who really cares. Any old axle ratio will work just fine. You guys don't even need to change the gear oil.

The aluminum plates, next to the rear sway bar, act as a reinforcement for the bushings on the rear cross-members. This worthwhile addition, sold by Vette Brakes & Products, costs very little and takes even less time to install. Nothing needs to be removed for its installation, and it's one of the easiest changes you can make to the Corvette rear suspension. The difference in performance may be small, but for so little money and effort, why not install them?

## Positraction

The Corvette Positraction is a robust unit. Very few people have problems with the Chevrolet version of a limited slip differential. The only common problem is that the positraction lube wears out, which is usually noticeable by a slight noise when you go around a corner, often at a slow speed. If this happens, the gear lube, or more specifically the Positraction additive, isn't providing proper lubrication for the clutches. Instead of working properly, the clutches are slipping and then engaging with a bang.

Changing the rear-axle oil on a regular basis could prevent this problem from occurring. But, make sure you use the correct type of fluid, since the normal gear oil you buy at K-Mart will only make the problem worse. Your Corvette needs gear oil designed for Positraction.

A second solution is to use the small bottles of Positraction additive. These little additive bottles are designed to turn normal gear oil into Positraction additive, and they work very well. In some cases I've simply put two of these into the rear axle, and the problem completely disappeared.

## Rear-Axle Codes

Corvette owners can easily locate the day, month, and factory where the rear axle was assembled. You can also easily determine the gear ratio. The gear ratio number is found on the bottom of the differential casing, next to the rear cover. A complete listing of the axle codes can be found in the appendix.

| **Example:** | AO 0621 W |
| --- | --- |
| AO | 3.70 Ratio/Positraction |
| 06 | Month of June |
| 21 | Twenty-first Day of the Month |
| W | Warren, Michigan, Plant |

The aftermarket differential cover has extra material on the sides, which prevents the ears that hold the rear spring in place from breaking. It may not be an original part, but it makes a great deal of sense if you're going to drive your Corvette in any form of motorsports.

# Chapter 22

# Interior

The worst part of a project car is when my friends come over and ask, "When is this supposed to be done?" When I tell them the completion date they simply shake their head and say, "No way."

My solution to that problem has always been to stop inviting people over to my garage. Each time I finish a task, I feel like I've put the hard part behind me and now I can do the easy stuff—like put the interior back together.

It certainly made sense to me that the interior should be the easy part. The people from Mid-America have been right on the other end of the phone to offer careful guidance. All the parts actually fit. Most importantly, there's not even any dirt to rub in your skin by this point in your Corvette project. You

should actually be working on a clean Corvette at this point.

Interiors should be the part you're most careful with since you have to look at this part as you drive down the road. Project Corvette had been designed for two things: The car would be brutally fast, which was the reason I spent so much time on the chassis and engine, and the car must look good, which is the reason I spent so much time on fiberglass repair and paint. When it came to working on the interior, I was working on the area I would be looking at while driving down the road, and the goal here was very simple—keep it stock.

## Interior Motives

When it comes to selecting new interior parts, you need to make some very firm decisions—decisions you'll be living with for more than a decade. The first problem is in getting all the colors to match. There's only one way to do this—buy all your interior parts from the same supplier.

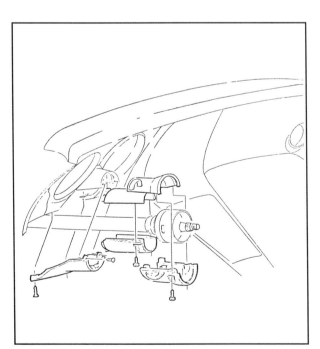

To remove a steering column you must first remove all the trim items. This is simply a matter of loosening a few screws. Just remember to keep a record of where all the screws came from.

On the earlier-model Corvettes, the panel below the column extends part way up the column. The thin steering wheel reminds you that you're driving a vintage car.

Notice the meaty steering wheel on this newer Corvette. Also notice the damage a key chain can do to a steering column.

No matter how careful you might be, it's virtually impossible to get all the colors and interior textures to match. Since there are a couple of different suppliers of Corvette interior parts, you'll naturally find a couple of different types of colors. The only way to be absolutely sure everything will match by the time you're done is to buy everything from the same supplier. This is a commitment you must make. It is the only way to keep your Corvette from looking like a Hyundai.

The best way to find a supplier is to ask people who have done the job before. Talk to them and look at their cars. If nothing else, you gain another good reason to attend a few more Corvette shows this Summer.

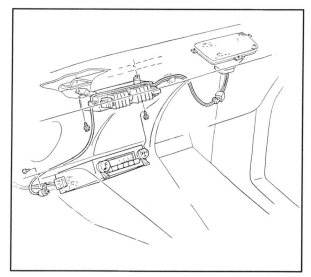

In 1972 and other years, the radio was actually in two separate pieces. There was the part you could see on the console, and another part hidden under the dash pad.

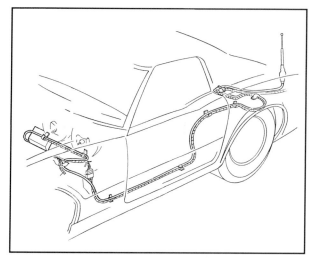

The radio antenna cable runs under the dash and the carpeting to the rear antenna. The cable runs parallel to the rear wiring harness.

## The Seats

Seats are a big deal. Next time you're walking around a Corvette show, take notice of all the ill-fitting seat covers. Very few people seem able to get the seats properly upholstered. The parts suppliers have convinced us it's no big deal to re-cover

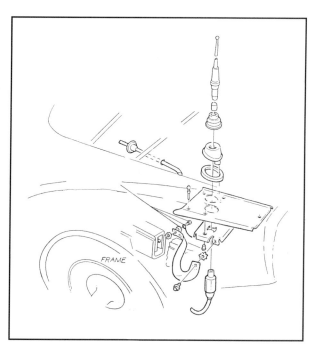

The cable runs through the rear bulkhead and into the rear antenna. The braided grounding strap is the most important part of this assembly. If you have trouble with the reception on your radio, check is the grounding strap connections first, and clean the frame rails as well as the attaching bolts.

In 1968, there was nothing but a flat panel in front of the passenger. A set of map pockets were added in 1969. The rarest part of this interior is the radio blanking plate, which is far more difficult to locate than the original radio. This Corvette was ordered with a radio delete option.

The glove box finally made its appearance in 1978. This seemingly minor item had been missing on the Corvette for the last fifteen years. The box can be removed to gain access to the rear of the dash panel.

Corvette seats. Even I believed that once upon a time.

Since I wanted a stock interior I called on M. F. Dobbins for advice. Dobbins has been involved with Corvette restorations longer than most of us have owned Corvettes. He's also one of the hobby's biggest sticklers for detail. If you have a question about what the correct item is on an older Corvette, Dobbins is the man to see. He's even written several books on the subject.

When someone asks an obscure Corvette question, I've heard people grudgingly say, "Only Dobbins would know the answer to that." This is the sort of person I need. Someone who is a recognized expert and willing to share that expertise with less knowledgeable people like myself.

Since I was after perfection, I asked Dobbins for help with the seat upholstery. Oddly enough, Dobbins couldn't meet his own standards in this case. His search for perfection, however, located a trim shop that could meet his level of perfection—Willow Grove Auto Top.

John Reilly, of Willow Grove Auto Top, agreed to take on the project. In the beginning I thought I could learn the secret tips from his decades of experience and simply pass them on to you in this book. In the end the only tip I can pass on is to tell you to simply send him your seats.

John mentioned that most of his Corvette seat work begins in the middle of his customer's upholstery work. Typically a disheartened Corvette owner toting a pair of ragged seats enters his shop after a few days of frustration with the project. The plea usually begins, "Can you help me?"

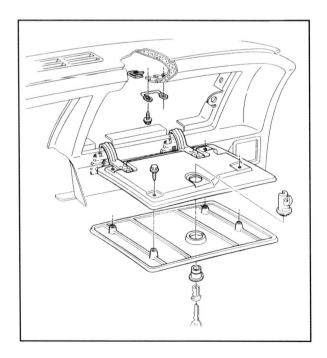

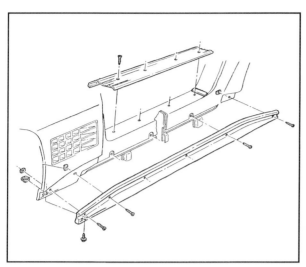

An easy way to dress up the interior of your Corvette is to replace the door sills. People have been scraping their feet over these sill plates for the last several decades. The best time to replace these plates is when you restore the carpeting. Make sure to place the carpeting high enough on the sill so the plate can properly clamp the carpeting to the body of the car.

This is normally the worst possible place to start an upholstery job. Better that you should simply let someone start from the very beginning. If Dobbins won't do his own upholstery work, what makes you believe you won't have any problem? When you

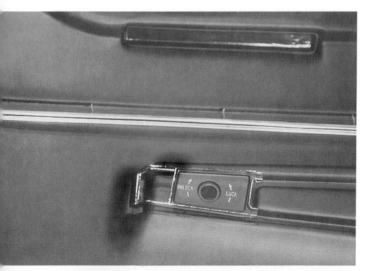

Corvette doors take an incredible amount of abuse. The expensive solution is to replace everything, including the panel, which would give you a show-quality interior. Or, you could simply remove the trim items and spray the door with the interior paint available from Mid-America. If you replace all the trim items, you'll end up with a very respectable interior. It won't be a show winner, but it'll be an improvement.

The armrest area seems to be one of the weakest areas on the doors. There's really no solution for the cracks in this area. The patch panels look just about as bad as a small crack. In 1978 Chevrolet made the armrest a separate item. The best solution for the pre-1978 Corvettes is to wait until you can fit new door panels into your budget. Always purchase door panels and armrests in pairs so both grain and color match.

turn the job over to a professional, all you need to do is get a second job to pay the bill.

It usually takes about six hours to do a pair of Corvette seats. Of course the Project Corvette virus hit Willow Grove Auto Top, and poor John spent over eight hours giving us an NCRS-quality job. The main thing I learned during this whole episode was that it's best to buy interior parts from a reputable suppli-

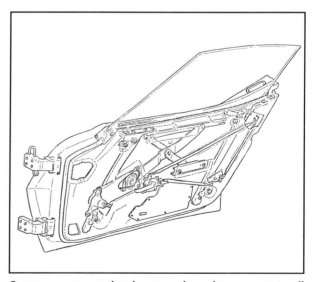

Once you remove the door panel you have access to all sorts of wonderful adjustments. It's also a time to clean up the old refuse left in the doors by previous owners.

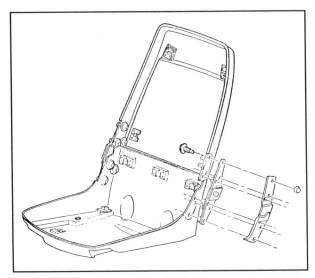

The seats were changed in 1978. They used a shell instead of the previous frame. Here you can see the new screw-on armrests introduced in 1978.

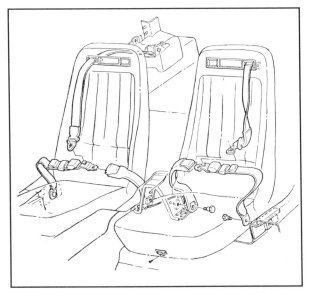

Seat belts have suffered over the past few decades. Not only do they generally look bad, but they're often so rotted that they're unsafe. New replica belt sets are available, but expensive. The seat-belt bolts are usually very difficult to remove. Make sure to use the proper socket so you don't strip the bolt head.

er and then locate a company that knows how to install them properly.

A lot of Corvette owners feel the need to replace the vinyl seats with leather. You already know leather covers cost a lot more to purchase, but you may not know they also cost more to install. Furthermore, leather covers may not look as nice when the upholstery is finished.

As you can see in the photos, a huge steam machine is used to shrink the vinyl seat cover to its final shape. This is how the upholstery shop gets that glove-like fit on your Corvette seats. Leather, however, does not shrink. The only way to get it to fit right is to pad out all the areas. Consequently, the quality of the fit is extremely important, and secondly, a perfect fit requires a lot more hand fitting. Done proper-

ly, it's going to cost you more money, so think carefully about how badly you want leather seats in your early version of the third-generation Corvette.

## Carpeting

Installing the carpeting was something I found I could do. It's easy to install. In fact, when you get it

The center console is often cracked, and many of the replacement consoles are not correct. If you want to match the original, take your old console to a major show and check out what the vendors are selling.

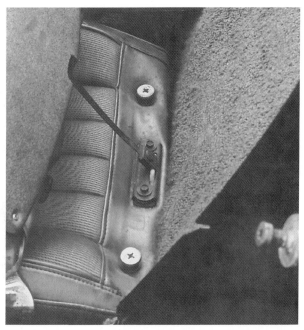

As the Corvette developed, a lot of items were changed. This seat mechanism was changed on the early cars. Make sure all the parts are present when you start shopping. These little items can eventually break your budget.

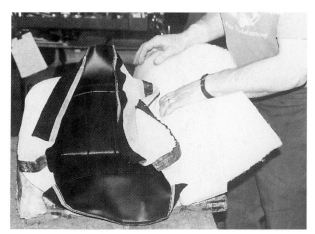

New padding is a key item for a quality seat. The padding gives the new covering an original look, not to mention a better feel.

from Mid-America it even comes with the backing/insulation installed. You only need to pay attention to the pattern.

Since some suppliers sell carpeting that is not the same as the original, it's best to locate owners of NCRS Duntov Corvettes or Bloomington Gold winners and ask them where they bought their carpet and whether they would purchase it from the same source again. You're probably only going to buy this carpeting once in your life, so you might as well buy the correct carpet the first time.

You should also purchase a complete carpet set. If you only buy a few pieces to cover the most highly worn spots, your Corvette will never have matching carpeting. The only way you can ensure the material, weave, and color will match is to buy a

Seat material and design changed on an annual basis. Good-looking seats are absolutely necessary in building a Corvette you can be proud of.

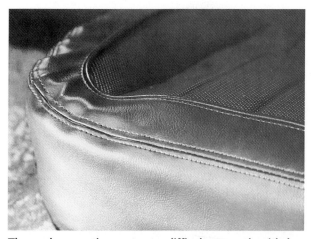

The early-seventies seats are difficult to work with because of how the various pieces are stitched together. Choose a quality upholstery shop and let them tell you which supplier offers the best product. They'll know which product is going to give you the quality you want.

A 5000rpm tachometer in a seventies Corvette. This shows what happened during the seventies—the old LT-1 engine didn't reach peak horsepower until 5600rpm. These tachometers were all electronic. The cable drive disappeared with the points ignition.

In 1978 the Corvette got little pictographs.

complete set from one supplier, on the same order form.

The door panels are another area for which you only have one choice. Break down and spend the money. Get the whole door panel, and forget about all the patch panels. While you're at it, purchase a new interior screw kit. Too often the previous owners took off the stock door panels so many times that the screws no longer hold them in place.

The early door panels are quite easy to replace. It's simply a matter of taking the screws out and pulling the panel off. The only reason to remove the

The center gauge would change as the third-generation Corvette matured.

Aftermarket radios have always been a problem in Corvettes. They lower the value of the car and add little in sound quality. The best solution is to keep the original radio and upgrade the speakers.

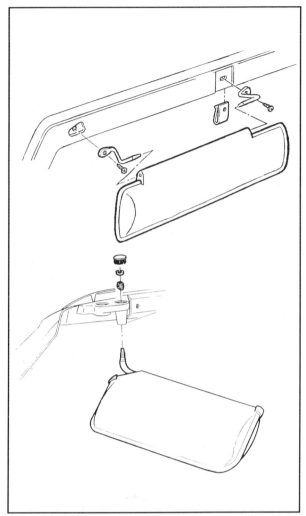

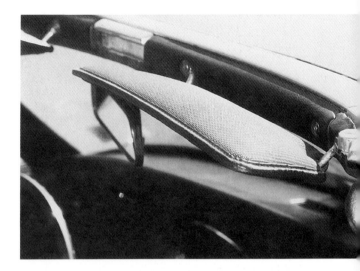

*Above and right,* the sun-visor design would change several times.

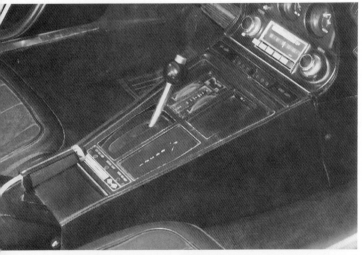

As rough as this center console looks, it can be cleaned up very nicely. All the parts are present, and the area simply needs a little detailing .

door panels is to replace the panels or make an adjustment on the actuation of the window glass.

When it comes to actually removing the glass from the windows, don't consider it for too long. Removing the side glass is a long involved process; avoid it if possible.

## Leave The Dash Alone

Going into the dashboard of your Corvette puts you into a new zone—The Aggravation Zone. There are very few reasons to take your dash apart. Even if you have a perfectly valid reason to start tearing it apart, you're going to regret the decision.

The right side of the dash is fairly simple. On the early cars, it's a matter of loosening a few screws. On the other hand, there is so little behind this panel, there's almost no reason to venture forth.

The left hand side of the dash, with the speedometer and the tachometer, is a lot more complicated. To start, you have to drop the steering column. Once you drop the column, the panel will come forward, along with all the wiring. This is where the problems begin. Before you actually remove the instruments, indeed even before you get this far, you better be sure the problem is actually in the instruments and not in the cables or cable drive gears.

The center section of the dash is where real problems begin, as this is the section where all the instruments reside. It's also inhabited by a lot of wires. While taking the panel out isn't all that difficult, putting it back properly will be, so be certain the problem exists in the instruments before you take on the challenge of the center section.

Instrument problems develop in only three areas. First, the sending unit may be defective, which means no electrical signal, or the wrong signal, is being sent to the instrument. Second, the wire to the instrument, or the path for the message, may be bro-

The power window switches moved around the interior as the third-generation Corvette matured.

Pedals are the one interior item everyone forgets. If you go to the trouble of replacing the carpeting, the pedals also deserve some attention.

ken. Third, the instrument may be broken. Determine where the problem is before you start tearing into the dash panels.

## The Parking Brake

You should not have to adjust the parking brake at the cables ending in the center console. Parking brake adjustment is normally done at the rear brake. If your parking brake is not working, do *not* start tearing the center console apart.

To adjust the parking brake at the rear brake, remove the rear wheels and see if the parking brake can be adjusted using the star wheel adjuster. Check your Haynes manual for the exact procedure. Also check the operation of the parking brake cable. If the previous owners did not use the parking brake in the last decade, they may be rusted. Try pulling on them and spraying them with WD-40. If you've led a good

life, they may start working. The other solution is to replace them.

Only when you've determined everything is fine in the rear brake area, should you start ripping into the center console.

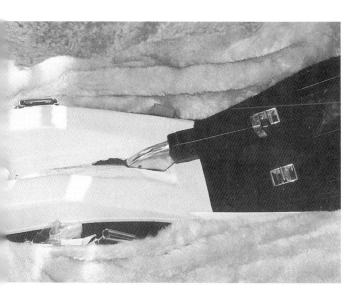

Prior to the 1978 installation of the glove box, these little compartments were the only storage area in your Corvette. The early doors were made from plywood and contained a number of informational decals. A previous owner decided these doors were also a good location for stereo speakers.

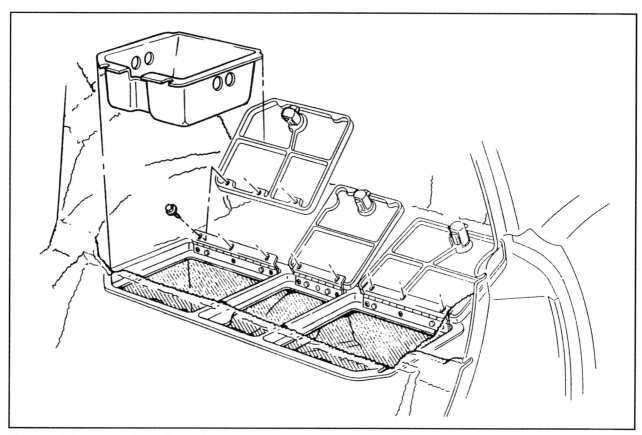

The wood doors were later changed to plastic covers.
The size and shape were retained.

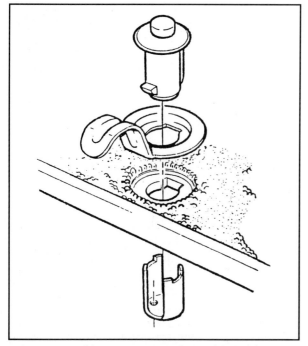

Latches are easy to remove and clean. Simply remove
the screw at the bottom, and the assembly comes apart.

*Chapter 23*

# Cooling System

The quest for coolness involves a lot more than purchasing a Georgio Armani suit. Coolness also involves driving your Corvette down the street without creating a cloud of water and antifreeze. An overheating Corvette is definitely *not* cool.

Let's take a minute to explain how your Corvette gets to an overheated state. Your Corvette's cooling system is really nothing more than a heat exchange system. Water circulates around the engine block and absorbs the heat from the engine. Approximately twenty-five percent of your engine's heat energy is absorbed by the cooling system. This hot water, combined with antifreeze, is circulated to the radiator where all of the heat is dissipated into the at-

mosphere. If you think of your radiator as a water-to-air heat exchanger, you're on the right track.

Your Corvette radiator works on the principle of heat transfer. If you remember high school physics, you remember that heat will always flow from the hotter object to the cooler object. The heat from the hot engine flows to the cooler water in the cooling system, and from there the heat flows into the atmosphere as the hot water passes through the radiator.

With this in mind, you can see water must be able to circulate freely around the engine block, absorbing as much of the engine's heat as possible. Secondly, you must make sure that as much air as possible can get to all this hot water as it passes

Radiators take a lot of abuse. Thirty years of neglect will take a toll on the cooling system. You'll need to decide whether you want an NCRS original numbers-matching radiator or a radiator that works more efficiently than the one Chevrolet installed at the St. Louis assembly plant. Note that the hood is removed. Anytime you have to get involved in serious cooling system work, you should consider removing the hood.

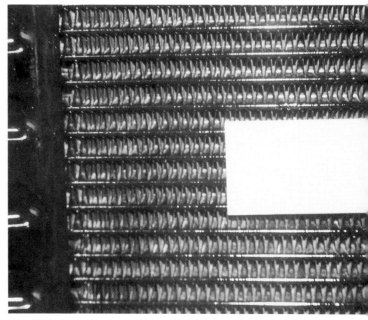

U.S Radiator makes a radiator that is close to the original but more efficient and cheaper in price than the old stock system. Don Armstrong uses more cooling fins for his radiators than the original Chevrolet radiator used.

This mess of hoses was in the original Project Corvette. When the original Corvette radiator expired, someone installed a totally inappropriate cooling system. Notice the radiator cap on both the radiator and the coolant recovery tank. Not a good idea.

The fan clutch is an important part of the cooling system. You only want to use the fan at slow speeds and in traffic, since at highway speeds the engine turns faster and more air is pushed through the radiator, causing the fan to disengage. This means more power for driving the car down the road. With the fan clutch, the radiator fan only works when you most need increased air flow.

through the radiator. How can such a simple system be so aggravating on a nice spring day?

The first line of defense for Corvette owners is to keep the radiator clean. Rust happens. If you keep enough water in contact with steel, as in the engine

block, rust is bound to form. Antifreeze has rust inhibitors, but in about two years the inhibitors have lost all effectiveness.

As rust forms, the size of the water passage is reduced. Think of it as a Corvette with clogged arteries. Now think of the roto-rooter man's job and you're starting to figure out the solution.

In the Corvette's case we're going to use chemicals to free up all the coolant passages. Several types of flushing solutions are available on the market. The strongest ones almost create holes in the cooling system, or in the radiatior. If the radiator is so clogged that only the strongest chemicals will work, you have nothing to lose by using the strongest solution. You're probably going to have to purchase a radiator anyway.

The best way to deal with cooling system problems is to use a mild flushing agent when you change the coolant. It's a lot easier to keep everything in top operating condition than it is to make repairs.

If all of the above fail, the next line of defense is U.S. Radiator in California. When you devote your whole life to building muscle-car radiators, you better be pretty good at it.

Don Armstrong understands Corvette owners want a stock-looking radiator but, at the same time, need an effective cooling system. Don and U.S. Radiator have made it possible for us to have both.

When we were working on Project Corvette, I asked Don to build a radiator that looked like a 1968 Chevrolet aluminum radiator but worked a lot better.

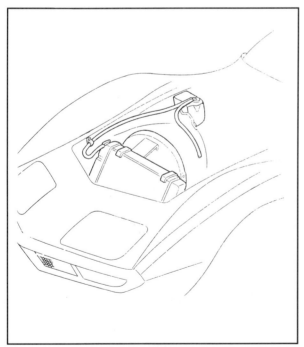

The purpose of the coolant recovery tank is to hold the overflow and recirculate it to the cooling system. The early C3 cars used aluminum tanks, which were replaced with plastic tanks when the system was revised in 1973.

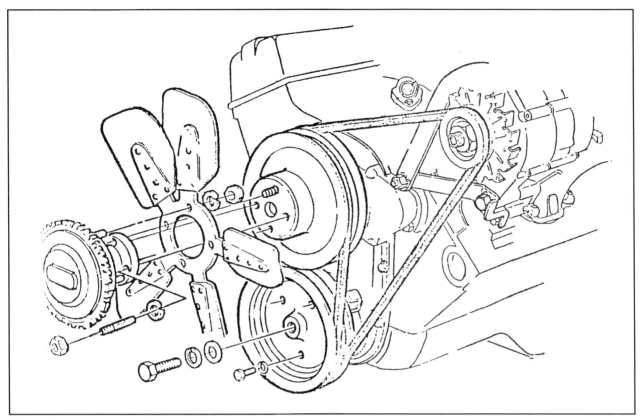

The biggest problem is that fan clutches wear out over time, losing about 200rpm each year. After twenty years you'll have a Corvette that overheats because the radiator fan won't operate when you get caught in traffic.

I wanted something to keep my Corvette cool and at the same time fool a novice NCRS judge.

Don explained that since the basic idea of a radiator is to send heat from the water to the atmos-

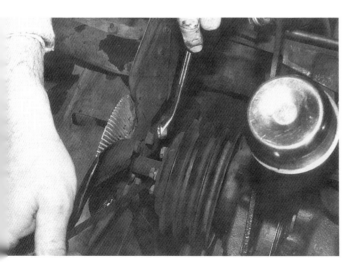

The fan clutch is easy to change. You may need to use a large screwdriver to wedge the water-pump shaft to keep the shaft from turning.

The ultimate Chevy water pump was designed by Drake Engineering, of Offenhauser fame. It flows more coolant and uses less horsepower than the stock unit. Unfortunately, the shaft length may not fit all applications.

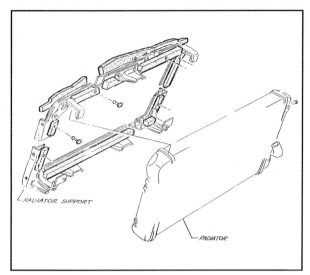

The foam that seals the radiator is an important part of your Corvette's cooling system. If you have to replace the radiator, call C Central and get new foam strips for reinstallation.

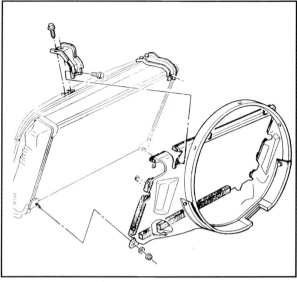

The fan shroud uses foam strips to seal the area where it meets the radiator. The entire system is engineered to bring cool air directly through the radiator. You don't want any air to escape.

phere, all we really want is for large amounts of coolant to come into contact with even larger amounts of cool air. The greater the surface area of the radiator, the easier it becomes for the heat to escape to the surrounding environment. One way to increase the radiator surface is to simply increase the number of cooling fins used per inch.

The purpose of the cooling fins is to have more surface for the air to touch. During the sixties, GM used only eight to fourteen fins per every inch of tubing. Most of the Corvettes built in the sixties and seventies have fourteen fins per inch, which means a new radiator will always be an improvement over the original.

If you have a good-quality radiator and you're still having problems, the next step is to check on the airflow to the radiator. It's essential that you get cool air to the radiator. If you have poor airflow, even the best radiator in the world won't help. Remember, we

The fan shroud is essential to operation of the cooling system. Only the L88 Corvette lacked a fan shroud, and we all know how often they overheated. Make sure you always use a shroud in a street Corvette.

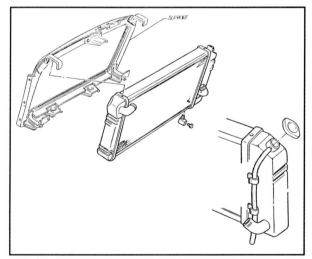

Make sure all the proper radiator supports are in place when you install the radiator. Check your copy of the *Assembly Instruction Manual* or talk to a very knowledgeable supplier.

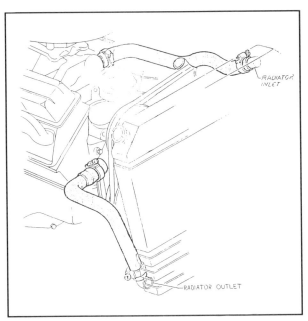

Make sure you use top-quality radiator hoses, and always use the molded hoses for the cooling system. The one-size-fits-all hose restricts coolant flow unnecessarily.

The small-block radiators, such as Project Corvette's, use a unique bottom hose arrangement. Very few radiators have ever used a similar hose connection. Make sure you're using the correct radiator and not some reject from an Impala.

need as much air as possible reaching the surface of the radiator.

All the C3 Corvettes used an engine-driven fan to increase the amount of air passing through the radiator. This fan creates negative pressure behind the radiator, and the negative pressure helps the air pass through the radiator. Your Corvette radiator shroud acts just like a wind tunnel. This wind tunnel effect is very important when you're driving around town. Since we can't depend on velocity to ram air through the radiator while driving at slow speeds, air has to be sucked in through the radiator.

The radiator shroud must be sealed along the edges to keep all the air going in the proper direction. Those little foam pieces stuffed between the radiator and the fan shroud act as the seals. When you remove your radiator, you should call C Central for new foam pieces. Why reinstall twenty-year-old parts?

One final item to remember concerning the radiator is the pressure cap. The radiator cap is a pressure valve. It's set to release the cooling system pressure at a predetermined level and is designed to be the weakest link in the cooling system. The radiator cap will reduce pressure before the hoses, or the radiator will blow.

A second feature of the radiator cap is that by allowing the pressure to reach a pre-determined maximum we can actually raise the temperature at which the coolant boils. We all know that water boils at 212° F. A 21lb pressure cap will raise this boiling point to 260° F.

Big blocks have always had a marginal cooling system. In early 1968 Chevrolet found that cutting a big hole below the grille helped a great deal. If you see this hole in your Corvette, it's not a homemade fix, it's a General Motors design. Yes, it does look just like something your cousin Ernie might try to solve an overheating problem.

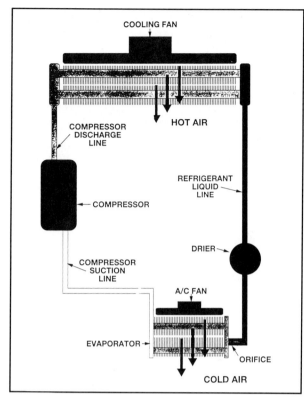

Your air conditioner works on the same principle as the cooling system. Heat will always flow to the cooler area. This is a basic description of how your air conditioner works.

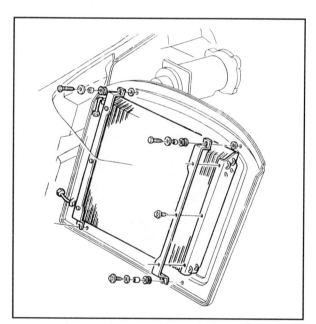

The air-conditioning condenser resides in front of your radiator. One secret to an effective air-conditioning system is to keep this condenser clean. You want to allow as much air as possible to flow into this area, especially if you use R-134A refrigerant.

Once you have a proper radiator, a working radiator cap, and an adequate amount of air passing through your Corvette radiator, make sure the water is moving through the system at an adequate speed. The water pump determines the speed and amount of water passing through the radiator. The easiest way to maximize the coolant flow through the radiator is to use the best possible water pump. Everyone has an opinion about pushing water through a small-block Chevrolet engine. The worst possible system is the stock numbers-matching Chevrolet water pump. The stock pump pushes roughly sixty percent of the water to the driver's side of the engine block. This obviously is not the best solution to prevent overheating.

One person who has taken the time to totally engineer a real solution to small-block cooling problems is John Drake of Drake Engineering. If you've spent most of your life designing Offenhauser engines, you probably approach the water circulation problem on a small-block Chevrolet as an engineer. You don't mess around with putting a different impeller in a stock Chevrolet housing, you make everything new.

A stock GM water pump eats about 4hp. The Drake Engineering takes only 2hp. Forget about electric water pumps. People who use electric water pumps have forgotten basic high school physics. Moving water takes energy—basic physics. If you use a mechanical water pump, the energy comes from the crankshaft pulley. If you use an electric water pump, the energy comes from the alternator. Guess

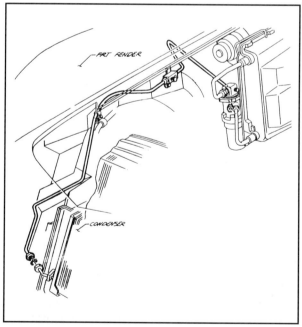

This shows the location of the line from the receiver-drier to the condenser.

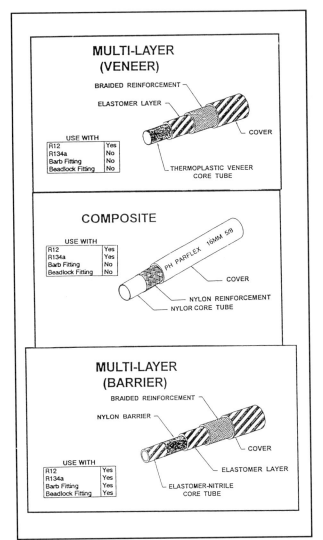

### MULTI-LAYER (VENEER)

BRAIDED REINFORCEMENT
ELASTOMER LAYER
COVER
THERMOPLASTIC VENEER CORE TUBE

| USE WITH | |
|---|---|
| R12 | Yes |
| R134a | No |
| Barb Fitting | No |
| Beadlock Fitting | No |

### COMPOSITE

PH PARFLEX 16MM 5/8
COVER
NYLON REINFORCEMENT
NYLOR CORE TUBE

| USE WITH | |
|---|---|
| R12 | Yes |
| R134a | Yes |
| Barb Fitting | No |
| Beadlock Fitting | No |

### MULTI-LAYER (BARRIER)

BRAIDED REINFORCEMENT
NYLON BARRIER
COVER
ELASTOMER LAYER
ELASTOMER-NITRILE CORE TUBE

| USE WITH | |
|---|---|
| R12 | Yes |
| R134a | Yes |
| Barb Fitting | Yes |
| Beadlock Fitting | Yes |

The biggest problem with R-134A refrigerant is that it leaks out of the older hoses. The molecular structure of R-134A is different from the old R-12. You may find it necessary to change your hoses. Everything else in the system should be just fine.

where the alternator gets its energy? Right, the crankshaft pulley. It takes the same amount of horsepower to turn an electric water pump as a mechanical water pump. Physics happens. There is no free energy in the world.

Another good part of the Drake pump is that all you folks out there with the late-model Corvettes can't use it. Since I'm stuck with a lousy selection of aftermarket wheels, you guys can have the bad water pumps.

An engine-driven fan is going to be more efficient than an electric fan, *unless* you use an underdriven fan pulley. These underdrive pulleys not only slow down the fan so it pulls less air, but they also slow down the water pump. This is a real problem

This is the old-style axial compressor used by General Motors until 1976.

with the underdriven pulley. The coolant is allowed to remain in the engine block so long that you can have an overheating problem. Generally this is of more concern for city driving, but if you drive your Corvette on the open road, there will seldom be a problem.

While you gain some horsepower with underdrive pulleys, you also increase your chances of overheating. Make sure you really want those extra 2hp when you install these fancy pulleys—there is a price.

Generally anything over 210-220° F is considered hot. Just to complicate things you have to keep in mind that anything below 180° F is considered too cool. There is an optimum temperature for your

GM switched to the radial style compressor in 1976. The main advantage was the lower weight.

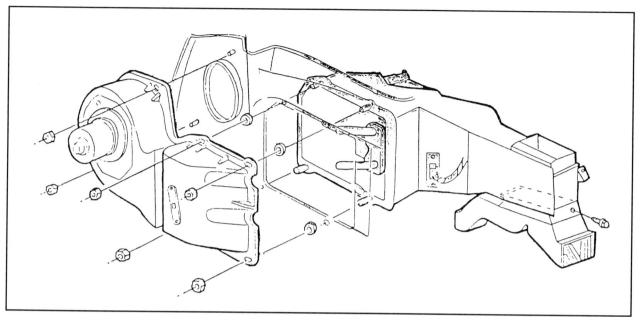

The heater blower and box bolt directly to the firewall. When you reinstall the heater box you should use a new gasket.

Corvette's water. If you run too cool, you can actually lower your engine's performance and increase the wear of the engine components. The optimum operating temperature for your engine is between 180° and 190° F.

The heater core fits in the opening closest to the center of the car, while the blower motor installs in the cover. It's best to install the heater core first and follow with the cover. Be careful not to damage the heater core when you make the installation.

## Disposing Of Antifreeze

Used antifreeze is a much bigger hazard to the environment than used motor oil. While a lot of local businesses will accept your used motor oil, very few will take your old antifreeze. When you empty your Corvette's radiator, you're dumping out water that is heavily contaminated with metal deposits that are both toxic and nonbiodegradable. Moreover, ethylene glycol is a toxic substance to begin with. Antifreeze also has a very sweet taste that household pets simply love. About four ounces will kill your neighbor's dog. If you neighbors already hate your Corvette, think how they'll feel when they find their pets missing.

Arco Chemical Company markets a non-toxic propylene glycol-based antifreeze called Sierra. However, used antifreeze is the real culprit. Pure ethylene glycol and propylene glycol are both biodegradable, but after several years in your cooling system, they're both a hazard to the environment. The best solution is to see if your local Chevrolet dealer will accept your used antifreeze. They already have a program in place to recycle their own cooling system sludge. For a small price they'll probably accept your waste.

## Keeping Warm

Before we leave the cooling system let's discuss the heater in your Corvette. It's really in the cooling system family. The heater system is basically a small radiator mounted to the firewall. There's a fan that blows air through the fins of this small radiator, and when the air arrives on the passenger side of the heater core it's been warmed by the heater core and makes your Corvette warm and comfy.

Think of your Corvette's heater system as simply a small auxiliary radiator. That's why you should always turn on the heater if your Corvette ever starts to overheat. The heater may provide just enough additional cooling capacity for you to make it home. It'll get awful hot inside your Corvette on the ride home, but it beats being stranded along the road.

There are really only two things that can go wrong with your heater system. First, the heater core, just like the radiator in the front of your Corvette, can develop a leak.

If you continually find wet carpeting in your Corvette, it's probably from a leaking heater core. If you turn on the defrosters and find a steamy, oily film covering the inside of your windshield, you definitely have a blown-out heater core.

The fix is very easy. Replace the heater core. Don't even consider having it repaired. The price of a new heater core is so low that a repair isn't worth considering.

If your cooling system is so bad that the heater core rusted out, you need to consider what other parts are going to blow up next.

Attaching a new heater core to your old rotted heater hoses is one of the dumber things you could do. Replace these hoses with nice new hoses. Also, check out the radiator; it may be getting ready to follow the heater core to Corvette heaven.

Another problem you may find in your heating system is a failed heater blower motor. Only two things can go wrong here, either the switch goes bad or the motor goes bad. Usually it's the fan motor—if you're lucky.

To test the fan motor, take a pair of jumper wires and put twelve volts of power directly to the heater blower fan. If the fan works you have a switch problem. If the fan doesn't work, you have a broken fan motor.

Heater blower motors are very inexpensive, especially the ones from Asia. If you want to maintain the originality of your Corvette, take the blower motor to any decent electrical shop. It'll cost more to repair the old motor than to buy a new one from Taiwan, but at least you'll be keeping as many original

Project Corvette had a perfectly good blower motor, but no air was getting to the heater vents. It seems several generations of mice had found a home in the heater, and they had moved a great deal of the carpeting to the heater box to make their new home a little more comfortable. This is what you can expect when you leave a Corvette stored in a barn for a decade.

parts as possible in your Corvette. Remember, we don't own Corvettes, we're simply their custodian for a period of time.

## We Don't Need Freon

Before Freon was finally removed from the market, we heard all sorts of stories about it—mainly bad stories. Now, several years later, we've discovered we can simply suck out all the old freon and install new PAG oil and R134.

Most people riding in your passenger seat will not even notice the difference between R12 (also known as Freon) and R134. While there may be a lot of technical answers as to how to deal with the R134 question, the real solution is to simply have your R12 system totally evacuated. You should then have new PAG oil installed and a full charge of R134 installed, assuming everything in your air conditioning system was already in good condition.

# Chapter 24

# Detailing

Washing your Corvette on Saturday morning is not the same as detailing your Corvette. I put washing under the category of routine maintenance. Saturday car washes are simply the first step in a comprehensive Corvette care program.

Washing is the process of removing all the surface dirt and crud. Cleaning your Corvette means returning your Corvette to the way it was when it was new, including the shiny paint, clean carpets, and an engine compartment that will impress the neighbors.

There's a tremendous amount of junk on the market when it comes to car care products. There's even more hype about what all these products can do. Over the past few years I've tried most of these products and settled on two companies that produce products that work—Meguiar's and Zymol.

The biggest factor, however, in a quality detailing job is work. A perfect professional detail for a ma-

jor car show can cost over $2,000, which is one more reason I've never entered a car at Pebble Beach. Remember, though, most of the $2,000 spent at Pebble Beach is for labor. At $50 an hour that's forty hours of hard work. Forty hours of dedication, perseverance, and attention to detail. If it takes a professional forty hours, consider how long it will take you to perform the same tasks. This is obviously serious business.

The first place to start detailing your Corvette is under the hood, because no matter how hard you try, you're going make a mess. Once you're under the hood, blow all the loose particles off the engine. The next step can involve different procedures dependent on the amount of dirt you find on your Bow-tie power.

In some cases you have to resort to engine degreaser or kerosene for the initial cleaning. After a re-

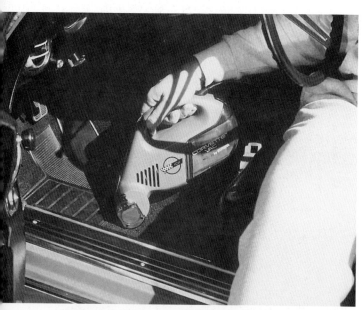

A clean Corvette requires a powerful vacuum cleaner. The real question is: "Will a Corvette Vac beat a Porsche Vac?"

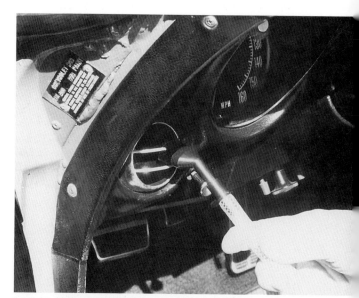

I might make fun of the Corvette Vac, but all its little attachments are very handy. Next time you think you're riding in a carefully detailed Corvette, look at the inside of the air vents. This is the true test of clean.

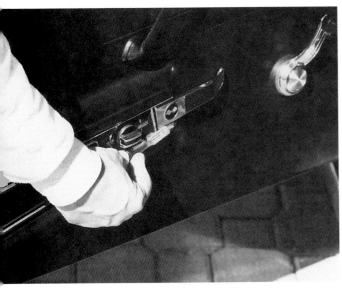

A toothbrush works wonders on the door panel trim. You can use soap and water, or you can just use a stiff bristle brush with no soap.

ally complete detailing effort, you shouldn't have to exercise that sort of cleaning power ever again. You never want to, either. Degreaser is very strong. If a cleaner has enough power to melt caked-on engine grease, you can easily imagine what it does to paint and aluminum.

The best underhood cleaner is actually alloy wheel cleaner. Zymol and P21S are two products I've used over the years, and both are strong enough to remove road dirt and brake dust yet mild enough to not harm the clear coat on most alloy wheels. They work just as well on your engine.

The best technique is to wet the engine compartment with a light mist and then spray with the alloy wheel cleaner. Then, using a soft paintbrush, clean all the little nooks and crannies that exist under your fiberglass hood. A final soft rinse with the hose should take care of all the residue. If you want to dry everything in a hurry, you might use an air hose from your compressor. At this point you should have an engine compartment that would impress most of your friends and neighbors.

The next step, should you decide to take it, is to use Meguiar's #42 Rubber Treatment on all the hoses that run around the engine compartment. This product gives you a nice flat finish on the hoses. There's none of the artificial gloss that comes with products like Armor-All.

## The Outside Gets a Bath

If you don't wash your Corvette at least once a week, you can skip this whole chapter. Washing your Corvette is the first step in a four-part detailing process.

Paintbrushes can do the same things as a toothbrush, except they work better on larger parts. Wrap the metal part of the paintbrush with masking tape. You certainly don't want to scratch the paint while you're trying to improve your Corvette's appearance.

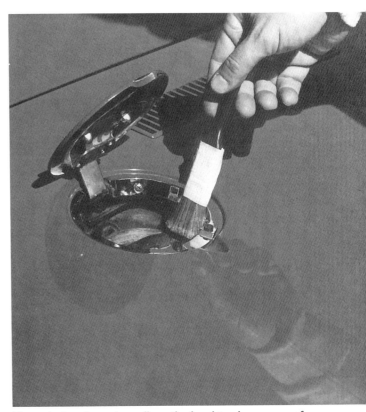

The paintbrush works well on the hard-to-clean areas of your Corvette.

Wax always seems to build up around the emblems, and your normal polishing rag does very little to remove all this wax. Your toothbrush is the secret tool for these areas.

Headlights are too often "out of sight, out of mind." Spend a little time and clean the headlights. Who knows, you might actually drive your Corvette at night.

The washing procedure involves getting rid of all the loose crud resting on the surface. The first step should be a really good pressure rinse with clear water. You want to flush as much debris from the car as possible. If you happen to pick up some sand and dirt in your wash rag later, it can cause some pretty severe damage.

Before you get around to applying soap, take a paint brush and clean all the crevices around the panels and in the grille. Make sure you have plenty of soap suds on the brush when you do this. You're trying to avoid getting anything on the wash rag that could cause paint scratches.

When you get around to applying the actual soap, use a product that's designed for cars. Dish soap is far too strong. You need something that is PH-balanced. Most of us will spend more time getting the surface of our Corvette to look right than we'll spend on our own skin. That's why I have a general rule that if the product label says anything about skin irritation, it certainly won't go on my Corvette. In fact I'm not as careful about my personal soap as I am about my Corvette soap. At this point I've found only two products that I actually trust. First is my old standby Zymol, and secondly, Meguiar's #00 Hi-Tech Wash.

If you aren't careful with bras, they'll flap in the breeze and rub right through your five-figure paint. Your solution for protecting the paint could easily end up doing a lot of damage. Also, on a long drive, road dirt can get up under the bra and scratch your paint. Basically, these protective bras can cause more problems than they eliminate.

Always wash your Corvette from the top down. First, you usually have more dirt on the bottom of the car than on the bottom. Top-down washing means you won't be dragging the dirt from the rocker panels up to the roof, where it can cause serious damage.

Next, clean the wheels and tires. A soft paintbrush works best for the wheels and gets around the trim rings and valve stems better than any rag. A soft scrub brush works wonders on the tires, but always avoid whitewall cleaners. If "prolonged exposure to the skin is harmful," do you really want it on your Corvette?

Once you complete the final washing, and drying with a soft terry towel, start checking the car for road tar and oil stains. There are several products available for cleaning off road tar and oil stains. My favorite is Zymol wax. Zymol wax cuts directly through the road tar. No other wax is as effective. Only kerosene works as well in taking off road tar and oil from a car's finish, but I certainly don't want to use kerosene on a weekly basis.

Next, use a mild abrasive on the surface of the paint. Meguiar's #7 Show Car Glaze is my personal favorite. Polish is designed to put very fine scratches in the surface of the paint. Polish actually creates very fine scratches that reflect light. This reflected light is what gives your Corvette that shine everyone admires. A quality shine is one where all the microscopic scratches are uniform. The goal is to have a consistent finish that shines when light strikes the surface. Contrary to popular opinion, wax does not provide the shine, polish does. That's why most of the pampered show cars are never waxed. Wax is only for protecting the surface, not making it shine.

Today's products are designed to be used in a specific sequence, mainly because the abrasive qualities vary from one product to another. It's always best to use the least abrasive product possible. The more abrasive a product is the quicker it will correct a defect in the surface of the paint but there will be more scratches and swirls that will have to be removed at the next step.

### The Neglected Corvette Surface

For the Corvette surface that's been neglected, although undamaged, it's going to take a lot of work to get it right. The most abrasive techniques are

Everyone makes some sort of vinyl and rubber conditioner. The real secret is finding a product that doesn't leave an artificial coating on the rubber, or vinyl. Some of the products contain too much alcohol, which gives that white finish after a few application. Meguiar's is one of the best products on the market. This is one of the few products that has no side effect.

called for in these cases. It's usually necessary to resort to 2000-grit sandpaper or sanding blocks. You could use 1000- or 1500-grit paper, but the chances of making a mistake are greater. Remember, since you're detailing your own Corvette, the labor is free.

Corvette alloy wheels are clear-coated to protect the shine. A lot of wheel cleaners eat directly through the clear-coat finish and expose the aluminum. Refinishing a wheel is an expensive proposition. P21S is one of the very few wheel cleaners recommended by Porsche and Mercedes, which have the same problem with clear coating. I even use P21S for engine compartment detailing, where it leaves a wonderful finish on the aluminum engine parts.

Detailing your Corvette is something you do for fun—right?

Get a bucket and a little bit of soap, and soak the paper for about ten minutes prior to using it. These fine sandpapers will wear out very quickly, so make sure you purchase enough of them. Also make sure you wash the surface of the car carefully before you start sanding, since any dirt particles can put some pretty impressive scratches in the paint.

When using sandpaper do not use your fingertips, instead wrap the paper around a sponge or semi-rigid sanding block. This technique distributes the downward pressure of your hand over the entire surface of the sanding paper. It also creates a smooth surface that will respond quickly to polishing.

Once you have a consistently smooth surface, return to the normal detail procedure with a fine polish. Most people prefer to keep the strokes parallel to the length of the car. Remember you're trying to create very fine uniform scratches.

## Has My Corvette Been Clear-Coated?

Most new cars have a coat of clear paint applied over the standard color coat. The purpose is to protect the color from the elements and add a high-gloss finish. Clear coating was never used on Corvettes until 1982, but it is showing up on a lot of

The real secret to a quality shine is the polish. Meguiar's #7 is the best hand-applied polish on the market. Polish, not wax, is what gives your Corvette a flawless shine.

Taking care of your Corvette's paint is really a three-part process. First, you need to select a quality soap for washing the car. Do not steal the dish soap from the under the kitchen sink, as this will not only get you in trouble with your wife, but the soap will attack the paint on your Corvette.

Corvettes that never had it originally, including Project Corvette. And if the clear coat is applied properly, no one will ever know it was used.

A recent NCRS national convention was literally overwhelmed with clear-coat paint, despite the fact that it is a violation of NCRS standards and can cost you some serious judging points. Standard procedure for NCRS meets is to simply get a soft white rag and ask the owner to polish the surface. If the color of the paint comes off on the polishing rag, there's no clear coat. If the rag comes off clean, the Corvette has clear-coat paint. I've actually seen owners rub straight through clear coat in an to effort to get full judging points, so be very careful with this technique.

Clear coat is nothing more than a high-tech solution for protecting the colored paint from oxidizing. Actually, it only makes the oxidizing less obvious. Now, the clear coat oxidizes. With today's modern paints you have to protect the clear coat and the color coat from acid rain, bird droppings, and industrial pollution. This is the purpose of wax.

## So What Does Wax Really Do?

Wax is really nothing more than a protective coat applied over a perfect surface. Despite its simple purpose, people disagree about every aspect of wax, except for the fact that a high-quality wax has a high carnauba base. And wax manufacturers guard their wax formulas as though they were military secrets.

The only thing I know about Zymol is that it's some mysterious combination of banana oil, coconut oil, carnauba fat, and other mixed vegetable oils. The end result is one of the best smelling waxes on the market.

One technique that works very well with Zymol is to apply the wax with your bare hand. Simply put some wax in the palm of your hand and spread it around, and you'll feel every single speck of dust on the Corvette's surface. Too often a rag will hold dirt, which can produce scratches. Using your hand eliminates that problem.

The best cloth to use for removing the wax is a cloth baby diaper. Cotton T-shirts will also work well, but you have to make sure you cut all the seams away. The threads can leave some very nasty scratches.

A 1in paintbrush works wonders for getting wax out of the emblems. The tip here is to cut the bristles to about one half the normal length. These stubby bristles can remove even the most stubborn wax particles. Just remember to wrap some tape around the metal part of the brush. You certainly don't want any new scratches at this point.

There's no way to predict how long wax will protect your finish. A good approximation is two to four months, depending on where you park your car, weather conditions, and how often you use a car cover.

If you drive your Corvette, plan on waxing the car at least four times a year, unless you use the Newton technique. Since I hate waxing a car I've developed a new procedure. Every week I polish and wax a different part of the car.

Once a week I clean my Corvette and select a single part of the car to be both polished and waxed. There's a check chart on the garage wall that shows which of the body parts was the last panel to get the treatment. It takes about two months to completely circle the car. The advantage is that you never have to spend half a day waxing, and you get to spend more time driving the car.

## Using Buffing Wheels

Professionals almost always use a buffing machine to polish paint. They have to. The less time they spend, the more money they make. The pros have to detail as many cars as possible each day. They also have a lot of experience with high-speed buffers. The average professional detailer uses a wheel more in one day than you do in the average year. If you're really fanatical you might use a buffing wheel once a month. But, my feeling is that a high-speed buffing wheel is a dangerous tool in the hands of an amateur.

You can do more damage in five minutes with a buffing wheel than a whole flock of pigeons resting on your paint job. The slightest mistake and you'll burn the paint right off the body. At some point you'll probably also rip the radio antenna and windshield wipers right off the car. Then when you're all done you'll have about a million swirls left in the paint that will let every parking lot attendant in town know you screwed up your paint job.

## Cleaning the Interior

The first step in cleaning the interior is to remove all the major dirt with a vacuum cleaner. The vacuum cleaner can be used not only for the carpets, but with a crevice tool you can clean all the dirt out of the seams and corners. One trick is to beat the carpet with your hand as you vacuum. This loosens the dirt and makes it easier for the vacuum cleaner to suck the dirt into the hose.

If you have stains on the carpet, I find that the carpet cleaners sold in the grocery stores for home carpeting work better than all the stuff sold in auto supply stores. They're also a lot cheaper.

The seats are another story. Actually two stories, depending on whether you have vinyl or leather. The vinyl is easy to clean—simply vacuum out all the crevices and clean the vinyl with soap and water. Meguiar's #42 Vinyl works wonders on the seats. With leather seats, vacuum first and then wash with saddle soap, which I've found is still the best cleaner. The next step is the tricky one—applying leather treatment. Avoid Lexol at all costs. For some reason it leaves a sticky film on the leather, and yes, I've read all the directions but still have the same problem.

Zymol leather treatment works better than anything else on the market. It's not cheap, but what Zymol product is? Zymol seems to soak into the leather better than any of the other products. Best of all, it doesn't rub off on your clothes the way Lexol does.

You should use Zymol leather conditioner at least every six months. The problem with leather is that it dries out and the character cracks, or patina begins. In the advanced stages there are big splits in the seats.

Remember you can always expect to pay a lot more to get leather seats upholstered than you pay for vinyl seats. More importantly, it's much more difficult to work with leather than vinyl. So, no matter what Zymol leather conditioner costs, it's still only a fraction of what a new seat is going to cost.

Fortunately everything else in the interior is

vinyl. The top of the dash is the most abused area in the Corvette interior. Here you have sun damage of the first order. The little carpeting covers that go over the dash are a good idea. They're called dash mats, and you can even get them with an embroidered Corvette logo, just in case you forget what sort of car you're driving. They're real ugly but, nonetheless, a good idea.

One last idea is to use a car cover to make sure none of the dreaded dust rests on your Corvette. Owning what may well be the world's largest collection of car covers, I feel more than qualified to address this issue.

The lightweight cotton covers are wonderful because they're lightweight and can be taken on and off your Corvette with very little effort. They can also be thrown in the home washer/dryer combination without a lot of trouble.

The next step up is the Evolution 4 material. These covers are big and heavy, but they work. If you take a lot of weekend trips they're great for outdoor parking situations. They'll even keep your car dry during a light rain. The only problem then will be what to do with a wet car cover on the drive home.

The advantage of the Evolution 4 for inside storage is that it'll protect your paint from minor scratches. The material is quilted heavily enough that should the garden rake have an encounter with your Corvette, the paint might survive.

The problem with the Evolution 4 cover is that you may have to take it to the laundromat for cleaning. They take up a lot of space in the washing machine and take forever to dry.

The most important place to keep your car covered is the garage. This sounds a little strange, but with a cover over it, your Corvette is ready to go at any time. The dust in the ordinary garage is phenomenal. Leave an uncovered Corvette in the average suburban garage and you'll find you have to wash the car every time you want to go for a drive.

Well, if you've done everything right so far, you're all set to enjoy your Corvette. It may have cost you a lot more than you ever imagined, but you'll still enjoy the car. Besides, Visa and MasterCard have raised your credit limit several times over the course of your personal Corvette adventure. The purveyors of plastic simply love Corvette projects.

Zymol is my favorite wax because it's easily applied with my bare hand. If you apply wax with your bare hand, instead of an applicator rag, you'll locate every flaw and blemish in your car.

Remember in the beginning I said the best Corvette was the one needing the least amount of work? Remember I said the cheapest Corvette would probably have the highest initial price? Now are you ready to believe me?

At any rate, the only thing left now is to take care of your Corvette. Maintain what you've created. Oh, and don't forget to drive it either. The people who put these cars away in hermetically sealed trailers are really missing all the fun. Or, perhaps, a very twisted notion of fun.

Detailing the Corvette is enjoyable. Driving the car is fun. That is what the dream is all about. Go ahead and drive your Corvette to work, then take an extra hour coming home the long way. When you reach the point where that's no longer fun, sell the car to someone who still believes in the dream. Corvettes are really all about mountain roads, the smell of misused tires and clutches, and more power than you're really comfortable driving.

# Color Combinations

## 1968

| Interior Color | Black | Red | Med Blue | Dark Blue | Dark Orange | Tobacco | Gunmetal |
|---|---|---|---|---|---|---|---|
| Vinyl | STD | 407 | 414 | 411 | 425 | 435 | 442 |
| Leather | 402 | 408 | 415 | n/a | 426 | 436 | n/a |

| Code | Color | Black | Red | Med Blue | Dark Blue | Dark Orange | Tobacco | Gunmetal |
|---|---|---|---|---|---|---|---|---|
| 900 | Tuxedo Black | x | x | x | x | x | x | x |
| 972 | Polar White | x | x | x | x | x | x | x |
| 974 | Rally Red | x | x | | | | | |
| 976 | LeMans Blue | x | | x | x | | | |
| 978 | International Blue | x | | x | x | | | |
| 983 | British Green | x | | | | | | |
| 984 | Safari Yellow | x | | | | | | |
| 986 | Silverstone Silver | x | | | | | | x |
| 988 | Cordovan Maroon | x | | | | | | |
| 992 | Corvette Bronze | x | | | | x | x | |

**Convertible Top:** Black (Standard)
White (RPO)
Sandalwood (RPO)

**Vinyl Roof:** Black Only (RPO CO8)

## 1969

| Interior Color | Black | Red | Bright Blue | Green | Saddle | Gunmetal |
|---|---|---|---|---|---|---|
| Vinyl | STD | 407 | 411 | 427 | 420 | 416 |
| Leather | 402 | 408 | 412 | 428 | 421 | 416 |

| Code | Color | Black | Red | Bright Blue | Green | Saddle | Gunmetal |
|---|---|---|---|---|---|---|---|
| 900 | Tuxedo Black | x | x | x | x | x | x |
| 972 | Can-Am White | x | x | x | x | x | x |
| 974 | Monza Red | x | x | | | x | |
| 976 | LeMans Blue | x | | x | | | |
| 980 | Riverside Gold | x | | | | x | |
| 983 | Fathom Green | x | | | x | x | |
| 984 | Daytona Yellow | x | | | | | |
| 986 | Cortez Silver | x | x | x | x | x | x |
| 988 | Burgandy | x | | | | x | |
| 990 | Monaco Orange | x | | | | | |

**Convertible Top:** Black (Standard)
White (RPO)
Sandalwood (RPO)

**Vinyl Roof:** Black Only (RPO CO8)

**1970**

| Interior Color | Black | Saddle | Red | Blue | Green | Brown |
|---|---|---|---|---|---|---|
| Vinyl | 400 | 418 | 407 | 411 | 422 | 414 |
| Deluxe* | 403 | 424 | — | — | — | — |

| Code | Color | Black | Saddle | Red | Blue | Green | Brown |
|---|---|---|---|---|---|---|---|
| 972 | Classic White | x | x | x | x | x | x |
| 974 | Monza Red | x | x | x | | | x |
| 975 | Marlboro Maroon | x | x | | | | x |
| 976 | Mulsanne Blue | x | | | x | | |
| 979 | Bridgehampton Blue | x | | | x | | |
| 982 | Donnybrooke Green | x | x | | | x | x |
| 984 | Daytona Yellow | x | | | | x | |
| 986 | Cortez Silver | x | x | x | x | x | x |
| 981 | Ontario Orange | x | x | | | | |
| 992 | Laguna Gray | x | x | x | x | x | x |
| 993 | Corvette Bronze | x | | | | | |

**Convertible Top:** Black (Standard)
White (RPO)
Sandalwood (RPO)

**Vinyl Roof:** Black Only (RPO CO8)

*The Deluxe Interior included leather seat trim, special cut pile carpeting on the floor and lower door side wall, wood grain insert on the floor console, and a wood grain insert on the door panels.

**1971**

| Interior Color | Black | Saddle | Red | Dark Blue | Green |
|---|---|---|---|---|---|
| Vinyl | 400 | 417 | 407 | 412 | 423 |
| Deluxe* | 403 | 420 | — | — | — |

| Code | Color | Black | Saddle | Red | Dark Blue | Green |
|---|---|---|---|---|---|---|
| 905 | Nevada Silver | x | | x | x | x |
| 912 | Sunflower Yellow | x | x | | | x |
| 972 | Classic White | x | x | x | x | x |
| 973 | Mille Miglia Red | x | | x | | |
| 976 | Mulsanne Blue | x | | | x | |
| 979 | Bridgehampton Blue | x | | | x | |
| 983 | Brands Hatch Green | x | | | | x |
| 987 | Ontario Orange | x | x | | | x |
| 988 | Steel Cities Gray | x | x | | | |
| 989 | Warbonnet Yellow | x | x | | | x |

**Convertible Top:** Black or White (available with any exterior color)

**Vinyl Roof:** Black only

*The Deluxe Interior included leather seat trim, special cut pile carpeting on the floor and lower door side wall, wood grain insert on the floor console, and a wood grain insert on the door panels.

**1972**

| Interior Color | Black | Saddle | Red | Blue |
|---|---|---|---|---|
| Vinyl | 400 | 417 | 407 | 412 |
| Deluxe* | 404 | 421 | — | — |

| Code | Color | Black | Saddle | Red | Blue |
|---|---|---|---|---|---|
| 912 | Sunflower Yellow | x | x | | |
| 924 | Pewter Silver | x | x | x | x |
| 945 | Bryar Blue | x | | | |
| 946 | Elkhart Green | x | x | | |
| 972 | Classic White | x | x | x | x |
| 973 | Mille Miglia Red | x | x | x | |
| 979 | Targa Blue | x | | | x |
| 987 | Ontario Orange | x | x | | |
| 988 | Steel Cities Gray | x | x | x | |
| 989 | Warbonnet Yellow | x | x | | |

**Convertible Top:**  Black or White (Available with any exterior color)

**Vinyl Roof:**  Black Only

*The Deluxe Interior included leather seat trim, special cut pile carpeting on the floor and lower door side wall, wood grain insert on the floor console, and a wood grain insert on the door panels. The seat and shoulder belts matched the interior colors ex- cepte for the blue interior. The seat belts were a darker shade of blue.

**1973**

| Interior Color | Black | Midnight Blue | Medium Saddle | Dark Saddle | Dark Red |
|---|---|---|---|---|---|
| Vinyl | 400 | 413 | 415 | 418 | 425 |
| Custom* | 404 | — | 416 | 422 | — |

| Code | Color | Black | Midnight Blue | Medium Saddle | Dark Saddle | Dark Red |
|---|---|---|---|---|---|---|
| 910 | Classic White | x | x | x | x | x |
| 914 | Silver Metallic | x | x | x | x | x |
| 922 | Medium Blue Metallic | x | x | x | | |
| 927 | Corvette Dark Blue Metallic | x | x | x | | x |
| 945 | Corvette Blue-Green Metallic | x | | x | x | x |
| 947 | Elkhart Green | x | | x | | |
| 952 | Yellow | x | x | | x | |
| 953 | Yellow Metallic | x | x | | | |
| 976 | Mille Miglia Red | x | x | x | x | x |
| 980 | Corvette Orange Metallic | x | | x | | |

**Convertible Top:**  Black (Standard)
White (RPO)

**Vinyl Roof:**  Black Only

*The Custom Interior included leather seat trim, special cut-pile carpeting on the floor and lower door side wall, wood grain in- sert on the floor console, and a wood grain insert on the door panels.

# 1974

| Interior Color | Black | Silver | Neutral | Dark Blue | Saddle | Dark Red |
|---|---|---|---|---|---|---|
| Vinyl | 400 | 406 | 408 | 413 | 415 | 425 |
| **Custom*** | 404 | 407 | — | — | 416 | — |

| Code | Color | Black | Silver | Neutral | Dark Blue | Saddle | Dark Red |
|---|---|---|---|---|---|---|---|
| 910 | Classic White | x | x | x | x | x | x |
| 914 | Silver Mist | x | x | x | x | x | x |
| 917 | Gray | x | x | x | x | x | x |
| 922 | Corvette Med. Blue | x | x | | x | | |
| 948 | Dark Green | x | x | x | | x | |
| 956 | Bright Yellow | x | x | x | | x | |
| 968 | Dark Brown | x | x | x | | x | |
| 974 | Medium Red | x | x | x | | x | x |
| 976 | Mille Miglia Red | x | x | x | | x | x |
| 980 | Orange | x | x | x | | x | |

*The Custom Interior included leather seat trim, special cut-pile carpeting on the floor and lower door side wall, wood grain insert on the floor console, and a wood grain insert on the door panels.

# 1975

| Interior Color | Black | Silver | Dark Blue | Neutral | Medium Saddle | Dark Red |
|---|---|---|---|---|---|---|
| Vinyl | 19V | 14V | 26V | 60V | 65V | 73V |
| **Custom*** | 192 | 142 | 262 | — | 652 | 732 |

| Code | Color | Black | Silver | Dark Blue | Neutral | Medium Saddle | Dark Red |
|---|---|---|---|---|---|---|---|
| 10 | Classic White | x | x | x | x | x | x |
| 13 | Silver | x | x | x | | x | x |
| 22 | Bright Blue | x | x | x | | | |
| 27 | Steel Blue | x | x | x | | | |
| 42 | Bright Green | x | x | | x | x | |
| 56 | Bright Yellow | x | | | x | x | |
| 67 | Medium Saddle | x | | | x | x | |
| 70 | Orange Flame | x | | | x | x | |
| 74 | Dark Red | x | x | | x | x | x |
| 76 | Mille Miglia Red | x | x | | x | x | x |

*The Custom Interior included leather seat trim, special cut-pile carpeting on the floor and lower door side wall, wood grain insert on the floor console, and a wood grain insert on the door panels.

## 1976

| Interior Color | White | Smoke-Gray | Black | Blue-Green | Light Buckskin | Dark Brown | Dark Firethorn |
|---|---|---|---|---|---|---|---|
| Vinyl | 15V | | 19V | 71V | 64V | | 71V |
| Leather | 112 | 152 | 192 | 322 | 642 | 692 | 712 |

| Code | Color | White | Smoke-Gray | Black | Blue-Green | Light Buckskin | Dark Brown | Dark Firethorn |
|---|---|---|---|---|---|---|---|---|
| 10 | Classic White | x | x | x | x | x | x | x |
| 13 | Silver | x | x | x | x | x | x | x |
| 22 | Bright Blue | x | x | x | | | | |
| 33 | Dark Green | x | x | x | x | x | | |
| 37 | Mahogany | x | x | x | | x | | x |
| 56 | Bright Yellow | | | | | | x | |
| 64 | Buckskin | x | | x | | x | x | x |
| 69 | Dark Brown | x | | x | | x | x | x |
| 70 | Orange Flame | | | x | | x | x | |
| 72 | Red | x | x | x | | x | | x |

## 1977

| Interior Color | Black | Red | Blue | Buckskin | Brown | Smoked Grey | White |
|---|---|---|---|---|---|---|---|
| Cloth | 19C | 72C | 27C | 64C | 69C | 15C | — |
| Leather* | 192 | 722 | 272 | 642 | 692 | 152 | 112 |

| Code | Color | Black | Red | Blue | Buckskin | Brown | Smoked Grey | White |
|---|---|---|---|---|---|---|---|---|
| 10 | Classic White | x | x | x | x | x | x | x |
| 13 | Silver | x | x | x | x | | x | x |
| 19 | Black | x | x | | x | | x | x |
| 26 | Corvette Light Blue | x | | | | | x | x |
| 28 | Corvette Dark Blue | x | | x | x | | x | x |
| 41 | Corvette Chartreuse | x | | | | | | x |
| 52 | Corvette Yellow | x | | | | x | | |
| 56 | Bright Yellow | x | | | | x | | |
| 66 | Corvette Orange | x | | | x | x | | |
| 72 | Medium Red | x | x | | x | | x | x |
| 80 | Corvette Tan | x | x | | x | x | | x |
| 83 | Corvette Dark Red | x | | | x | | x | |

*Leather seats were standard for the first time in 1977. The cloth-leather combination was offered as an option at no additional cost.

**1978**

| Interior Color | Black | Red | Dark Blue | Dark Brown | Light Beige | Silver* | Mahogany | Oyster |
|---|---|---|---|---|---|---|---|---|
| Cloth | 19C | 72C | 29C | 69C | 59C | 15C | 76C | 12C |
| Leather | 192 | 722 | 929 | 692 | 592 | 152 | 722 | 122 |

| Code | Color | Black | Red | Dark Blue | Dark Brown | Light Beige | Silver* | Mahogany | Oyster |
|---|---|---|---|---|---|---|---|---|---|
| 10 | Classic White | x | x | x | x | x | | x | x |
| 13 | Silver | x | x | x | | | | x | |
| 13/07 | Silver Anniversay | x | x | | | | | | x |
| 19 | Black | x | x | | | x | | x | x |
| 26 | Corvette Light Blue | | | x | | | | | |
| 52 | Corvette Yellow | x | | | x | | | | x |
| 59 | Corvette Light Beige | x | | x | x | | | x | |
| 72 | Corvette Red | x | x | | | x | | | x |
| 82 | Corvette Mahogany | x | | | x | x | | x | x |
| 83 | Corvette Dark Blue | | | x | | x | | | x |
| 89 | Corvette Dark Brown | | | | x | x | | | x |

* Available with RP01YZ87 (Pace Car) only.

**1979**

| Interior Color | Oyster | Black | Dark Blue | Dark Green | Light Beige | Red |
|---|---|---|---|---|---|---|
| Cloth | 12C | - | 29C | 49C | 59C | - |
| Leather | 122 | 192 | 292 | 492 | 592 | 722 |

| Code | Color | Oyster | Black | Dark Blue | Dark Green | Light Beige | Red |
|---|---|---|---|---|---|---|---|
| 10 | Classic White | x | x | x | x | x | x |
| 13 | Silver | x | x | x | x | | x |
| 19 | Black | x | x | | | x | x |
| 28 | Corvette Light Blue | x | x | x | | | |
| 52 | Corvette Yellow | x | x | | | x | |
| 58 | Corvette Dark Green | x | x | | x | x | |
| 59 | Corvette Light Beige | | x | | x | x | x |
| 72 | Corvette Red | x | x | | | x | x |
| 82 | Corvette Dark Brown | x | x | | | x | |
| 83 | Corvette Dark Blue | x | x | x | | x | x |

**1980**

| Interior Color | Black | Oyster White | Midnight Blue | Dark* Green | Doeskin | Red | Dark Claret |
|---|---|---|---|---|---|---|---|
| Cloth | 12C | 29C | 49 | NA | 79C | | |
| Leather | 192 | 122 | 292 | 492 | 592 | 722 | 792 |

| Code | Color | Black | Oyster White | Midnight Blue | Dark* Green | Doeskin | Red | Dark Claret |
|---|---|---|---|---|---|---|---|---|
| 10 | Classic White | x | x | x | | x | x | x |
| 13 | Silver | x | x | x | | | x | x |
| 19 | Black | x | x | x | | x | x | |
| 28 | Dark Blue | x | x | x | | x | x | |
| 47 | Dark Brown | x | x | | | x | | |
| 52 | Yellow | x | x | | | | | |
| 58 | Dark Green | x | x | | | x | | |
| 59 | Frost Beige | x | | x | | x | x | x |
| 76 | Dark Claret | x | x | | | x | | x |
| 83 | Red | x | x | | | x | | |

* Dark Green was available—just never used.

## 1981

| Interior Color | Dark | Dark Blue | Camel | Med. Red | Dark Red | Silver Gray |
|---|---|---|---|---|---|---|
| Cloth | 19C | 29C | 64C | 67C | | |
| Leather | 192 | 292 | 642 | 752 | 672 | 152 |

| Code | Color | Dark | Dark Blue | Camel | Med. Red | Dark Red | Silver Gray |
|---|---|---|---|---|---|---|---|
| 06 | Mahogany Metallic | | | x | | x | |
| 10 | White | x | x | x | x | x | x |
| 13 | Silver Metallic | x | x | | x | | x |
| 19 | Black | x | | x | x | | x |
| 24 | Bright Blue Metallic | x | x | x | | | |
| 28 | Dark Blue Metallic | | x | x | | | x |
| 52 | Yellow | x | | x | | | |
| 59 | Frost Beige | | | x | x | x | |
| 75 | Spectra Red | x | | x | | | x |
| 79 | Maroon Metallic | x | | x | | | x |
| 84 | Charcoal Metallic | x | | x | | | x |
| 33/38 | Silver/Dark Blue | | x | | | | x |
| 33/39 | Silver/Charcoal | x | | | | | x |
| 50/74 | Beige/Dark Bronze | | | x | | | |
| 80/98 | Autumn/Dark Claret | | | | | x | x |

## 1982

| Interior Color | Charcoal | Silver Gray | Dark Blue | Silver Green | Silver Beige | Camel | Dark Red |
|---|---|---|---|---|---|---|---|
| Cloth | - | 13C | 22C | - | - | 64C | 74C |
| Leather | 182 | 132 | 222 | 402 | 592 | 642 | 742 |

| Code | Color | Charcoal | Silver Gray | Dark Blue | Silver Green | Silver Beige | Camel | Dark Red |
|---|---|---|---|---|---|---|---|---|
| 10 | White | x | x | x | x | | x | x |
| 13 | Silver | x | x | x | x | | x | x |
| 19 | Black | x | x | | x | | x | x |
| 24 | Silver Blue | x | x | | | | | |
| 26 | Dark Blue | | x | x | | | x | |
| 31 | Bright Blue | x | x | x | | | x | |
| 39 | Charcoal | x | x | | | | | x |
| 40 | Silver Green | x | | | x | | | |
| 56 | Gold | x | | | | | x | |
| 59 | Silver Beige | | | | | x | | |
| 70 | Red | x | x | | | | x | x |
| 99 | Dark Claret | | x | | | | x | x |
| 10/13 | White/Silver | x | x | | | | | |
| 13/39 | Silver/Charcoal | x | x | | | | | x |
| 13/99 | Silver/Dark Claret | | x | | | | | x |
| 24/26 | Silver Blue/Dark Blue | | x | x | | | | |

# Options List

## 1968 Corvette Options

| RPO # | DESCRIPTION | QTY. SOLD | PRICE |
|---|---|---|---|
| — | Genuine Leather Seats | 2,429 | $79.00 |
| A01 | Tinted Glass, All Windows | 17,635 | 15.00 |
| A02 | Tinted Glass, W/S Only | 5,509 | 10.55 |
| A31 | Power Windows | 7,065 | 57.95 |
| A82 | Headrests | 3,197 | 42.15 |
| A85 | Shoulder Belts (Std./Cpe) | 350 | 26.35 |
| C07 | Hardtop | 8,735 | 231.75 |
| C08 | Vinyl Covering for Hrdtp | 3,050 | 52.70 |
| C50 | Rear Window Defroster | 693 | 31.60 |
| C60 | Air Conditioning | 5,664 | 412.90 |
| F41 | Special Front and Rear Susp | 1,758 | 36.90 |
| G81 | Positraction (All Ratios) | 27,008 | 46.35 |
| J50 | Power Brakes | 9,559 | 42.15 |
| J56 | Special Heavy Duty Brakes | 81 | 384.45 |
| K66 | Transistor Ignition System. | 5,457 | 73.75 |
| L36 | 427ci, 390bhp Engine | 7,717 | 200.15 |
| L68 | 427ci, 400bhp Engine | 1,932 | 305.50 |
| L71 | 427ci, 435bhp Engine | 2,898 | 437.10 |
| L79 | 327ci, 350bhp Engine | 9,440 | 105.35 |
| L88 | 427ci, 430bhp Engine | 80 | 947.90 |
| L89 | Alum. Heads with L71 | 641 | 805.75 |
| M20 | 4-Spd Man. Trans | 10,760 | 184.35 |
| M21 | 4-Spd Man. Trans (close ratio) | 12,337 | 184.35 |
| M22 | 4-Spd Man. Trans (c.r. h.d.) | 80 | 263.30 |
| M40 | Turbo Automatic Trans | 5,063 | 226.45 |
| N11 | Off Road Exhaust System | 4,695 | 36.90 |
| N36 | Telescopic Steering Column. | 6,477 | 42.15 |
| N40 | Power Steering | 12,364 | 94.80 |
| P01 | Bright Metal Wheel Covers | 8,971 | 57.95 |
| PT6 | Red Stripe Tires (F70x15) | 11,686 | 31.30 |
| PT7 | White Stripe Tires (F70x15) | 9,692 | 31.30 |
| UA6 | Alarm System | 388 | 26.35 |
| U15 | Speed Warning Indicator | 3,453 | 10.55 |
| U69 | AM-FM Radio | 24,609 | 172.75 |
| U79 | AM-FM Radio (stereo) | 3,311 | 278.10 |

## 1969 Corvette Options

| RPO # | DESCRIPTION | QTY. SOLD | PRICE |
|---|---|---|---|
| — | Genuine Leather Seats | 3,729 | $79.00 |
| A01 | Tinted Glass, All Windows | 31,270 | 16.90 |
| A31 | Power Windows | 9,816 | 63.20 |
| A82 | Headrests | 38,762 | 17.95 |
| A85 | Shoulder Belts (Std./Cpe) | 600 | 42.15 |
| C07 | Hardtop | 7,878 | 252.80 |
| C08 | Vinyl Covering for Hrdtp | 3,266 | 57.95 |
| C50 | Rear Window Defroster | 2,485 | 32.65 |
| C60 | Air Conditioning | 11,859 | 428.70 |
| F41 | Special Frt. and Rear Susp | 1,661 | 36.90 |
| G81 | Positraction (All Ratios) | 36,965 | 46.35 |
| J50 | Power Brakes | 16,876 | 42.15 |
| J56 | Special Heavy Duty Brakes | 115 | 384.45 |
| K50 | Engine Block Heater | 824 | 10.55 |
| K66 | Transistor Ignition System | 5,702 | 81.10 |
| L36 | 427ci, 390bhp Engine | 10,531 | 221.15 |
| L68 | 427ci, 400bhp Engine | 2,072 | 326.55 |
| L71 | 427ci, 435bhp Engine | 2,722 | 437.10 |
| L88 | 427ci, 430bhp Engine | 116 | 1,032.15 |
| L89 | Alum. Heads with L71 | 390 | 832.05 |
| L46 | 350ci, 350bhp Engine | 12,846 | 131.65 |
| MA6 | Heavy Duty Clutch | 102 | 79.00 |
| M20 | 4-Spd Man. Trans | 16,507 | 184.80 |
| M21 | 4-Spd Man. Trans (close ratio) | 13,741 | 184.80 |
| M22 | 4-Spd Man. Trans (c.r. h.d.) | 101 | 290.40 |
| M40 | Turbo Automatic Trans | 8,161 | 221.80 |
| N14 | Side Mount Exhaust System | 4,355 | 147.45 |
| N37 | Telescopic Steering Column | 10,325 | 84.30 |
| N40 | Power Steering | 22,866 | 105.35 |
| PO2 | Bright Metal Wheel Covers | 8,073 | 57.95 |
| PT6 | Red Stripe Tires (F70x15) | 5,210 | 31.30 |
| PT7 | White Stripe Tires (F70x15) | 21,379 | 31.30 |
| PU7 | White Letter Tires (F70x15) | 2,398 | 33.15 |
| TJ2 | Front Fender Louver Trim | 11,962 | 21.10 |
| UA6 | Alarm System | 12,436 | 26.35 |
| U15 | Speed Warning Indicator | 3,561 | 111.60 |
| U69 | AM-FM Radio | 33,871 | 172.75 |
| U79 | AM-FM Radio (stereo) | 4,114 | 278.10 |
| ZL1 | Special Alum. Block L88 | 2 | 4,718.35 |

## 1970 Corvette Options

| RPO # | DESCRIPTION | QTY. SOLD | PRICE |
|---|---|---|---|
| — | Custom Interior Trim | 3,191 | $158.00 |
| A31 | Power Windows | 4,813 | 63.20 |
| A85 | Shoulder Belts (Std./Cpe) | 475 | 42.15 |
| C07 | Hardtop | 2,556 | 273.85 |
| C08 | Vinyl Covering for Hardtop | 832 | 63.20 |
| C50 | Rear Window Defroster. | 1,281 | 36.90 |
| C60 | Air Conditioning | 6,659 | 447.65 |
| G81 | Optional Rear Axle Ratio | 2,862 | 12.65 |
| J50 | Power Brakes | 16,876 | 42.15 |
| LS5 | 454ci, 390bhp Engine | 4,473 | 289.65 |
| L46 | 350ci, 350bhp Engine | 4,910 | 158.00 |
| LT1 | 350ci, 370bhp engine | 1,287 | 447.60 |
| M21 | 4-Spd Man. Trans (close ratio) | 4,383 | 0.00 |
| M22 | 4-Spd Man. Trans (c.r. h.d.) | 25 | 95.00 |
| M40 | Turbo Automatic Transmission | 5,102 | 0.00 |
| NA9 | California Emissions | 1,758 | 39.90 |
| N37 | Telescopic Steering Column | 5,803 | 84.30 |
| N40 | Power Steering | 11,907 | 105.35 |

| RPO # | DESCRIPTION | QTY. SOLD | PRICE |
|---|---|---|---|
| PO2 | Deluxe Wheel Covers | 3,467 | 57.95 |
| PT7 | White Stripe Tires (F70x15) | 6,589 | 31.30 |
| PU7 | White Letter Tires (F70x15) | 7,985 | 33.15 |
| TS6 | Heavy Duty Battery (std/LS5) | 165 | 15.80 |
| UA6 | Alarm System | 6,727 | 31.60 |
| U69 | AM-FM Radio | 14,529 | 172.75 |
| U79 | AM-FM Radio (stereo) | 2,462 | 278.10 |
| ZR1 | Special Purpose Engine Pkg | 25 | 968.95 |

## 1971 Corvette Options

| RPO # | DESCRIPTION | QTY. SOLD | PRICE |
|---|---|---|---|
| — | Custom Interior Trim | 2,602 | $158.00 |
| A31 | Power Windows | 6,192 | 79.00 |
| A85 | Shoulder Belts (Std./Cpe) | 677 | 42.00 |
| CO7 | Hardtop | 2,619 | 274.00 |
| CO8 | Vinyl Covering for Hrdtp | 832 | 63.00 |
| C50 | Rear Window Defroster | 1,598 | 42.00 |
| C60 | Air Conditioning | 11,481 | 459.00 |
| G81 | Optional Rear Axle Ratio | 2,395 | 13.00 |
| J50 | Power Brakes | 13,558 | 47.00 |
| LS5 | 454ci, 390bhp Engine | 5,097 | 295.00 |
| LS6 | 454ci, 425bhp Engine | 188 | 1,221.00 |
| LT1 | 350ci, 330bhp engine | 1,949 | 483.00 |
| M21 | 4-Spd Man. Trans (close ratio) | 2,387 | 0.00 |
| M22 | 4-Spd Man. Trans (c.r. h.d.) | 130 | 100.00 |
| M40 | Turbo Automatic Trans | 10,060 | 0.00 |
| N37 | Telescopic Steering Column | 8,130 | 84.30 |
| N40 | Power Steering | 17,904 | 115.90 |
| PO2 | Deluxe Wheel Covers | 3,007 | 63.00 |
| PT7 | White Stripe Tires (F70x15) | 6,711 | 28.00 |
| PU7 | White Letter Tires (F70x15) | 12,449 | 42.00 |
| TS6 | Heavy Duty Battery (std/LS5/LS6) | 1,455 | 15.80 |
| UA6 | Alarm System | 8,501 | 31.60 |
| U69 | AM-FM Radio | 18,078 | 178.00 |
| U79 | AM-FM Radio (stereo) | 3,431 | 283.00 |
| ZR1 | Special Purpose LT1 Engine Pkg | 8 | 1,010.00 |
| ZR2 | Special Purpose LS6 Engine Pkg | 12 | 1,747.00 |

## 1972 Corvette Options

| RPO # | DESCRIPTION | QTY. SOLD | PRICE |
|---|---|---|---|
| — | Custom Interior Trim | 8,709 | $158.00 |
| AV3 | Three Point Seat Belts | 17,693 | ——— |
| A31 | Power Windows | 9,495 | 85.35 |
| A85 | Shoulder Belts (Std./Cpe) | 749 | 42.15 |
| CO7 | Hardtop | 2,646 | 273.85 |
| CO8 | Vinyl Covering for Hrdtp | 811 | 158.00 |
| C50 | Rear Window Defroster | 2,221 | 42.15 |
| C60 | Air Conditioning | 17,011 | 464.50 |
| G81 | Optional Rear Axle Ratio | 1,986 | 12.65 |
| J50 | Power Brakes | 18,770 | 47.40 |
| K19 | Air Injection Reactor | 3,912 | ——— |
| LS5 | 454ci, 270bhp Engine | 3,913 | 294.90 |
| LT1 | 350ci, 255bhp engine | 1,741 | 483.45 |
| M21 | 4-Spd Man. Trans (close ratio) | 1,638 | 0.00 |
| M40 | Turbo Automatic Trans | 14,543 | 0.00 |
| N37 | Telescopic Steering Column | 12,992 | 84.30 |
| N40 | Power Steering | 23,794 | 115.90 |
| PO2 | Deluxe Wheel Covers | 3,593 | 63.20 |

| RPO # | DESCRIPTION | QTY. SOLD | PRICE |
|---|---|---|---|
| PT7 | White Stripe Tires (F70x15) | 6,666 | 30.35 |
| PU7 | White Letter Tires (F70x15) | 16,623 | 42.65 |
| TS6 | Heavy Duty Bat. (std/LS5/LS6) | 2,969 | 15.80 |
| U69 | AM-FM Radio | 19,480 | 178.00 |
| U79 | AM-FM Radio (stereo) | 7,189 | 283.35 |
| YF5 | California Emission Test | 1,967 | 15.80 |
| ZR1 | Special Purpose LT1 Engine Pkg | 20 | 1,010.05 |

## 1973 Corvette Options

| RPO # | DESCRIPTION | QTY. SOLD | PRICE |
|---|---|---|---|
| — | Custom Interior Trim | 13,434 | $154.00 |
| A31 | Power Windows | 14,024 | 83.00 |
| A85 | Shoulder Belts (Std./Cpe) | 788 | 41.00 |
| CO7 | Hardtop | 1,328 | 267.00 |
| CO8 | Vinyl Covering for Hrdtp | 323 | 62.00 |
| C50 | Rear Window Defroster | 4,412 | 41.00 |
| C60 | Air Conditioning | 21,578 | 452.00 |
| G81 | Optional Rear Axle Ratio | 1,791 | 12.00 |
| J50 | Power Brakes | 24,168 | 46.00 |
| LS4 | 454ci, 275bhp Engine | 4,412 | 250.00 |
| L82 | 350ci, 250bhp engine | 5,710 | 299.00 |
| M21 | 4-Spd Man. Trans (close ratio) | 3,704 | 0.00 |
| M40 | Turbo Automatic Trans | 17,927 | 0.00 |
| N37 | Telescopic Steering Column | 17,949 | 82.00 |
| N40 | Power Steering | 27,872 | 113.00 |
| PO2 | Deluxe Wheel Covers | 1,739 | 62.00 |
| PT7 | White Stripe Tires (GR70x15) | 19,903 | 32.00 |
| PU7 | White Letter Tires (GR70x15) | 4,541 | 45.00 |
| T60 | Heavy Duty Bat. (std/LS4) | 4,912 | 15.00 |
| U79 | AM-FM Radio (stereo) | 12,482 | 273.00 |
| UF1 | Map Light (on rearview mirror) | 8,186 | 5.00 |
| YF5 | California Emission Test | 1,967 | 15.00 |
| YJ8 | Cast Aluminum Wheels (4) | 4 | 175.00 |
| Z07 | Off Road Suspension/Brake Pkg | 45 | 369.00 |

## 1974 Corvette Options

| RPO # | DESCRIPTION | QTY. SOLD | PRICE |
|---|---|---|---|
| — | Custom Interior Trim | 19,959 | $154.00 |
| A31 | Power Windows | 23,940 | 86.00 |
| A85 | Shoulder Belts (Std./Cpe) | 618 | 41.00 |
| CO7 | Hardtop | 2,612 | 267.00 |
| CO8 | Vinyl Covering for Hrdtp | 367 | 329.00 |
| C50 | Rear Window Defroster | 9,322 | 43.00 |
| C60 | Air Conditioning | 29,397 | 467.00 |
| FE7 | Gymkhana Suspension | 1,905 | 7.00 |
| — | Optional Rear Axle Ratio | 1,219 | 12.00 |
| J50 | Power Brakes | 33,306 | 49.00 |
| LS4 | 454ci, 270bhp Engine | 3,494 | 250.00 |
| L82 | 350ci, 250bhp engine | 6,690 | 299.00 |
| M21 | 4-Spd Man. Trans (close ratio) | 3,494 | 0.00 |
| M40 | Turbo Automatic Trans | 25,146 | 0.00 |
| N37 | Telescopic Steering Column | 27,700 | 82.00 |
| N41 | Power Steering | 35,944 | 117.00 |
| QRM | White Striped Tires (GR70x15) | 9,140 | 32.00 |
| QRZ | White Letter Tires (GR70x15) | 24,102 | 45.00 |
| UO5 | Dual Horns | 5,258 | 4.00 |
| U58 | AM-FM Radio (stereo) | 19,581 | 276.00 |
| U69 | AM-FM Radio | 17,374 | 173.00 |

| RPO # | DESCRIPTION | QTY. SOLD | PRICE |
|---|---|---|---|
| UA1 | Heavy Duty Bat. (std/LS4) | 9,169 | 15.00 |
| UF1 | Map Light (on rearview mirror) | 16,101 | 5.00 |
| YF5 | California Emission Test | — | 20.00 |
| Z07 | Off Road Suspension/Brake Pkg | 47 | 400.00 |

## 1975 Corvette Options

| RPO # | DESCRIPTION | QTY. SOLD | PRICE |
|---|---|---|---|
| — | Custom Interior Trim | — | $154.00 |
| A31 | Power Windows | 28,745 | 93.00 |
| A85 | Shoulder Belts (Std./Cpe) | 646 | 41.00 |
| CO7 | Hardtop | 2,407 | 267.00 |
| CO8 | Vinyl Covering for Hrdtp | 279 | 350.00 |
| C50 | Rear Window Defroster | 13,760 | 46.00 |
| C60 | Air Conditioning | 31,914 | 490.00 |
| FE7 | Gymkhana Suspension | 3,194 | 7.00 |
| — | Optional Rear Axle Ratio | 1,969 | 12.00 |
| J50 | Power Brakes | 35,842 | 50.00 |
| L82 | 350ci, 250bhp engine | 2,372 | 336.00 |
| M21 | 4-Spd Man. Trans (close ratio) | 1,057 | 0.00 |
| M40 | Turbo Automatic Trans | 28,473 | 0.00 |
| N37 | Telescopic Steering Column | 31,830 | 82.00 |
| N41 | Power Steering | 37,591 | 129.00 |
| QRM | White Striped Tires (GR70x15) | 5,233 | 35.00 |
| QRZ | White Letter Tires (GR70x15) | 30,407 | 48.00 |
| UO5 | Dual Horns | 22,011 | 4.00 |
| U58 | AM-FM Radio (stereo) | 27,701 | 284.00 |
| U69 | AM-FM Radio | 12,902 | 178.00 |
| UA1 | Heavy Duty Bat. (std/LS4) | 16,778 | 15.00 |
| UF1 | Map Light (on rearview mirror) | 21,676 | 5.00 |
| YF5 | California Emission Test | 3,037 | 20.00 |
| Z07 | Off Road Suspension/Brake Pkg | 144 | 400.00 |

## 1976 Corvette Options

| RPO # | DESCRIPTION | QTY. SOLD | PRICE |
|---|---|---|---|
| — | Custom Interior Tri | — | $164.00 |
| A31 | Power Windows | 38,700 | 107.00 |
| C49 | Rear Window Defroster | 24,960 | 78.00 |
| C60 | Air Conditioning | 40,787 | 523.00 |
| FE7 | Gymkhana Suspension | 5,368 | 35.00 |
| — | Optional Rear Axle Ratio | 1,371 | 13.00 |
| J50 | Power Brakes | 46,558 | 59.00 |
| L82 | 350ci, 210bhp engine | 5,720 | 481.00 |
| M21 | 4-Spd Man. Trans (close ratio) | 2,088 | 0.00 |
| M40 | Turbo Automatic Trans | 36,625 | 0.00 |
| N37 | Telescopic Steering Column | 41,797 | 95.00 |
| N41 | Power Steering | 46,385 | 151.00 |
| QRM | White Striped Tires (GR70x15) | 3,992 | 37.00 |
| QRZ | White Letter Tires (GR70x15) | 39,923 | 51.00 |
| U58 | AM-FM Radio (stereo) | 34,272 | 281.00 |
| U69 | AM-FM Radio | 11,083 | 187.00 |
| UA1 | Heavy Duty Bat. (std/LS4) | 25,909 | 16.00 |
| UF1 | Map Light (on rearview mirror) | 35,361 | 10.00 |
| YF5 | California Emission Test | 3,527 | 50.00 |

## 1977 Corvette Options

| RPO # | DESCRIPTION | QTY. SOLD | PRICE |
|---|---|---|---|
| A31 | Power Windows | .44,341 | $116.00 |
| B32 | Color Keyed Floor Mats | 36,763 | 22.00 |
| C49 | Rear Window Defogger | 30,411 | 84.00 |
| C60 | Air Conditioning | 45,249 | 553.00 |
| D35 | Sport Mirrors | 20,206 | 36.00 |
| FE7 | Gymkhana Suspension | 5,368 | 35.00 |
| G95 | Optional Rear Axle Ratio | 972 | 14.00 |
| J50 | Power Brakes | 46,558 | 59.00 |
| K30 | Speed Control | 29,161 | 88.00 |
| L82 | 350ci, 210bhp engine | 6,148 | 495.00 |
| M21 | 4-Spd Man. Trans (close ratio) | 2,060 | 0.00 |
| M40 | Turbo Automatic Trans | 41,231 | 0.00 |
| NA6 | High Alt. Emiss Equip. | — | 22.00 |
| N37 | Telescopic Steering Column | 46,487 | 165.00 |
| QRZ | White Letter Tires (GR70x15) | 46,227 | 57.00 |
| UA1 | Heavy Duty Battery | 32,882 | 17.00 |
| U58 | AM-FM Radio (stereo) | 18,483 | 281.00 |
| U69 | AM-FM Radio | 4,700 | 187.00 |
| UM2 | AM-FM Radio/8-Track | 24,603 | 414.00 |
| V54 | Luggage/Roof Panel Rack | — | 73.00 |
| YF5 | California Emission Test | 3,527 | 73.00 |
| YJ8 | Cast Aluminum Wheels (4) | 12,646 | 321.00 |
| ZN1 | Trailer Package | 289 | 83.00 |
| ZX2 | Convince Group | 40,872 | 22.00 |

## 1978 Corvette Options

| RPO # | DESCRIPTION | QTY. SOLD | PRICE |
|---|---|---|---|
| 1YZ87/78 | | Pace Car | 6,502 |
| | $13,653.31 | | |
| A31 | Power Windows | 36,931 | 130.00 |
| AU3 | Power Door Locks | 12,187 | 120.00 |
| B2Z | Silver Anniversary Paint | 15,283 | 399.00 |
| C49 | Rear Window Defogger | 30,912 | 95.00 |
| CC1 | Removable Glass Panels | 972 | 349.00 |
| C60 | Air Conditioning | 37,638 | 605.00 |
| D35 | Sport Mirrors | 38,405 | 40.00 |
| FE7 | Gymkhana Suspension | 12,590 | 41.00 |
| G95 | Optional Rear Axle Ratio | 382 | 15.00 |
| J50 | Power Brakes | 46,558 | 59.00 |
| K30 | Cruise Control | 31,608 | 99.00 |
| L82 | 350ci, 220bhp engine | 12,739 | 525.00 |
| M21 | 4-Spd Man. Trans (close ratio) | 3,385 | 0.00 |
| M40 | Turbo Automatic Trans | 38,614 | 0.00 |
| NA6 | High Alt. Emiss. Equip. | — | 33.00 |
| N37 | Telescopic Steering Column | 37,858 | 175.00 |
| QRZ | White Letter Tires P255/60R15 | 18,296 | 216.32 |
| QRZ | White Letter Tires P255/70R15 | 36,203 | 51.00 |
| UA1 | Heavy Duty Battery | 28,243 | 18.00 |
| UM2 | AM-FM Stereo Radio/Tape | 20,899 | 419.00 |
| UP6 | AM-FM Stereo Radio/CB | 7,138 | 638.00 |
| U58 | AM-FM Stereo Radio | 10,189 | 286.00 |
| U69 | AM-FM Radio | 2,057 | 199.00 |
| U75 | Power Antenna | 23,069 | 49.00 |
| U81 | Dual Rear Speakers | 12,340 | 49.00 |
| YF5 | California Emission Test | — | 75.00 |
| YJ8 | Cast Aluminum Wheels (4) | 28,008 | 340.00 |
| ZN1 | Trailer Package | 978 | 89.00 |
| ZX2 | Convince Group | 37,222 | 84.00 |

## 1979 Corvette Options

| RPO # | DESCRIPTION | QTY. SOLD | PRICE |
|---|---|---|---|
| A31 | Power Windows | 20,631 | $141.00 |
| AU3 | Power Door Locks | 9,054 | 131.00 |
| CC1 | Removable Glass Roof Panels | 14,480 | 365.00 |
| C49 | Rear Window Defogger | 1,587 | 102.00 |
| C60 | Air Conditioning | 47,136 | 635.00 |
| D35 | Sport Mirrors | 48,211 | 45.00 |
| D80 | Spoilers (frt. & rear) | 6,853 | 265.00 |
| FE7 | Gymkhana Suspension | 12,321 | 49.00 |
| F51 | H.D. Shock Absorbers | 2,164 | 33.00 |
| G95 | Optional Rear Axle Ratio | 428 | 19.00 |
| K30 | Cruise Control | 34,445 | 113.00 |
| L82 | 350ci, 225bhp engine | 14,516 | 565.00 |
| M21 | 4-Spd Man. Trans (close ratio) | 4,062 | 0.00 |
| M40 | Turbo Automatic Trans | 41,454 | 0.00 |
| NA6 | High Alt. Emiss Equipment | — | 35.00 |
| N37 | Tilt/Tele. Steering Column | 47,463 | 190.00 |
| QRZ | White Letter Tires P255/60R15 | 17,920 | 226.20 |
| QRZ | White Letter Tires P255/70R15 | 29,603 | 54.00 |
| UM2 | AM-FM Stereo Radio/Tape | 21,435 | 228.00 |
| UP6 | AM-FM Stereo Radio/CB | 4,483 | 439.00 |
| U58 | AM-FM Stereo Radio | 9,256 | 90.00 |
| U75 | Power Antenna | 35,730 | 52.00 |
| U81 | Dual Rear Speakers | 37,754 | 52.00 |
| UA1 | Heavy Duty Battery | 3,405 | 21.00 |
| YF5 | California Emission Test | — | 83.00 |
| ZN1 | Trailer Package | 1,001 | 98.00 |
| ZQ2 | Pwr. Door Locks & Windows | 28,465 | 272.00 |
| ZX2 | Convince Group | 41,530 | 94.00 |

## 1980 Corvette Options

| RPO # | DESCRIPTION | QTY. SOLD | PRICE |
|---|---|---|---|
| AU3 | Power Door Lock | 32,692 | $140.00 |
| CC1 | Removable Glass Roof Panels | 19,695 | 391.00 |
| C49 | Rear Window Defogger | 36,589 | 109.00 |
| FE7 | Gymkhana Suspension | 9,907 | 55.00 |
| F51 | H.D. Shock Absorbers | 1,695 | 35.00 |
| K30 | Cruise Control | 30,821 | 123.00 |
| LG4 | 305ci, 180bhp engine | 3,221 | -50.00 |
| L82 | 350ci, 230bhp engine | 5,069 | 595.00 |
| MM4 | 4-Spd Man. Trans (close ratio) | 5,726 | 0.00 |
| MX1 | Turbo Automatic Trans | 34,838 | 0.00 |
| N90 | Aluminum Wheels (4) | 34,128 | 407.00 |
| QXH | White Letter Tires P255/60R15 | 13,140 | 426.16 |
| QGB | White Letter Tires P225/70R15 | 26,208 | 62.00 |
| UM2 | AM-FM Stereo Radio/Tape | 15,708 | 155.00 |
| UN3 | AM-FM Radio w/Cassette | 15,148 | 168.00 |
| UP6 | AM-FM Stereo Radio/CB | 2,434 | 439.00 |
| U75 | Power Antenna | 32,863 | 52.00 |
| UL5 | Radio Delete | 201 | -126.00 |
| U81 | Dual Rear Speakers | 36,650 | 52.00 |
| UA1 | Heavy Duty Battery | 1,337 | 22.00 |
| V54 | Roof Panel Carrier | 3,755 | 125.00 |
| YF5 | California Emission Test | 3,221 | 250.00 |
| ZN1 | Trailer Package | 796 | 105.00 |

## 1981 Corvette Options

| RPO # | DESCRIPTION | QTY. SOLD | PRICE |
|---|---|---|---|
| AU3 | Power Door Lock | 32,692 | $140.00 |
| CC1 | Removable Glass Roof Panels | 19,695 | 391.00 |
| C49 | Rear Window Defogger | 36,589 | 109.00 |
| FE7 | Gymkhana Suspension | 9,907 | 55.00 |
| F51 | H.D. Shock Absorbers | 1,695 | 35.00 |
| K30 | Cruise Control | 30,821 | 123.00 |
| LG4 | 305ci, 180bhp engine | 3,221 | -50.00 |
| L82 | 350ci, 230bhp engine | 5,069 | 595.00 |
| MM4 | 4-Spd Man. Trans (close ratio) | 5,726 | 0.00 |
| MX1 | Turbo Automatic Trans | 34,838 | 0.00 |
| N90 | Aluminum Wheels (4) | 34,128 | 407.00 |
| QXH | White Letter Tires P255/60R15 | 13,140 | 426.16 |
| QGB | White Letter Tires P225/70R15 | 26,208 | 62.00 |
| UM2 | AM-FM Stereo Radio/Tape | 15,708 | 155.00 |
| UN3 | AM-FM Radio w/Cassette. | 15,148 | 168.00 |
| UP6 | AM-FM Stereo Radio/CB | 2,434 | 439.00 |
| U75 | Power Antenna | 32,863 | 52.00 |
| UL5 | Radio Delete | 201 | -126.00 |
| U81 | Dual Rear Speakers | 36,650 | 52.00 |
| UA1 | Heavy Duty Battery | 1,337 | 22.00 |
| V54 | Roof Panel Carrier | 3,755 | 125.00 |
| YF5 | California Emission Test | 3,221 | 250.00 |
| ZN1 | Trailer Package | 796 | 105.00 |

## 1982 Corvette Options

| RPO # | DESCRIPTION | QTY. SOLD | PRICE |
|---|---|---|---|
| AG9 | Power Driver's Seat | 22,585 | $197.00 |
| AU3 | Power Door Locks | 23,936 | 140.00 |
| CC1 | Removable Glass Roof Panels | 14,763 | 443.00 |
| C49 | Rear Window Defogger | 19,886 | 129.00 |
| DG7 | Electric Sport Mirrors | 20,301 | 125.00 |
| D84 | Two-Tone Paint | 4,871 | 428.00 |
| FE7 | Gymkhana Suspension | 5,457 | 165.00 |
| K35 | Cruise Control | 24,313 | 165.00 |
| N90 | Aluminum Wheels (4) | 16,844 | 458.00 |
| QXH | White Letter Tires P255/60R15 | 19,070 | 542.52 |
| QGR | White Letter Tires P225/70R15 | 5,932 | 80.00 |
| UM4 | AM-FM Stereo Radio/Tape | 923 | 386.00 |
| UM3 | AM-FM Stereo Radio w/Cassette | 20,355 | 423.00 |
| UN5 | AM-FM Stereo Radio/CB/Cassette | 1,987 | 755.00 |
| U58 | AM/FM Stereo Radio | 1,533 | 101.00 |
| U75 | Power Antenna | 15,557 | 60.00 |
| UL5 | Radio Delete | 150 | -124.00 |
| VO8 | Heavy Duty Cooling | 6,006 | 57.00 |
| V54 | Roof Panel Carrier | 1,992 | 144.00 |
| YF5 | California Emission Test | 4,951 | 46.00 |

**The Gear Ratios**

If positraction is not indicated, it was not used (3.36, for example, means a 3.36 ratio without positraction). Also, 1973–75 is inclusive, meaning that 1973, 1974, and 1975 were all the same.

**1968–69**

| Ratio/Posi | Code |
|---|---|
| 3.36 | AK |
| 3.08 Positraction | AL |
| 3.36 Positraction | AM |
| 3.55 Positraction | AN |
| 3.70 Positraction | AO |
| 4.11 Positraction | AP |
| 3.70 | AS |
| 3.08 Positraction H.D | AT |
| 3.36 Positraction.H.D | AU |
| 3.08 Positraction | AV |
| 3.08 Positraction.H.D | AW |
| 2.73 Positraction.H.D | AY |
| 3.55 Positraction.H.D | AZ |
| 3.70 Positraction.H.D | FA |
| 4.11 Positraction.H.D | FB |
| 4.56 Positraction | FC |

**1970**

| Ratio/Posi | Code |
|---|---|
| 3.36 | CAK |
| 3.08 Positraction | CAL |
| 3.36 Positraction | CAM |
| 3.55 Positraction | CAN |
| 3.70 Positraction | CAO |
| 4.11 Positraction | CAP |
| 3.70 | CAS |
| 3.08 Positraction H.D | CAT |
| 3.36 Positraction.H.D | CAU |
| 3.08 Positraction | CAV |
| 3.08 Positraction.H.D | CAW |
| 2.73 Positraction.H.D | CAY |
| 3.55 Positraction.H.D | CAZ |
| 3.70 Positraction.H.D | CFA |
| 4.11 Positraction.H.D | CFB |
| 4.56 Positraction | CFC |
| 3.36 Positraction | CLR |

**1971**

| Ratio/Posi | Code |
|---|---|
| 3.55 Positraction | AA |
| 3.70 Positraction | AB |
| 4.11 Positraction | AC |
| 4.56 Positraction | AD |
| 3.08 Positraction | AW |
| 3.36 Positraction | AX |
| 3.36 Positraction | LR |

**1972**

| Ratio/Posi | Code |
|---|---|
| 3.55 Positraction | AA |
| 3.70 Positraction | AB |
| 4.11 Positraction | AC |
| 3.08 Positraction | AW |
| 3.36 Positraction | AX |
| 3.36 Positraction | LR |
| 2.73 Positraction | AV |

**1973–75**

| Ratio/Posi | Code |
|---|---|
| 3.36 Positraction | AX |
| 3.36 Positraction | LR |
| 4.11 Positraction | AC |
| 3.70 Positraction | AB |
| 3.55 Positraction | AA |
| 3.08 Positraction | AW |
| 2.73 Positraction | AV |

**1976**

| Ratio/Posi | Code |
|---|---|
| 3.08 Positraction | OA |
| 3.36 Positraction | LR |
| 3.55 Positraction | OB |
| 3.70 Positraction | OC |

**1977**

| Ratio/Posi | Code |
|---|---|
| 3.08 Positraction | OA |
| 3.36 Positraction | OD |
| 3.55 Positraction | OB |
| 3.70 Positraction | OC |

**1978**

| Ratio/Posi | Code |
|---|---|
| 3.08 Positraction | OK |
| 3.36 Positraction | OM |
| 3.55 Positraction | OH |
| 3.70 Positraction | OJ |

**1979**

| Ratio/Posi | Code |
|---|---|
| 3.36 Positraction | OM |
| 3.55 Positraction | OH |
| 3.70 Positraction | OJ |

**1980**

| Ratio/Posi | Code |
|---|---|
| 3.07 Positraction | DANA |

**1981**

| Ratio/Posi | Code |
|---|---|
| 2.87 Positraction w/auto trans | OM |
| 2.72 Positraction w/manual trans | OH |

**1982**

| Ratio/Posi | Code |
|---|---|
| 2.87 Positraction | OJ |

**Torque Settings**

Front Suspension

|  | Ft./lbs |
|---|---|
| Front Wheel Bearings | 12 |
| (.001-.005 end play) | |
| Upper Ball joint nut | 70 |
| Lower ball joint nut | 90 |
| Ball joint attaching nuts | 28 |

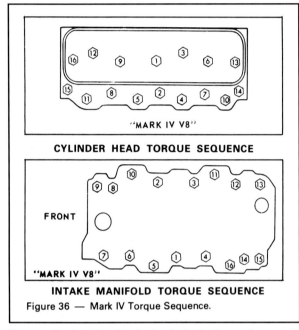

**CYLINDER HEAD TORQUE SEQUENCE**

**INTAKE MANIFOLD TORQUE SEQUENCE**

Figure 36 — Mark IV Torque Sequence.

Torque the head and cylinder bolts in the orders specified above.

| Steering arm to spindle | 70 |
|---|---|
| Upper control arm to frame | 55 |
| Upper control arm shaft bolts | 60 |
| Lower Control arm shaft to cross member: | |
| Front bolt | 70 |
| Rear bolt | 90 |
| Lower control arm shaft bolts | 60 |
| Upper shock mounting bolt | 12 |
| Lower shock mounting bolt | 18 |
| Sway bar bracket bolts (frame mounts) | 15 |
| Wheel nuts | 80 |

Rear Suspension

| Control arm front pivot bolt | 50 |
|---|---|
| Shock mount bolt(upper) | 50 |
| Shock mount bolt(lower) | 35 |
| Leaf spring anchor plate(Vette Products) | 30 |
| Strut rod bracket to differential | 35 |
| Sway bar bracket bolts(to frame) | 25 |
| Brackets to hub carrier | 25 |
| Sway bar link brackets | |
| 1/2" bolts | 55 |
| 3/8" bolts | 35 |
| Differential cross member/frame | 30 |
| Differential/spring bolts | 2- |
| Wheel nuts | 80 |

Rear Axle

| Differential cover bolts | 50 |
|---|---|
| Driveshaft to to pinion flange | 15 |
| Differential front mounting bolt | 65 |

Brake System

| Master Cylinder Bolts | 24 |
|---|---|
| Caliper mounting bolts (all) | 70 |

# SPECIFICATIONS

### BOLT TORQUES (FT. LBS.)

| Stabilizer Shaft | | Drive Spindle Support | |
|---|---|---|---|
| Bracket to Frame | 150 in. lb. | to Torque Arm | 30 |
| Bracket to Torque Arm | 150 in. lb. | Strut Rod | |
| Link Bushing Bolts | 25 | to Spindle Support | 75* |
| Jounce Bumper to Frame | 20 | Bracket to Carrier | 20 |
| Carrier To Frame | 90 | Camber Cam Nut | 120 |
| Carrier Front Support | | Torque Arm To Frame | 34* |
| to Crossmember | 65 | | |
| Drive Spindle Nut | 100* | Spring Link Bolt | Install Nut to expose hole |
| Rear Spring to Carrier | 50 | to Torque Arm | then insert cotter pin. |
| Shock Absorber | | Axle Drive Shaft | |
| Lower | 35 | Automatic | 150 in. lbs. |
| Upper | 35 | Manual | 20 |

*Plus additional torque necessary to line up cotter pin hole.

| | |
|---|---|
| Caliper housing bolts (rear) | 40 |
| Caliper housing bolts (front) | 130 |

Driveshaft And Rear Axles

| | |
|---|---|
| Universal joint U-bolts | 15 |
| Axle shaft to wheel spindle flange | 75 |
| Axle shaft to differential side yoke | 15 |
| Camber cam bolt | 65 |
| Differential mounting bracket | 60 |

Engine and Transmission Mounts

| | |
|---|---|
| Flywheel housing to Engine | 30 |
| Exhaust manifolds | 20 |
| Water pump bolts | 30 |
| Flywheel bolts | 60 |
| Spark plugs | 25 |
| Distributor Clamp | 25 |
| Intake Manifold | 30 |
| Thermostat Housing | 30 |
| Water Outlet | 30 |
| Water Pump | 30 |
| Connecting Rod Cap | 45 |

| | |
|---|---|
| Cylinder Head | 65 |
| Main Bearing Cap | 80 |
| Outer Bolts | 70 |
| Oil Drain Plug | 20 |

Clutch

| | |
|---|---|
| Flywheel to engine | 30 |
| Pressure plate bolts | 30 |

Manual Transmission

| | |
|---|---|
| Case to clutch housing | 55 |
| Mount bolts | 40 |
| Cross-member to frame nuts | 25 |
| Shifter levers to shafts | 20 |
| Drain plug | 30 |

Body

| | |
|---|---|
| Body mount Bolts | 45 |
| Front bumper bolts | 18 |
| Door hinge bolts | 27 |

Engine

| | |
|---|---|
| Exhaust manifolds | 20 |
| Fuel pump bolts | 35 |
| A.I.R. manifold bolts | 15 |
| Starter bolts | 30 |

## SPECIFICATIONS

### BOLT TORQUES

| | |
|---|---|
| Ball Joint Stud Nuts* | |
| Upper Stud | 70 N·m (50 ft. lbs.) |
| Lower Stud | 110 N·m (80 ft. lbs.) |
| Joint to Upper Arm | |
| (Service Replacement) | 35 N·m (25 ft. lbs.) |
| Steering Arm Nuts | 95 N·m (70 ft. lbs.) |
| Control Arm Pivot to Frame | |
| Upper | 70 N·m (50 ft. lbs.) |
| Lower (nut only) | See Below |
| Cross Shaft Bolts | 70 N·m (50 ft. lbs.) |
| Shock Absorber | |
| Upper End | 10 N·m (90 in. lbs.) |
| Lower End | 17 N·m (150 in. lbs.) |
| Stabilizer Bar | |
| Link Nuts | 24 N·m (18 ft. lbs.) |
| Bracket Bolts | 140 N·m (120 in. lbs.) |
| Lower Control Arm Shaft to Crossmember | |
| Front | 95 N·m (70 ft. lbs.) |
| Rear | 130 N·m (95 ft. lbs.) |
| Mounting Bolts Disc Brake Caliper | 95 N·m (70 ft. lbs.) |
| Wheel Bearing Adjustment** | |
| Preload | |
| End Movement | |

*Plus additional torque to align cotter pin hole.
1/16 turn maximum.
NEVER back off to align cotter pin.
**See Procedure in FRONT SUSPENSION Section.

### TORQUE SPECIFICATIONS

| | |
|---|---|
| Crankcase Front Cover | 80 lb. in. |
| Flywheel Housing Cover | 80 lb. in. |
| Oil Filter Bypass Valve | 80 lb. in. |
| Oil Pan To Crankcase (1/4-20) | 80 lb. in. |
| Oil Pump Cover | 80 lb. in. |
| Rocker Arm Cover | 45 lb. in. |
| Camshaft Sprocket | 20 lb. ft. |
| Oil Pan To Crankcase (5/16-18) | 165 lb. ft. |
| Clutch Pressure Plate | 30 lb. ft. |
| Distributor Clamp | 25 lb. ft. |
| Flywheel Housing | 30 lb. ft. |
| Manifold (Exhaust) | 20 lb. ft.* |
| Manifold (Inlet) | 30 lb. ft. |
| Thermostat Housing | 30 lb. ft. |
| Water Outlet | 30 lb. ft. |
| Water Pump | 30 lb. ft. |
| Connecting Rod Cap | 45 lb. ft. |
| Cylinder Head | 65 lb. ft. |
| Main Bearing Cap | 80 lb. ft. @ |
| Oil Pump | 65 lb. ft. |
| Rocker Arm Stud | 50 lb. ft. |
| Flywheel | 60 lb. ft. |
| Torsional Damper | 60 lb. ft. |
| Temperature Sending Unit | 20 lb. ft. |
| Oil Filter | 25 lb. ft. |
| Oil Pan Drain Plug | 20 lb. ft. |
| Spark Plug | 17-27 lb. ft. |

* Inboard bolts 30 lb. ft.
@ Outer bolts (L82) 70 lb. ft.

# Parts Suppliers

**American Racing Equipment**
19067 South Reyes Ave.
Rancho Dominguez, CA 90221
(800) 3215489
The American Racing Torque Thrust wheel is the only wheel that looks right on the early C3 Corvette. When Chevrolet was creating show platforms in the early seventies they used this very same wheel, and most of the racers in the early seventies used them. Just make sure that you order the eight inch version, not the 8 1/2 as I did.

**American Racing Products (ARP)**
250 Quail Court
Santa Paula, CA 93060
(800) 826-3045
This is the hardware company. If you're building a Corvette motor then keep this phone number handy. The only thing more expensive than ARP bolts is having your engine blow up because you used an inferior product.

**Andover Automotive**
P.O. Box 2651
Columbia, MD 21045
(800) 447-3520
A whole junk yard of Corvette parts. Imagine just being able to work in a place like this. Andover stocks a tremendous amount of quality used parts for the Corvette. Get to know these people.

**Auto Accessories of America**
Box 427
Boalsburg, PA 16827
(814) 364-2141
This is a full service Corvette parts company.

**Brass Works**
289 Prado
San Luis Obispo, CA 93401
(805) 544-8841
These are the best Chevrolet water pumps on the market. They may not have matching numbers but they'll certainly keep your motor cool.

**Cagle Fuel Regulators**
P.O. Box 2536
Rolling Hills, CA 90274
(310) 377-7501
The guys at RHS swear by these fuel regulators. A lot of your carburetion problems can be solved with a fuel regulator. They may not fit into a perfectly stock NCRS engine compartment but if they solve your fuel pressure problem who cares?

**Caledonia Classic Cars**
9595 Cherry Valley Road S.E.
Caledonia, MI 49316
(800) 245-5224
Gary runs one of the best Corvette restoration facilities in the country. He offers rebuilding services for a lot of your Corvette's components, as well as a fantastic number of hard core Corvette parts.

**C Central**
5865 Sawyer Road
Sawyer, MI 49125
(616) 426-3342
C Central sells real parts. There are no shirts in their catalog - just some of the best reproduction parts on the market. They've developed a corner on the exhaust and muffler market. It's gotten to the point where a lot of other Corvette suppliers sell C Central exhaust products as their own parts. Why not buy from the original?

**Coker Tire**
1317 Chestnut Street
Chattanooga, TN 37402
(800) 251-6336
These are the reproduction tire people. If you want the original look on your Corvette you have to call Coker.

**Competition Cams**
3406 Democrat Road
Memphis, TN 38118
(800) 999-0853
This is the best camshaft company in the country. They have the facilities to develop the best equipment for your Corvette. They also care about having you as a customer.

**The Eastwood Company**
580 Lancaster Ave.
Malvern, PA 19355
(800) 345-1178(215)
    This the largest restoration supplies company in the world. They not only have the greatest selection of supplies, but they have a knowledgeable staff to help you.

**Eckler's**
P.O. Box 5637
Titusville, FL 32783-5637
(407) 269-9680
    Eckler's began as a fiberglass company. In the past decade they've become a full line parts operation. They still have the best selection of retail fiberglass on the market.

**Edelbrock Corp.**
2700 California Street
Torrance, CA 90503
(310) 781-2222
    Edelbrock is the industry leader for emissions legal induction systems. They were the first company to recognize that our Corvettes must be good citizens as well as fast.

**Energy Suspension**
960 Calle Amanecer
San Clemente, CA 92672
(714) 361-3935
    Energy Suspension is the world's largest manufacturer of polyurethane suspension bushing. They are also the leader in quality. Call them if you're doing any suspension work.

**Fast Blast**
143 Conchester Highway
Twin Oaks, PA 19014
(610) 485-2501
    Fast Blast removed the paint from Project Corvette. What was then an advanced technique has rapidly become the standard procedure for paint removal.

**Uniroyal Goodrich**
1 Parkway South
Greenville, South Carolina 29615
(803) 458-6957
    BF Goodrich has become the Corvette tire. It seems that at least half of the Corvette owners switch to BF Goodrich tires when the time comes for new rubber. The secret seems to be that they offer a quality tire that is just a little more reasonably priced than the guys with the blimp.

**Goodyear Tire and Rubber Co.**
1144 East Market Street
Akron, Ohio 44398-6020
(216) 796-2936
    Goodyear has always been the original equipment Corvette tire. They've lost the edge in the replacement market, but they still produce a quality product.

**Grant Products**
700 Allen Ave.
Glendale, CA 91201
(213) 849-3171
    These are the steering wheel people. They produce a complete range of replacement steering wheels and accessories.

**Gulstrand Engineering**
11924 West Jefferson Boulevard
Culver City, CA 90230
(310) 391-7108
    Dick Gulstrand is Mr. Corvette performance. Project Corvette even took styling cues from the old James Garner racing team that Dick managed in the late sixties.

**Mr. Gasket**
8700 Brook Park Road
Clevelend, Ohio 44129
(216) 398-8300
    I'm always amazed at how many small companies operate under the Mr. Gasket banner. These include Lakewood, Hays, Accel and Hurst.

**Hooker Headers**
1009 West Brooks Street
Ontario, CA 91761
(714) 983-5871
    These are the headers you grew up with. They are also the headers used by most racers. Hooker produces the best quality headers on the market. If you just have to have a set of headers call Hooker.

**Jet Coatings**
55 East Front Street/Suite A200
Bridgeport, PA 19405
(215) 277-2444
    We used Jet Coating on Project Corvette. This is rapidly becoming the standard finish on aftermarket pipes and headers. It may not look stock, but it sure holds up a lot better than the stock finish.

**Koni Shocks**
8085 Production Ave.
Florence, KY 41042
(606)727-5000
    Koni has been the industry standard for several decades. You can probably buy shocks that are just as good, but why not purchase from the industry leader? I've installed Konis on all three of my personal cars.

## Legendary Corvette
903 Easton Road
Warrington, PA 18972
(215) 766-2323

Legendary Corvette has been working with fiberglass for several decades. They know as much about fiberglass as any company in the world.

## M.F. Dobbins
16 East Montgomery Avenue
Hatboro, PA 19040
(215) 4430779

Dobbins was the first to reproduce decals and placards for the area under your Corvette's hood. He also has a small restoration shop which turns out Bloomington Gold Corvettes on a regular basis.

## Meguiar's
17991 Mitchell South
Irvine, CA 92714
(800) 854-8073

Professional detail shops feel this is the finest line of car care products. If there is any problem with Meguiar's product line it's that they make so many products that it's hard to ascertain the correct product for you application.

## Mid-America
One Mid-America Place
P.O. Box 1368
Effingham, IL 62401
(800) 637-5533

This is my favorite full-service Corvette supplier. Mid-America is owned by a family of Corvette nuts who also happen to make a living selling Corvette parts. They know about your Corvette because they own Corvettes.

## Moroso Performance Products
80 Carter Drive
Guilford, CT 06437
(203) 453-6906

Moroso carries Herb Adams, or VSE, suspension equipment for Corvettes.

## Motorbooks International
PO Box 1
Osceola, WI 54020
(800) 826-6600

These are good people, and not just because they published this book. If it's a book about cars they sell it. Make sure that you get on their mailing list. If a new Corvette book is released, they'll be selling it first.

## Paragon
8040 Jennings Road
Swartz Creek, MI 48473
(800) 882-4688

Paragon manufacturers most of their products. Everything they sell is a correct reproduction part.

## Performance Friction
83 Carbon Metallic Highway
Clover, South Carolina 29710
(800) 521-8874

Here's a company that developed a better brake pad and went on to dominate the field. If there's a race anyplace in world you can be sure that most of the cars have Performance Friction brake pads installed.

## M. Parker
374 N. Cooper Road, Unit C-7
Berlin, NJ 08009
(609) 753-0350

M. Parker makes most of the reproduction wiring harnesses in the United States. Their products are so accurate that even NCRS judges can't tell an M. Parker harness from the Chevrolet original.

## Racing Head Services
3410 Democrat Road
Memphis, TN 38118
(800) 333-618

RHS has cornered the market on high performance street motors. They use a very simple formula. They offer the best performance, and the best endurance, for the most reasonable price. They've simply blown the corner speed shop out of the market when it comes to street motors. They'll also take your original Corvette motor and massage extra horsepower out of all that GM steel. The best part is that they know how to create horsepower and still keep the car looking NCRS stock.

## Stage 8 Locking Fasteners
15 Chestnut Ave.
San Rafael, CA 94901
(800) 843-7836

Stage 8 has developed a system of locking bolts for your Chevrolet engine. The most useful ones are for the headers.

## U.S. Radiator
6710 S. Avalon Blvd.
Los Angles, CA 90003
(213) 778-5525

These are the radiator experts. U.S. Radiator not only makes most of the reproduction radiators in the country, but they can also make a custom radiator for your Corvette. The best part is that you get all this expertise, and craftsmanship, for about the same price that you'll give your Chevrolet dealer for a not quite right radiator.

## Van Steel
1141-A Court Street
Clearwater, FL 34616
(813) 443-2245

Art Dorsett has been rebuilding Corvette rear bearing assemblies for several decades. I doubt if anyone can match his company's experience when it comes to Corvette rear axle units.

**Vette Brakes**
74790-30th Avenue North
St. Petersburg, FL 33710
(800) 237-9991
      Vette Brakes & Products is the leading Corvette brake company in the United States. They also carry a line of suspension parts for street driven Corvettes. The best part is they are extremely helpful in offering advice.

**Herb Adams**
VSE
23865 Fairfield
Carmel, CA 93923
(408) 649-8423
      Herb Adams is one of the best chassis guys around. Moroso has handled his chassis parts for a long time. The parts are quality and they tend to be a little more robust than the average Corvette chassis parts.

**Vibratech / Fluid Damper**
537 E. Delvan Ave.
Buffalo, N.Y. 14211
(716) 895-5404
      The industry standard when it comes to front engine dampers.

**ZIP Products**
1250 Commercial Center
Mechanicsville, VA 23111
(800) 962-9632
      ZIP started out reproducing Corvette fuel lines. They are now a full service Corvette parts company.

**Zymol**
50 West Pond Road
North Branford, CT 06471
(800) 999-5563
      Zymol has made the finest, if not the most expensive, wax for over a decade. They have a complete line of car products, but the wax is really the reason you know the name Zymol.

# Index